James Conway, Julius Pottgeisser

Sermons for Sundays and Chief Festivals of the Ecclesiastical Year

Vol. 2

James Conway, Julius Pottgeisser

Sermons for Sundays and Chief Festivals of the Ecclesiastical Year
Vol. 2

ISBN/EAN: 9783744742184

Printed in Europe, USA, Canada, Australia, Japan

Cover: Foto ©Lupo / pixelio.de

More available books at **www.hansebooks.com**

SERMONS

FOR

The Sundays and Chief Festivals

OF

THE ECCLESIASTICAL YEAR

WITH TWO COURSES OF

LENTEN SERMONS

AND

A TRIDUUM FOR THE FORTY HOURS

BY

REV. JULIUS POTTGEISSER, S.J.

Rendered from the German

BY

REV. JAMES CONWAY, S.J.

VOL. II

Sermons for Festivals, Lenten Sermons, Forty Hours

FOURTH EDITION

NEW YORK, CINCINNATI, CHICAGO

BENZIGER BROTHERS

PRINTERS TO THE | PUBLISHERS OF
HOLY APOSTOLIC SEE | BENZIGER'S MAGAZINE

Permissu Superiorum.

Imprimatur.
✠ MICHAEL AUGUSTINE,
Archbishop of New York.
NEW YORK, July 21, 1889.

Copyright, 1889, by BENZIGER BROTHERS.

CONTENTS OF VOL. II.

	PAGE
FEAST OF THE IMMACULATE CONCEPTION.—Cause of our Joy	5
CHRISTMAS DAY.—The Birth of Our Lord	14
FEAST OF ST. STEPHEN, THE FIRST MARTYR.—A most Glorious and Fruitful Death	23
NEW YEAR'S DAY.—Good Use of Time	32
FEAST OF THE EPIPHANY.—Vocation to the Faith	43
FEAST OF THE MOST HOLY NAME OF JESUS.—Sanctity and Power of the Holy Name	53
FEAST OF THE PURIFICATION OF THE BLESSED VIRGIN.—The Self Sacrifice of the Mother of God	62
FEAST OF ST. JOSEPH.—St. Joseph's Holiness	72
FEAST OF THE ANNUNCIATION.—Generosity of the Mother of God	80
GOOD FRIDAY.—The Passion of Our Lord	88
EASTER SUNDAY.—The Resurrection of Our Lord	102
EASTER MONDAY.—Our own Resurrection	112
FEAST OF THE ASCENSION.—On Heaven	120
WHITSUNDAY.—Mission of the Holy Ghost	131
WHITMONDAY.—Baptism	141
FEAST OF THE MOST HOLY TRINITY.—Belief in the Mystery of the Trinity	149
FEAST OF CORPUS CHRISTI.—The Real Presence	158
FEAST OF THE SACRED HEART OF JESUS.—Devotion to the Sacred Heart	171
FEAST OF ST. PETER AND ST. PAUL.—St. Peter the Visible Head of the Church	183
FEAST OF THE ASSUMPTION.—Mutual Reception of Mother and Son	194

	PAGE
FEAST OF THE NATIVITY OF THE BLESSED VIRGIN.—Confidence in the Mother of God	204
FEAST OF ST. MICHAEL THE ARCHANGEL.—Devotion to St. Michael	213
FEAST OF THE HOLY ROSARY.—Excellence of the Devotion of the Rosary	222
FEAST OF THE GUARDIAN ANGELS.—Devotion to our Guardian Angels	233
FEAST OF ALL SAINTS.—The Reward of Sanctity	243
ALL SOULS' DAY.—Devotion to the Suffering Souls	252
FEAST OF THE DEDICATION OF A CHURCH.—A Day of Joy and Gratitude	262

LENTEN SERMONS.

FIRST COURSE: ON PRAYER.

FIRST SERMON.—Necessity of Prayer	273
SECOND SERMON.—Efficacy of Prayer	284
THIRD SERMON.—Requisites of Fruitful Prayer	293
FOURTH SERMON.—Time and Place of Prayer	303
FIFTH SERMON.—Apostleship of Prayer	313

SECOND COURSE: ON SUFFERING.

FIRST SERMON.—Sources of Sufferings	325
SECOND SERMON.—Fruits of Sufferings	334
THIRD SERMON.—Remedies against Sufferings	344
FOURTH SERMON.—Remedies against Sufferings (Continued)	353
FIFTH SERMON.—Remedies against Sufferings (Continued)	362

TRIDUUM FOR THE ADORATION OF THE FORTY HOURS.

FIRST DAY.—The Good Shepherd Dwells amid His Sheep	373
SECOND DAY.—The Good Shepherd Feeds His Sheep	383
THIRD DAY.—The Good Shepherd Sacrifices Himself for His Sheep	393
ALPHABETICAL INDEX	405

Feast of the Immaculate Conception.

CAUSE OF OUR JOY.

"I will put enmities between thee and the woman, and thy seed and her seed ; she shall crush thy head."—Gen. iii. 15.

CHILDREN whose mother has been distinguished by some great mark of honor naturally rejoice as often as they recall to mind her prerogative ; and the greater this distinction is, the greater is their joy. The cause of their joy is, on the one hand, the love which they bear towards their mother, and, on the other hand, the advantages which thence accrue to themselves. How great, then, should be our joy to-day, when we commemorate the first great prerogative of our holy Mother Mary— her Immaculate Conception ! Mary, the Mother of God, is our Mother, and her Immaculate Conception, which we celebrate on this day, is her most glorious prerogative ; a prerogative which is peculiar to her alone, which is dearest to her heart of all the honors that God has lavished upon her, which is the source of all her greatness ; a prerogative which is at the same time her victory and her crown—a victory over sin and a crown of heavenly beauty and loveliness. Hence we see that this mystery of the Immaculate Conception is represented under the figure of the Blessed Virgin with the serpent writhing beneath her foot, and on her head a crown of twelve stars. The serpent is the figure of sin, and the crown of stars symbolizes the immaculate and heavenly splendor in which the Mother of God was arrayed from the first moment of her existence. And this glorious distinction of our holy Mother is not only the glory and the honor of us, her children, but is also the source of the greatest spiritual advantages to us.

Therefore, in order that we may rejoice to-day as becomes the privileged children of such a privileged Mother, I shall endeavor briefly to show you that the *Immaculate Conception* of the Mother of God is—

1. *A source of honor to our holy Mother;*
2. *A source of spiritual blessings to us, her children.*

I. THE HONOR OF OUR HOLY MOTHER.

1. That the Immaculate Conception is the source of the highest honor to the Mother of God follows, first of all, from the *nature of this holy mystery.* For, what do we understand by the mystery of the Immaculate Conception? It is a privilege by which the Blessed Virgin Mary, alone of the descendants of Adam, has been preserved from original sin, and entered into existence adorned with sanctifying grace and all the supernatural gifts of original justice. Recall to mind how our first parents, after they had been created by God in justice and sanctity and placed in the Paradise of pleasure, listened to the evil suggestion of the serpent, transgressed the commandment of God, and thus made themselves guilty of a grievous sin. Recall to mind how, in consequence of this sin, they were stript of sanctifying grace, deprived of the friendship of God and the inheritance of His heavenly kingdom, subjected to the degrading law of concupiscence and sufferings and privations of every description, and finally sentenced to the horrors of death. Recall to mind, moreover, how this sin of our first parents, with all its baleful consequences, has passed upon all their posterity, so that all men are conceived in sin, born into this world as children of wrath, excluded from the happiness of heaven, and amenable to eternal damnation. Recall to

mind all this; and then judge for yourselves whether or not the Immaculate Conception, which has exempted the Blessed Mother of God alone of all humanity from this universal curse, and adorned her in the first instant of her existence with original justice, is not a most singular and glorious prerogative of our holy Mother.

2. The greatness of this prerogative and the consequent honor accruing from it to our blessed Lady will also appear from the *cause* why Almighty God conferred this distinction upon His holy Mother. The cause of this privilege manifestly was that she was destined to be the Mother of His only-begotten Son; for it was befitting that, as the Royal Prophet says, the Most High should sanctify His own tabernacle (Ps. xlv. 5). And how did He accomplish this? He certainly provided for the most suitable decoration of the temple of His divine Son. And what ornament did He choose? Evidently the All-powerful and All-wise, who had all resources at His disposal, chose that which would make her most worthy to be the Mother of God. And what ornaments are befitting the Mother of Sanctity, and Justice, and Purity? Is it earthly greatness? Is it a perishable crown? Is it queenly dignity and honors? No, beloved brethren; the choice of the Most High was original justice and sanctity, the prerogative of the Immaculate Conception. The Eternal Wisdom itself has given preference to this before all other honors and distinctions. This grand prerogative must, then, be the most suitable ornament for the future Mother of God; an ornament which is in keeping with her unspeakable dignity. This being the case, is it not evident that the Immaculate Conception is a prerogative whose worth surpasses all understanding, and that it, accordingly, confers the highest conceivable honor on our holy Mother?

3. If we, furthermore, consider the *effects* which the Immaculate Conception produced in the Blessed Virgin, we must come to the same conclusion—that this glorious mystery has conferred upon her the highest honor imaginable. To be brief, I shall consider only one of these marvellous effects—the unspeakable *beauty* which it shed upon the soul of our blessed Mother.

In order, in some degree, to make you understand the surpassing lustre of this supernatural beauty, I must briefly draw your attention to the beauty which sanctifying grace, even in its ordinary, or *lowest degree*, diffuses upon the soul. This beauty is so great that it surpasses all imagination. A soul which is adorned with sanctifying grace, though it be only in the lowest grade, is infinitely more beautiful than sun, and moon, and stars; more beautiful than heaven and earth, and the whole universe with all the grandeur it displays. For, great as is the beauty of the universe, yet it is merely natural, while the beauty of a sanctified soul is supernatural. As grace surpasses nature, as heaven surpasses earth, as eternity surpasses time, in the same degree does the beauty of the soul in sanctifying grace transcend all created beauty of the universe. It is so great that it charms the angels of heaven; so great that the infinite God Himself, the uncreated beauty, contemplates it with unspeakable complacency. Grace is that glorious wedding garment (Matt. xxii. 11) which adorns the sanctified souls on earth and the blessed in heaven, which renders the soul worthy to dwell among the angels and saints in heaven, and to appear before the throne of the Most High. Nay, St. Thomas does not hesitate to call sanctifying grace the radiance of the light of the divine countenance, by which the soul becomes partaker of the beauty of God Himself. And St. Brigit of Sweden in her Revelations says that, if a mortal eye could only behold one ray of the divine light of grace, this one ray would make the heart of the beholder burst with pure love of God.

But if even the lowest grade of sanctifying grace sheds such beauty and splendor on the soul, what shall we say of that divine lustre which was diffused in the soul of the Mother of God by that *high degree* of sanctity which was bestowed on her at her creation by Him that was to become her son? That beauty not even the tongues of angels could describe. So wondrously beautiful was this privileged soul, thus adorned with supernatural grace, that the eyes of the adorable Trinity—of the Father, her Creator and Father; of the Son, that soon was to be her son; of the Holy Ghost, who had then espoused her to Himself—rested upon her with infinite delight, and that the whole court of heaven broke out into the words: " Thou art all fair, O my love, and there is not a spot in thee "(Cant. iv. 7). Who is this that cometh up from the desert, leaning upon her beloved?"(Ibid. viii. 5.) " Thou art the glory of Jerusalem; thou art the joy of Israel; thou art the honor of our people " (Jud. xv. 10).

Whatever view, then, we may take of the mystery of the Immaculate Conception of the Mother of God; whether we consider its nature, its cause, or its effects, we come to the same conclusion, that it is a jewel of incomparable worth, that it is a prerogative which far surpasses mortal understanding. Have we not reason, then, to rejoice with all our hearts and to congratulate our holy Mother on this grand privilege which God has conferred upon her? Have we not reason, also, to congratulate ourselves that we may with truth call such a privileged creature our Mother? Is not her honor our honor? But we have reason, also, to rejoice in her Immaculate Conception because it is, moreover—

II. A SOURCE OF SPIRITUAL BLESSINGS FOR US.

The mystery of the Immaculate Conception is for us the source of spiritual blessings in two ways: first, because it imparts to us a rich store of *salutary instruction;* and, secondly, because it opens to us a rich *treasury of graces.*

1. *A source of instruction.* The first lesson which this holy mystery conveys to us is the importance and *value of the grace of God.* For, is it not manifest that what God prizes highest is most important and valuable? And does the mystery of the Immaculate Conception not show us in the clearest light that God values grace above all things? Is it not evident that He chose the choicest and most costly for the first gift which He bestowed on her who was destined to be His Mother? And this gift was grace, and grace alone. Grace is, therefore, of infinitely more value than all the goods, and honors, and pleasures of this world taken together. Should we not, then, make every sacrifice to secure such a treasure? And if we have the happiness to possess this inestimable treasure, should we not employ all care to preserve it, and, therefore, at all costs and hazards, endeavor to lead an unsullied, a truly Christian life?

The second lesson, which we learn from this holy mystery, is that the beauty in which Almighty God delights is not the external and visible beauty of the body but the internal, invisible beauty of the soul—*purity of heart.* For, do we not see at once in the mystery of the Immaculate Conception how little account God makes of external beauty, and how pleasing to Him, on the other hand, is the inward beauty of the soul, the immaculate purity of the heart? Was it not with this interior beauty that He adorned His holy Mother through the prerogative of her Immaculate Conception, that she might become a worthy habitation for His only-begotten Son? He may have added outward beauty, but of this there is not a single mention made in Revelation; for, when the Holy Ghost calls her "fair" and "all fair" these words refer not to the outward graces of the body, but to the inward purity and lustre of her immaculate soul. But it goes without saying that this inward beauty consists, above all, in the freedom from sin, both mortal and venial; for it is only sin that can defile the soul.

Finally, this mystery teaches us that we should be most *solicitous to cultivate this inward beauty* of the soul, the purity of the heart. Or, is it not befitting that we, who are the children of the Immaculate Virgin, should endeavor to please and honor our spotless Mother? But how could we do that, if we led an impure and sinful life? What delight can the heart of a stainless and more than angelic Mother have in impure and sin-stained children—children whose souls are defiled and disfigured with the hideous leprosy of sin? Are such vile and degenerate children an honor to their heavenly Mother? Must she not rather be ashamed of such degraded children? Let us, then, beloved brethren, in order to be true children of our Immaculate Mother, children on whom she may look with delight, carefully avoid the occasions of sin, fortify ourselves with prayer, and good works, and the frequent reception of the sacraments. These are the means of preserving and increasing the inward beauty of our souls and making ourselves worthy children of the Mother of beauteous love.

2. *A source of graces.* The Immaculate Conception of the Mother of God is for us a rich source of graces, if we venerate this holy mystery with true devotion, that is, if we have confident recourse to it with prayer

and other pious works, and particularly endeavor to honor it by purity of life.

That this is an undoubted fact, beloved brethren, even *reason* itself, enlightened as it is by faith, assures us. For, who does not see that the Mother of God has a special predilection for, and lavishly bestows her favors upon, such of her children as try to give her most joy, and are most anxious to honor her? And do we not belong to this class of her children when we make her Immaculate Conception, which is the most precious ornament in her glorious crown, the object of our especial veneration and devotion?

And does not *experience* teach us this same truth? From the many facts which I might advance in proof of this assertion, I shall, for the sake of brevity, mention only one, of which I myself was witness. It is now some twenty years ago that in a village on the Rhine a laborer who had long neglected his religious duties was taken with a serious illness. Though it was soon manifest that there was no hope of recovery, he obstinately refused to see the priest or receive the sacraments. Just at the time I happened to be in the neighborhood, and heard of the sad state of the dying man. I went to see him, but could effect nothing. I could only recommend him to God and, therefore, took refuge to the Immaculate Conception. Before leaving the house I advised the pious nurse, who waited on him from charity, and was much concerned for his soul, secretly to put a medal of the Immaculate Conception around his neck. She did so, and in a very short time the patient opened his eyes and said to the nurse: "I think it would be well to send for the priest; I want to make my confession." In a moment the priest was at hand; the sick man confessed his sins as best he could. In the meantime the joyous news was circulated in the village; the people assembled in the church and accompanied the Blessed Sacrament to the patient's house; and fortified with all the sacraments, amid the prayers of his pious neighbors and the consoling words of the priest, he died a peaceful and, as we may hope, a happy death. And this, beloved brethren, is not the only fact of the kind that I myself have witnessed. Now, if our blessed Mother, even in cases in which very little has been done in honor of her Immaculate Conception, has not seldom obtained such signal graces from Almighty God, what may we not expect from her if during our whole lives we have tried to do all in our power to honor this holy mystery! May we not confidently hope that she will obtain for us the inestimable grace of a happy death?

Let us, then, beloved brethren, to-day, on the glorious feast of her Immaculate Conception, renew ourselves in this devotion, which is so pleasing to her and so fruitful for us. Let us endeavor in future to give joy to our holy Mother by often devoutly recalling the mystery of her Immaculate Conception, by availing ourselves of it as a shield against the onslaughts of the enemies of our souls, and by carefully endeavoring to preserve the purity of our hearts; and our spotless Mother, who is so tender-hearted and generous, and so faithful in rewarding the least things we do to her honor, will amply repay our love and devotion. She will be our protection in life, our comfort in **death, and our joy and delight in eternity.** Amen.

Christmas Day.

THE BIRTH OF OUR LORD.

"You shall find the infant wrapped in swaddling clothes, and laid in a manger."—Luke ii. 12.

BEHOLD the sign by which the shepherds were to recognize the Saviour of the world—a strange sign, forsooth! You shall find a child; so weak and helpless, that it is wrapped in swaddling clothes; so poor, that a lowly manger is its cradle. But is not He, who is here announced, the Messias promised by God; the object of the faith, and hope, and longing of the patriarchs of old; the object of the rites, ceremonies, and sacrifices of the Old Law; the soul and centre of the entire divine worship of the chosen people of God? Is it not He whom the prophets had foretold as the personal wisdom and power of the Most High, as the King of heaven and earth, as the Deliverer and Redeemer of the whole human race? How can the crib and the swathing bands, which betoken abject poverty and helpless weakness, be the sign by which this great King is to be recognized?

Beloved brethren, this was the objection of the Jews and heathens of old against the great mystery which we celebrate to-day; and the same is the objection of the enlightened pagans of our own day against the Godhead of Jesus Christ. The Divine Majesty, they say, could not possibly debase Himself so low: no; if the Godhead would have deigned to descend upon this earth, they imagine, He would have done so in a way that would be more befitting His greatness and majesty; He would have appeared surrounded with such splendor and glory as would command the awe and reverence of all men. O proud unbelief, is that the reputed wisdom of which thou boastest? How foolish is thy wisdom! How contemptible are the thoughts and sentiments which thou judgest so sublime!

That you may see the folly of unbelief, whether old or new, and admire the power and wisdom of God in the mystery of the crib, and that you may thus be strengthened in your faith in the divinity of Jesus Christ, I mean to show you to-day that the circumstances of the birth of our blessed Lord were for Him, as our God and Redeemer, the most befitting; because as God He could not have chosen a manner more worthy of His infinite majesty, and as our Redeemer He could not have selected a means better suited to His end. Therefore I say that *the circumstances* of the birth of Jesus Christ were—

1. *Most befitting the greatness of God;*
2. *Best suited for the end of our redemption.*

I. MOST BEFITTING THE GREATNESS OF GOD.

1. Jesus Christ as the Son of God could not on entering the world have chosen circumstances more worthy of His infinite greatness, because the *utmost poverty*, in which He was born, best harmonizes with the *immense riches* which He possesses as the Supreme Lord of heaven and earth. This assertion may seem contradictory at first sight; yet it is most true, and not at all difficult to understand. For, first of all, it goes without saying that in God there can be no desire for earthly goods; for, one can have a desire only for that which one does not possess, and God, as the Supreme Good and sum-total of all goods in Himself, possesses all

things in infinite fulness. As God, in His own infinite riches, therefore, is absolutely self-sufficient and independent of all earthly goods, it is plain that those circumstances of His birth which manifest in the clearest light His infinite riches, His independence of His creatures, and the absence of all desire of created things, are most befitting His dignity as God. Now, there is evidently nothing which displays more clearly this absolute self-sufficiency and independence of the Son of God than the abject poverty of His birth. For this poverty was voluntary, self-imposed. Could He not have been born amid abundance and luxury, if He only desired? This depended entirely on His free choice. But, of His own free will He renounced all riches and even the most necessary comforts this earth can bestow. Does He not thus plainly show that He had no desire for earthly goods? Now, I ask you, beloved brethren, would He have given the same evidence of His independence of all earthly goods if He had been born amid all comforts and luxuries? Certainly not. The utmost poverty, therefore, in which our blessed Lord was born, is most in keeping with the infinite greatness, dignity, and riches of the Divine Majesty and Supreme Good.

2. Jesus Christ as God could not have chosen more becoming circumstances on His appearance in this world, in the second place, because the *weakness*, which is manifested in His childhood, is best in harmony with His divine *omnipotence*, and displays this attribute in the clearest and most striking manner. By assuming the weakness and helplessness of childhood, He shows us to evidence that the work which He came to perform—viz., the attainment of the loftiest and most arduous end without the employment of any natural or human means—was one which could be realized only

by infinite power, therefore, that His work was a supernatural and divine work.

And, in fact, what was the object of His mission? It was, first of all, to be acknowledged and adored as God by men. Can you imagine a more arduous task? And what means did He employ for this end? No human means whatever. He purposely excluded all natural means, by choosing a state of utter helplessness. Is not earthly greatness—power, riches, and outward pomp—the ordinary means of influencing and securing the respect and awe of a generation of men that is sunk in worldliness and sensuality? If Jesus Christ, therefore, desired to use the means suggested by human prudence for the attainment of His end, He would have to be born of some powerful sovereign, in a grand palace, surrounded by all the wealth and pageant of a kingly court.

But where is the royal state of this new-born king? Enter in spirit, beloved brethren, into that lowly stall of Bethlehem. What do you behold there? On the one side, the dumb cattle fastened to the manger; on the other, the holy Virgin, poor, friendless, and unknown; and St. Joseph, the humble carpenter. Come nearer, and cast a reverent glance into that lowly manger; and behold a helpless babe, wrapt in swaddling clothes and laid on a handful of coarse straw; His tiny hands and His tender limbs trembling in the winter's cold! But in this weakness and littleness what power and greatness! Was it not this helpless little babe that pulled down the temples and idols of the false gods, and set up His sanctuaries and altars on their ruins? Is this not the child before whom the mighty of this world bow the knee in adoration, at whose feet kings and emperors lay down their crowns and sceptres? Was it not this child who peopled the cloisters and the deserts with His followers, for whose sake millions of every age and condition have joyfully shed their blood? Is it not to this tiny babe that to-day the whole Christian world prostrate themselves in adoration? What power, what omnipotence dwells in this helpless weakness!

Jesus Christ, the Son of God, could not, therefore, have chosen for His entrance into this world circumstances more suitable and more in keeping with His divine attributes; because His poverty and weakness manifest in the most striking manner the infinite riches and power of His Godhead. And is this not a palpable solution of all the difficulties of unbelievers, old and new? Are not His outward poverty and weakness the strongest evidence of His divinity? Is not, therefore, the mystery of the crib well calculated to strengthen our faith in the Godhead of Jesus Christ? How great, then, was the blindness of the Jews and Gentiles of old; how great is the folly of modern unbelievers, who reject the Godhead of Jesus Christ for that very reason which displays it in the most brilliant light; who make that a pretext of their unbelief which must confirm every thinking mind in the faith in the divinity of our blessed Lord! But as His lowliness and weakness were most befitting the greatness and omnipotence of the Son of God, so they were also—

II. BEST SUITED FOR THE END OF OUR REDEMPTION.

Jesus Christ, as the *Redeemer* of mankind, had a twofold task to perform. The first was to make *satisfaction* to the divine justice for our sins; the second, to encourage us by His *example* to walk upon the way to heaven. Now, it is manifest that the circumstances which Christ our Lord chose for His entrance into this world were the most suitable for the attainment of this twofold end and, consequently, for the work of Redemption, which He came to accomplish.

1. It was best suited for the *satisfaction* of the divine justice. For satisfaction can be rendered only by suffering, by self-denial; in short, by penal works. But, beloved brethren, can you imagine circumstances connected with greater sufferings, privations, humiliation, self-denial, than those of the birth of Jesus Christ?

Prominent in the line of sufferings are poverty, contempt, and bodily discomfort. In the birth of our Divine Saviour all these three kinds of suffering were represented in the highest degree. Here we see the utmost *poverty*. He is born in a stable; a manger is His cradle; and poor, homely swaddling clothes are His apparel. He suffered the profoundest *humiliation*. "He came into His own, and His own received Him not" (John i. 2). He was rejected in His own city of Bethlehem as an outcast from human society; He is forced to seek shelter among the beasts of the field, in a lowly and abandoned stable. His parents, though of royal descent, are humble and unknown; His companions are the irrational animals. He was subjected to the greatest imaginable bodily *discomfort*. Or, can we picture to ourselves a greater discomfort for this tender babe than to be born in a cold and damp cave, in the chill of the winter's night; to be laid in a rude, cold manger, on a bed of straw, with hardly enough clothing to cover His naked limbs, warmed only by the breath of the dumb cattle? And all this suffering, this abject poverty, this contempt and humiliation, all these keen privations were the more painful to Him, because, unlike other children, who have not consciousness and the use of reason, nor the full use of their senses, He had from the first moment of His human existence full consciousness, and a perfect use of His reason and of His senses. Has ever a human being come into this world amid such hardships and sufferings? The Redeemer of the world could not, therefore, have chosen for His birth circumstances better suited to give satisfaction to the divine justice for our sins.

2. Neither could He have chosen a course more efficacious to encourage us by His *example* manfully to walk on the way of our salvation. For, which is the true way to salvation? Is it not the way of self-denial and mortification? To attain to our salvation we must keep the commandments. But that is impossible unless we wage a continual warfare against our own passions; that is, unless we walk constantly on the way of self-abnegation and mortification. And what are the obstacles which we have to overcome in order to walk constantly on the path to heaven? They are the illusions and allurements of the world—of that world which is described by the Apostle as the threefold concupiscence: the concupiscence of the eyes, the concupiscence of the flesh, and the pride of life. It is this world which Christ has condemned, but to which our hearts are so immoderately attached, that blinds and befools us; which, by deceit and illusion, by force and guile, diverts us from the way of self-denial, the true path of salvation, and deludes us into the broad way of avarice, lust, and pride, and finally leads to destruction. But this is the world which Jesus Christ, Our Saviour, has conquered by the very circumstances of His nativity. He exposed its deceits, destroyed its illusions, overcame its tyranny, and robbed it of all its deceitful charms.

And these circumstances of His birth, beloved brethren, are not the work of chance, but the result of His free choice. If He was born in poverty, contempt, and suffering, He Himself so willed and pre-ordained it. He, therefore, chose privations, and humiliations, and hardships in preference to riches, honors, and enjoyments. These latter He renounced altogether; He despised them. But if He despised and condemned them, He despised and condemned also the attachment to them. Jesus Christ, therefore, by the circumstances of His birth displayed His utter contempt and expressed His solemn condemnation of all the riches, honors, and pleasures of this world, of all that this world can bestow, and pronounced the sentence of reprobation on the attachment to this world. He has condemned the world in the face of all mankind and declared it to be the mammon of iniquity, and the pomp and snares of the evil one. Christ, therefore, by the very manner of His birth, clearly revealed the character of this world before the eyes of all men, covered it with shame and confusion, and stript it of all its power and attractions. Has He not, therefore, in His very birth, disarmed the world, the greatest enemy of our salvation? Has He not thus smoothed for us the arduous way to heaven, and mightily encouraged us to walk manfully on the way of self-denial, the only way that leads to eternal life?

Now, beloved brethren, shall we, illumined as we are by the divine light which beams forth from the crib of our new-born Saviour, shall we further esteem those things which Christ, the Son of God, has despised and renounced? Can we still retain in our hearts an immoderate attachment to those things which the Eternal Wisdom condemns and declares to be the pomps and snares of Satan? Will you not, then, my dear friends, to-day, in the presence of the poverty, humiliations, and privations of the crib, make the firm resolve earnestly to combat your worldly desires.

especially those which are the chief cause of your sins? Or, will you still persevere in your attachment to that wicked world which Jesus Christ has exposed and branded as a vile and deceitful fraud? What answer does your heart give to this question? When you behold your God as an infant child in the crib; when you look at His tears, and see how He lovingly stretches out His tiny hands to you; does your heart then not urge you to show some gratitude for such excessive love? But if there is any gratitude in your hearts, can you, then, refuse to follow His example, and at least to banish from your hearts the spirit of this world, the spirit of avarice, pride, and lust, and to put on the true spirit of Jesus Christ, detachment from the mammon of this world, true humility, and self-denial? Make, then, to-day, beloved brethren, this generous resolution before the crib of your Infant Saviour, and lay it at the feet of the Divine Child. It will be to Him the most pleasing gift you can bestow, and for you it will be a pledge of that salvation which He came to bring into the world. Amen.

Feast of St. Peter, the First Martyr.

A MOST GLORIOUS AND FRUITFUL DEATH.

"And they stoned Stephen, invoking and saying: Lord Jesus, receive my spirit."—Acts vii. 58.

OF the life of St. Stephen, the first martyr, whose feast we celebrate to-day, little is known to us; and that little is confined to his ministry as the first deacon of the Church, and to his glorious martyrdom. We need not, however, regret this fact very much, as his death, which is minutely described in the Acts of the Apostles, is of such a character as to eclipse every feature of his life, and engross all our attention. We shall, therefore, to-day dwell chiefly on St. Stephen's illustrious martyrdom; and we shall see that his was—

1. *A most glorious death;*
2. *A most fruitful death.*

I. A GLORIOUS DEATH.

The illustrious death of our first martyr may be considered under two different aspects: *in itself*, and in its *circumstances*. Whichever view we take of it, we must pronounce it most glorious.

1. Considered *in itself*, the martyrdom of St. Stephen secures for him the first place among the most illustrious of the confessors of Christ. To convince ourselves of this fact we need only recall the history of his triumphant victory, as it is recorded in the pages of Holy Scripture. Stephen, whom the apostles had chosen as a man full of faith and the Holy Ghost, and ordained deacon of the Church, worked great signs and wonders to confirm the truth which he preached.

Therefore some, belonging to the Synagogue, arose and disputed with him. But as they could not withstand the truth and spirit that spoke in him, they sought false witnesses against him. Thus they stirred up the people, and the ancients, and the scribes against him ; and coming together, they brought him before the Council. Here St. Stephen, challenged by the high priests, addressed them ; and, after reminding them of the ingratitude with which their forefathers had returned the countless favors and wonders which God had worked in their behalf, he exclaimed : " You stiff-necked and uncircumcised in heart and ears, you always resist the Holy Ghost ; as your fathers did, so do you also. Which of the prophets have not your fathers persecuted ? And they have slain them who foretold of the coming of the Just One ; of whom you have been now the betrayers and murderers ; who have received the law by the disposition of angels, and have not kept it " (Acts vii. 51-53).

Now, hearing this, they were stung to the heart and gnashed their teeth against him, but he, full of the spirit of God, raised his eyes to heaven and saw the glory of God and Jesus standing at the right hand of God, and said : " Behold, I see the heavens opened and the Son of Man standing at the right hand of God." But they cried out with a loud voice, and stopped their ears, and rushed upon him with one accord ; and having cast him out of the city, they stoned him, while he prayed and said : " Lord Jesus, receive my spirit !" And falling upon his knees, he cried out with a loud voice: " Lord, lay not this sin to their charge !" And having said this, he fell asleep in the Lord.

Such, in a few words, is the history of the heroic martyrdom of St. Stephen. Considered in itself, then, in this unvarnished narrative, does it not entitle him to the first place among the most glorious of the martyrs of Christ, on account of the wonderful *patience and charity* displayed in it? So deeply were those two virtues rooted in his heart that neither the cruel torments of the most dreadful execution could shake his patience, nor the fiendish fury of his executioners extinguish his love. Therefore, while writhing under a shower of stones, he lifts up his eyes to heaven and prays for his enemies, saying: "Lord, lay not this sin to their charge!"

But, if we further consider the circumstances of St. Stephen's martyrdom, we shall behold it surrounded with additional glory.

2. The *circumstances* of the martyrdom of St. Stephen may be summarized in the one fact, that he was the protomartyr, as he is called, or the first martyr; for, although many, both in the Old and in the New Dispensation, had died for the faith before him, yet he is justly considered and styled the *first martyr.* In the New Testament we find only the Holy Innocents, who suffered death for the faith before him. But as these were incapable of personal merit, and were saved only by the baptism of blood, they cannot come into consideration where there is question of personal distinction and rank.

The case of the *martyrs of the Old Law* is similar. They, too, it is true, suffered for the faith. But for what faith? For a faith which, by its antiquity and by the number and prestige of its followers, had grown venerable and taken deep root in the hearts of God's people; a faith which numbered among its adherents the holy patriarchs and prophets, kings and leaders anointed by the hand of the Most High, and a long line of venerable pontiffs and priests. St. Stephen, on the other hand, suffered for a faith that was still in its infancy; a faith whose founder had been ignominiously put to the death of the cross; a faith whose preachers were twelve humble and ignorant fishermen; a faith whose followers, few in number, were of the poorest and lowest classes.

Besides, the faith for which the martyrs of the Old Testament died was the *faith of their childhood*, which they had imbibed at their mothers' breast; a faith to which birth, education, and customs had formed them. In short, all circumstances combined to impress upon them the loyalty to their faith: the veneration for their forefathers, who adhered to it; the reverence for their parents, from whom they had inherited it; the love for their countrymen, who professed it. St. Stephen, on the other hand, died for a faith in which he was neither born nor educated; for a new faith, contradicting the faith of his childhood which he accepted at a later stage of his life. The martyrs of the Old Law, therefore, who suffered under such encouraging circumstances, cannot be brought into comparison with St. Stephen, who lacked all those assuring conditions. With perfect right, then, in accord with all Christendom of all ages, we yield to St. Stephen the glorious palm of the protomartyr—the first martyr of Jesus Christ, not only in time, but also in rank and dignity. And from this circumstance, as from a common source, naturally spring all the other features which add to the glory of his martyrdom.

As the first martyr he could not cheer himself by the *example of others*. And we all know the power of example. How often has it not happened that through the example of one brave warrior, who fearlessly exposed himself to the onset of the enemy, an all but lost field was won? And what courage does it not infuse into the breast of the soldier, when at the storming of a fortress he sees his comrades bravely take their stand upon the rampart? It is much more arduous, says St. Chrysostom, to undertake an unknown journey, which no one has yet attempted, than one that has been explored by many travellers. Think of the difficulty of the first sea voyage—how the friends and relatives of those stout-hearted seamen stood upon the seashore and wept, raising their cries of anguish to heaven, when first they saw the feeble crafts breast the sea! It was the first voyage, a journey which no one had yet attempted. What made this voyage so arduous was the circumstance that the seafarers had as yet no example before them. Now you may judge for yourselves, beloved brethren, whether the martyrdom of St. Stephen, who had no precedent, was not incomparably more heroic, and therefore more glorious, than that of his followers upon the same blood-stained path.

Another circumstance which rendered the combat of St. Stephen more arduous was that he had to suffer his cruel martyrdom under bitter and apparently everlasting reproach. For, being the first and without precedent, he could not have known the glory with which the Church here on earth would surround her holy martyrs. How could he even suspect that the galling ignominy in which he died would be changed into universal honor and glory? Had he not, on the contrary, reason to fear that the reproach of his death would cling to his memory forever? But every one knows how much the hope of future honor contributes to constancy in suffering. How much more arduous, then, and how much more glorious on that account was the triumph of the first martyr than that of his successors, since he alone of all the confessors of Christ lacked this hope of the Church's honors!

A third circumstance, which is at the same time the most honorable and glorious of all in the case of the First Martyr, is that he was the first directly to follow Jesus Christ on the way of His passion, the first generously to compensate the death of his Saviour with his own death; and thus, as an humble deacon, he led the way for all, even for the apostles themselves. " He has shown the way to the apostles in his blissful and glorious death," says St. Maximus, " and thus he became the first in suffering, who was the last in rank; he became a teacher in his death, who was a disciple in order." How glorious, therefore, is the crown of St. Stephen, which is radiant with so many costly gems which grace no other martyr of the Old or New Testament!

Whether we view the martyrdom of St. Stephen in itself or in its circumstances, we find it to be one of surpassing glory. But if we further consider it we shall find it to be one of extraordinary fruits and blessings.

II. A FRUITFUL DEATH.

1. The first fruit of the martyrdom of St. Stephen, according to the teaching of the holy Fathers of the Church, was the *conversion of St. Paul.* In a sermon on St. Stephen St. Bernard says: " No less by the touch of St. Stephen's garments than by his prayers was St. Paul converted." St. Augustine is no less explicit in his teaching on this point. In a sermon on the same martyr he says: " In order that you may understand, my brethren, how powerful the intercession of St. Stephen is, let us return to that youth whose name was Saul, who watched the garments of the executioners while St. Stephen was being stoned. If St. Stephen had not so prayed, the Church would have no St. Paul. But Paul was raised up, because the prayer of St. Stephen, who was prostrated on the earth, was heard " (Serm.

ccclxxxii-4). St. Chrysostom is of the same opinion with St. Augustine. After narrating how St. Stephen had prayed for those who had stoned him, he continues: "Therefore the persecutor [Saul] has become a preacher of the Gospel; for he was immediately converted after St. Stephen had been stoned to death. The Lord heard his prayer, because Stephen was worthy to be heard, both on account of the future virtue of Paul and in virtue of his own prayer. 'Lord, lay not this sin to their charge,' prayed St. Stephen. And what followed? One source was closed, that of Stephen; and another was opened, from which flowed copious streams. For, no sooner was the mouth of Stephen closed in death than the trumpet of Paul resounded" (De ferendis reprehens. et de mut. nom. iii.) Finally, St. Fulgentius, in a sermon on St. Stephen, says: "In virtue of his love St. Stephen conquered the cruel persecutor Saul, his adversary on earth he changed into a friend and companion in heaven." Similar testimonies we find in the Fathers generally; but what we have quoted is sufficient to convince any one who is able to appreciate the testimony of those learned and saintly men that the conversion of the Apostle of the Gentiles was due to the prayers and sufferings of the First Martyr.

The same truth, which the Fathers derived from the narrative of the Scripture, has been revealed by God to some of his favored servants. Thus Cornelius à Lapide relates of St. Mary of Oignie that she once saw in a vision how St. Stephen at his death obtained from God the conversion of St. Paul, as a reward for his prayer, and how again he assisted St. Paul when the latter was beheaded for Christ, and bore his soul in triumph before the throne of God.

And how fruitful was the death of St. Stephen even

in this one respect—as the cause of Saul's conversion! What evil did it not prevent! Picture to yourselves, beloved brethren, all the evil which Saul would have caused, had he not been converted—Saul, a man of such ability for evil as well as good; a man of such wonderful energy; a man who, according to the testimony of Holy Scripture, breathed wrath and vengeance against the Church of God. And what good has it not brought about! What wonderful fruits has not St. Paul produced in the Church! He it was who, though, as he says himself, the last and the least of the apostles, worked more than all the rest; who brought the heathens into the bosom of the Church; who implanted the spirit of the Gospel in the hearts of all; who peopled heaven with myriads of saints. And all this is due, in the first place, to the dying prayer of St. Stephen. Is it not true, then, that the death of St. Stephen was a fruitful one?

2. But this was not the only fruit of the martyrdom of our saint. There are other fruits, no less striking and marvellous—*numerous miracles* and *a remarkable spread of Christianity among the heathen.* This is a fact based on historical documents.

St. Augustine, after relating in his famous work *De Civitate Dei* a large number of miracles tested by himself, which had been wrought by the intervention of St. Stephen, exclaims: "What shall I do? For, if I were to relate all the miraculous cures which have been wrought by the glorious St. Stephen in our own and the Calamese colony alone, many volumes would not suffice to contain them." With regard to the propagation of Christianity through the merits and intercession of St. Stephen, we have likewise the authority of St. Augustine; and the history of the conversion of Hungary, which was brought about by the wonderful interposition of the Protomartyr, is an eloquent testimony to the same fact.

From what I have said, beloved brethren, you have perceived how Almighty God has honored St. Stephen, and how eagerly He consequently desires that we should honor him. Now, in no way can we show greater honor to our great patron than by putting great confidence in him and imitating the example of his virtues; for by our confidence we actually profess our belief in his power and goodness, and by imitating him we profess a true admiration and just appreciation of his heroic sanctity.

Let us, then, with firm confidence have recourse to him in all our necessities. We may rely upon the promptness and power of his intercession. He who prayed for his bitterest enemies and obtained such favors for them, unasked, will not fail to come to the aid of his friends who invoke his intercession. But let us, above all, endeavor to imitate his virtues, particularly his charity and gentleness. If we do so, we may in all our wants, and especially at the hour of our death, count on his powerful assistance and hope once to crown our lives with a blissful death, confidently repeating with him: "Lord Jesus, receive my soul!" Amen.

New Year's Day.

GOOD USE OF TIME.

"He gave Himself for us that He might redeem us from all iniquity, and might cleanse to Himself a people acceptable, a pursuer of good works."—Tit. ii. 14.

GOD in His love and mercy has granted us to begin a new year. May this year be for all of you a happy and fruitful one! This is my sincere and heartfelt wish and prayer for each and all of you. But in order that my good wishes, which are certainly also your wishes, may be fulfilled, you must, according to the words of my text, make a good use of the time which Almighty God in His goodness has given you, for the performance of good works. Therefore, that I might not stop at good wishes alone, however sincere, but that I might contribute my share towards the fulfilment of those wishes, I have chosen for the subject of to-day's discourse *the good use of time*. And in reference to this important point I would put before you two chief considerations:

1. *The motives of making a good use of our time;*
2. *The practical manner of improving our time.*

I. MOTIVES.

The chief motive which should impel us to make a good use of our time is evidently its *value*. Now, its value may be determined by its usefulness, its duration, and the task which we are called to accomplish within its limits. Considering time under these three aspects, we shall find that its usefulness is exceedingly great,

Good Use of Time. 33

that its duration is short and uncertain, and that the work to be achieved within its compass is of the greatest moment.

1. *Usefulness.* The utility of time is exceedingly great, because without time the greatest *benefits of God would be fruitless* for us. God's favors are only then of use to us when we avail ourselves of them to gather from them the fruits of salvation. For what purpose does God bestow His blessings upon us? Is it not that we may use them for our sanctification, for the promotion of the work of our salvation? But for this use of God's blessings time is necessary. Without time, therefore, all God's favors would be useless for us: the Incarnation of the Son of God; His life, passion, and death; His Church, His sacraments, His doctrine; His merits, satisfactions, and graces—all would be fruitless. Since this is the case, since without time all the graces and blessings of God would be useless and utterly lost for us, is not the value of time infinitely great—so great and important, as far as we are concerned, as are the work of our Redemption and all the numberless graces which God has bestowed on us for our salvation? Do we not see this in the sad instance of the fallen angels? What is it that makes their lot infinitely more miserable than that of our first parents? It is the fact that Almighty God in His infinite justice gave them no time for conversion and penance. Oh, how happy would those fallen spirits not be if God had given them only one moment for repentance! But for them time was no more! And such a treasure, of such infinite value as time is, we should recklessly squander, or allow to go unused!

But time is, moreover, exceedingly valuable, because *it enables us daily to acquire new treasures* for heaven. According to the unanimous teaching of the Fathers and divines of the Church, we may at every moment which we employ for the honor of God or for the benefit of our neighbor obtain new graces. But every new grace which we obtain procures for us a higher degree of glory in heaven, which infinitely surpasses all the treasures of earth. The saints of God are great and happy only in as far as they have used their time here below to accumulate grace and merit. What would they be now if they had not made a better use of their time than we do? They would be just on the same level with us, and the Church would be silent of their good works and merits.

Time is, therefore, the most valuable good of earth, because it alone enables us to heap up treasures of incorruptible wealth for eternity, and because without time the greatest favors of God would be of no avail for us. Should we not, therefore, endeavor with all earnestness to use our time profitably? But the value of time depends not only on its usefulness, but also on its brief duration.

2. *Shortness.* When I say that time is short, I do not speak of that period of your lives which is already past. I do not say that your life has been short, and that you have had thus far little time to attend to the business of your salvation. God may have already given you many years, and have incessantly urged you to employ them in the work of your salvation. If you have followed His holy inspirations, and earnestly labored in the work of your salvation, you have already accumulated no small treasure against the day of account. If you have not, your time has been lost. Neither do I speak of the future, nor imply that you have but a short time to live, for God alone, who is master of life and death, knows what time He has allotted for you in this world. No, beloved brethren;

I here speak of the time of which alone you can dispose; and that is only *the present*. For, of the future, which does not yet exist, you can no more dispose than you can of the past, which no longer exists. Both are alike beyond your reach.

But the *present time is exceedingly short*, unspeakably short. Its duration is not even of a second; it is only the instant. Hardly has it begun when it is past and gone—gone forever, never to be recalled, never to be used again. Now, what follows from this? It follows that it should be our earnest endeavor to use the present moment, because, otherwise, fleeting as it is, it will escape our grasp, pass us unused, and be lost in the ocean of the past. Is this not really the case, beloved brethren? Have you not often made this sad experience in your past lives? How many days, and weeks, and months, and years have you lost, because you have run recklessly through the routine of life, from day to day, unconcerned about the use of time, thinking only how to while it away in all manner of useless pastimes and even sinful amusements!

That is all very true, some one will say; but it is not so bad after all; we can easily make up for lost time; we have a hopeful *future* before us. To this I answer, first of all, that, even in the case that you could count on the future, you should nevertheless endeavor with all care to improve the present; for, the future, be it ever so long, *will pass rapidly*, and if we fail to turn the present to good account we run the risk at the end of our lives to be found with empty hands. For, the future will for most of us pass quicker than the past, as the greater number of us have run more than the half of life's course. And how quickly have not the past years of your life glided away! Does it not seem to you almost like a dream that has vanished?

Even so, if not more quickly, the future will pass away, and before we are aware death will stand at our door and knock. Do not forget, beloved brethren, death is on his way and keeps pace with the fleeting years. May it not perhaps surprise us, and find us unprepared? Should we not, then, though we could count on a long future, yet set earnestly to work and improve the present moment?

But how much more is it necessary for us to do so since the future is altogether *uncertain*, and we can by no means rely upon it? The present, which is so short and fleeting, is, after all, the only time we can dispose of; and hence it is that Almighty God continually urges us to hasten, and not to allow ourselves to be delayed by the vain things of this world, but to strive with all earnestness after things eternal. That is the reason why the Apostle repeatedly admonishes us that time is short. Yes, beloved brethren, time is short, and before you are aware you will stand at the end of your earthly career. That is also the reason why the evil one so incessantly labors to ensnare you and drag you to your ruin, because he knows well that time is short. And yet, short as is the time allotted us, the task which we have to perform within its narrow limits is most important and arduous.

3. *The task to be accomplished.* What is the task of this life? It is the *working of our salvation*. Here the soul itself, which is of more value than the whole visible universe, is at stake. Our own soul, that is, our own self is at stake. Eternity is at stake—an eternity of weal or woe! Is not, therefore, our task a most *important* one?

And how *arduous* is the task! For, to accomplish this task and to save our souls, we must make satisfaction to the divine justice for our sins, that God may pardon the guilt and remit the eternal punishment due to them. We must procure a fund of merit large enough to purchase eternal happiness, an everlasting crown, a kingdom without end—an inheritance that has cost the Son of God three and thirty years of privations and hardships, yea, even His life and the last drop of His precious blood. And to accomplish all this we have only the present moment at our disposal. How solicitous should we be, then, to use every moment while it is yet within our grasp!

Or, what think you, beloved brethren, if a man is involved in a *law-suit*, in which his honor, his fortune, and his life are at stake, and has to defend himself personally, and knows not the day when the trial will come off, will he fail to be prepared to meet his accusers? Will he recklessly abandon himself to idleness, and squander his valuable time? If he did so, would you not pronounce him guilty of the greatest folly? But are not all of us involved, I will not say in a similar law-suit, but in a much more dangerous one—in a suit in which there is question, not of our temporal property and earthly life, but of the eternal destiny of our souls? And must not each one of us appear in the defence of his own cause? And is not the day of the awful trial totally unknown to us? May we not be called to account at any moment?

And *how do we behave* in this uncertainty? Are there not many amongst us who, instead of using their precious time to prepare themselves against the day of account, think only of amassing money and procuring comfortable and honorable circumstances for themselves and their families? "Thou fool," says our blessed Lord, "this night do they require thy soul of thee; and whose shall those things be which thou hast provided?" (Luke xii. 20.) Yea, this very night, beloved brethren, your eternal lot may be cast, while all your thoughts are engrossed in the concerns of this world! O unspeakable blindness! The more I reflect upon it the more inconceivable it becomes to me. For, how is it possible that Christians who believe in an eternity; who know that in a short time they are to be landed upon its shores, to be eternally happy or eternally miserable; who know that the world with all its vanities is like smoke that vanishes, and that all earthly things can contribute nothing, absolutely nothing, to their true happiness—how is it possible that they entirely lose sight of eternity, think only of this present life, speak only of the goods of earth, and consider them alone worthy of their love and esteem? O unhappy souls who are burning in hell's flames at this moment, what say you of this incomprehensible blindness? Oh, how eagerly would you now, if you could, use that time which so many Christians so recklessly squander!

But what I have said suffices to convince you of the necessity of making a proper use of the time that God has given us for the work of our salvation; let us now, further, consider how we should use it.

II. MANNER.

From the great stress which I have laid on the use of the present moment you will probably expect from me only a few hints on the manner of profitably using the *present*. I shall, however, go farther, and show that you can also turn to account the lost time of the past, and even the future, which does not yet exist, and perhaps never shall exist for you.

1. *The past.* To begin with the past, it is already gone, and yet it remains to some extent. For, its memory still lives within us, and that is enough to make

it, in some way, fruitful for us. In fact, the fruits which the remembrance of ill-spent time produces in a sincerely contrite soul are so great that they often outweigh all former losses.

The first and chief fruit of the remembrance of the past is a true and hearty *sorrow* for our sins. This disposition of the soul is so pleasing to Almighty God that it moves Him, not only to extend to us His friendship anew, but also to lavish His choicest graces upon us. Another fruit of inestimable value is the *knowledge of ourselves*—a knowledge of our own weakness and helplessness, whence originates true humility, which is the foundation and at the same time the ornament of all Christian virtues. A third no less valuable fruit is the deep sense of our indebtedness to the infinite goodness and *mercy of God*, which, notwithstanding our manifold and grave offences, has borne with us so long and spared us so lovingly. What an incentive to love God with our whole heart and to consecrate ourselves entirely to His service! *Patience* in sufferings is also a precious fruit of the remembrance of the past. For we can hardly seriously think of our past sins without awaking within us the consciousness that we owe to God's justice satisfaction for them, and that the sufferings of this life afford us the best opportunity of discharging this debt to God. Lastly, the remembrance of the past is well calculated to arouse in us great *zeal* and fervor in the performance of good works, in order to make up for the neglect of the past. You see, then, beloved brethren, that even from the culpable neglect and sinful errors of the past we may gather a plentiful harvest of good fruits.

2. *The present.* With regard to the good use of the present, be not afraid that I shall require of you to spend all your time in prayer and works of piety. No,

beloved brethren; for that is by no means necessary, nor is it even possible. We cannot dispense with the duty of providing for the necessaries of this life and managing the various affairs connected with this duty. It is sufficient if in the management of our temporal affairs we do not exclude or neglect the ordinary prayers and practices of piety of a good Christian.

But, in order that the time which you devote to your secular business may not be fruitless for the next life, it is necessary to be in the *state of grace* and to sanctify your actions with a *good intention*, as I have had more than once occasion to impress upon you. If you perform your daily works, not from the impulse of avarice, or from other natural motives, but for the honor and glory of God, or from sense of duty toward Him, they change their nature and become supernatural. Begin the day, then, with a good intention and renew the same, from time to time, during the course of the day. That is the secret which enables us to turn all things that we touch in this world into gold and precious stones, to add to the splendor of our eternal crown. And that is all that is necessary for the fruitful use of the present.

3. *The future.* But how can we profitably use the future, which does not yet exist, and perhaps never will exist for us? The fruitful use of the future depends altogether on the state in which we exist—whether in the state of sin, or in the state of grace.

Now, as regards *the sinner*, if he is only of good will, he may still, in a short time, obtain the merits of a long life spent in the service of God. For this end he needs only arise *at once* from the state of sin, reconcile himself at once with God by a good confession, and begin without delay manfully to serve God with his whole heart. Thus he shows the good will, if possible, to serve God faithfully for a long life. For, as he who delays his conversion to God from day to day, from week to week, and from year to year, manifestly declares his will to begin to serve God as late as possible, and to serve Him as short a time as possible, so he who immediately and without any delay begins to serve God proves that it is his will to serve Him as long as possible. But Almighty God in His goodness takes the will for the deed. Though such a fervent, penitent sinner, therefore, may have but a short time to live, yet he can, at the end of his short life, have accumulated the merits of a life of many years spent in the service of God. And is it such a hard task for the sinner at once to make a good confession, and to begin without delay to serve God?

But, with regard to *the just*, who have already for a considerable time served God—and to this class, I have reason to hope, most of you belong—to make a proper use of the future, they must, above all, endeavor to give a *good example* to their neighbors. For, as bad example draws our neighbor into sin, and easily spreads evil, and continues indefinitely to produce its evil fruits, so good example is productive of good fruits and continues to diffuse its sweet odor and its blessings long after the giver has sunk into his grave. But, though he is no more, his work remains, and there is no doubt that its merits belong to him. Do you not see, then, that by your good example you turn the future to good account, and multiply your merits? May you not thus easily make a profitable use of the future?

And you, Christian parents, particularly, have a most effectual means of improving the future and making it fruitful. This means is *the education of your children*. Faithfully employ this means,—which, for the rest, is your bounden duty—and you shall have a share in the good works of your children and children's children. You shall continue for generations after generations by their lips to praise and magnify God, and by their Christian lives and virtues to honor and serve Him. Thus, beloved brethren, we can add to the short and evil days of this life, and, to a certain extent, turn all futurity to our advantage.

Let us, then, my dear friends, one and all set earnestly to work and make a good use of the valuable time that God has given us for the work of our salvation. Then the good wishes for the new year which I expressed to you in the beginning will be realized. You will soon make up for what you have lost by your neglect in the past; you will in a short time amass a large treasure of merits for the next life, and secure true happiness in this life; and when your last hour shall come, you will not appear with empty hands, but will joyfully come before the tribunal of God, bearing the sheaves of a rich harvest. Amen.

Feast of the Epiphany.

VOCATION TO THE FAITH.

"Arise, be enlightened, O Jerusalem; for thy light is come, and the glory of the Lord is risen upon thee."—Is. lx: 1.

TO-DAY, beloved brethren, we commemorate an occasion which should be doubly dear to us—the Epiphany, or manifestation of Our Lord—the day on which the royal sages of the East, the firstlings of the heathen nations, acknowledged Christ Our Lord in the crib, as the king of nations, as true God and true man. It is, then, the origin of our faith and the source of our hope that we celebrate to-day; and certainly, if ever, to-day our hearts should glow with love and gratitude to Our Lord and Redeemer. In order to awake this sense of love and gratitude, therefore, let us consider the manner in which the heathen nations, and with them we ourselves, have been called to the faith; and, following the words of the epistle of the day let us see how through Christ, His Son, God called the apostles, and through the apostles all nations, into the bosom of His Church, into the true faith; in other words, let us consider—

1. *The vocation of the apostles;*
2. *The vocation of the nations through the apostles.*

I. VOCATION OF THE APOSTLES.

1. The epistle of to-day, which is taken from the prophet Isaias, begins with the words: "*Surge, Jerusalem.*" Arise, Jerusalem! What is here meant by

Jerusalem? Whom does the prophet address? Doubtless those few faithful Jews who followed Christ, and among them the first *the apostles*. Before the coming of Christ the name of Jerusalem designated the whole Jewish nation, as all the Jews belonged to the chosen people of God; but after they had denied our blessed Lord before Pilate and expressed their adherence to the Roman emperor in preference to the Son of God made man, God also denied and abandoned them, and the prophecy of Daniel was fulfilled: "The people that shall deny Him shall not be His" (Dan. ix. 26). Hence you see that only those who professed the faith of the patriarchs and prophets and adhered to Jesus Christ, whom they had foretold, deserved to be called by the name of the holy and chosen city of Jerusalem; and to these belong, in the first instance, the apostles; but, in the second place, also those who through them embraced the true faith of Christ.

Let us, then, rejoice, beloved brethren, that we, too, belong to the inhabitants of the Holy City, and let us not be alarmed or misled if we see that many fall off from the faith and Church of Christ. For, as then so many Scribes and Pharisees, so many of the priests and people, apostatized, while the true Jerusalem did not perish, but continued to exist in the few faithful followers of Christ; so now, how great soever may be the number of apostates, the Church, the true Jerusalem, stands, and will continue to stand unto the end of the world. For the Church is that Jerusalem whose foundations are on the holy mountains. She stands on the unshaken rock to which Christ has said: "Thou art Peter, and on this rock I will build My Church" (Matt. xvi. 18).

2. The words of the prophet are, therefore, in the first instance, directed to the apostles. And what is

the divine message addressed to them in this place? "*Surge,*" Arise! He addresses them as a messenger would address one who is pining in the squalid dungeon of a prison, to whom he brings the joyous message of freedom: rejoice, my friend, arise; the days of thy confinement are past and gone; the hour of thy release is at hand. The import of the message, therefore, is this: Addressing himself to the apostles, as I have said, the prophet says: I bring you tidings of great joy. You shall arise from the slavery and degradation of sin to the highest grade of sanctity; you shall be exalted from the lowly and contemptible estate of poor fishermen to the dignity of apostles of the Messias; you shall be delivered from the slavery of the law and the spirit of fear, and raised to the freedom and dignity of the children of God, to be ruled by the spirit of hope and love. And in this consisted the exaltation of the apostles. They were raised to the highest degree of sanctity, to the apostolate of the whole world, and inspired with the unwavering hope of the inheritance of God's eternal kingdom.

But, *how* were the apostles promoted to this dignity? Did God first enrich them with money and the goods of this world? By no means; for, money and other earthly treasures cannot confer true dignity, true greatness. To be great it is not necessary to be free from poverty; but he who is truly great cannot be the slave of poverty. There are poor people who continually complain, murmur against the rich, and try all means, lawful and unlawful, to enrich themselves. These are slaves of poverty and the most wretched of men. They, too, bear their cross; but it is not the cross of Christ; it is the cross of the impenitent thief. Such poor are beggars in body and spirit, and make themselves miserable in this life and in the life to come.

But there are other poor people, who possess nothing, and desire to possess nothing, well knowing that they have a rich Father in heaven, who will provide for His children, and that an eternal inheritance is in store for them. These are not slaves of poverty; they triumph over poverty, because they avail themselves of it as a means to secure the imperishable treasures of heaven. It is not earthly goods, therefore, which renders a man truly great and honorable, but heroic, Christian virtue. This is the way by which the apostles arrived at their greatness. God bestowed on them, not great wealth, but great love. He did not exempt them from suffering, but taught them to suffer willingly and joyfully. He gave them greatness of soul and abundance of supernatural grace; and fitted out with these supernatural resources, they despised and trod under foot this world with all its pomp and pleasures. Poor despised fishermen though they were, Almighty God gave them a nobility of heart and soul that raised them high over the great and mighty of this world. In this consisted their exaltation. This is what is contained in the word of the prophet, "*Surge*," arise!

3. But the prophet adds: "*Illuminare*," be enlightened. What is the meaning of this word? As the apostles were raised from the lowly estate of poor fishermen to a rank of true nobility, so they were also brought out of the darkness of ignorance into the radiant light of true wisdom—of poor, simple, and ignorant men they were by divine inspiration made the greatest and wisest of theologians, the princes of doctors in the Church of God. And whence comes this light upon the apostles? The prophet tells us: "Thy light is come, and the glory of the Lord is upon thee." This light is Christ Himself, the Eternal Wisdom, the splendor and glory of the Father. Therefore the prophet adds:

"The Lord shall arise upon thee, and His glory shall be seen upon thee." Therefore Christ says of Himself: "I am the Light of the world" (John viii. 12). He is, therefore, the Light that cometh to illumine the Holy City, to illumine the apostles, and through them to enlighten us—the true Light, "that enlighteneth every man that cometh into this world." He is the Light by His divine nature; He is the Light by His humanity. Before becoming man He could not be our Light, because as God we could not see Him. But since He clothed Himself with our nature, and thus veiled, as it were, His divine splendor, He who was the Light of the blessed angels became also our Light, according to the words of the Holy Ghost, "And all flesh shall see the salvation of God" (Luke iii. 6).

4. After thus announcing the Light that was to enlighten the apostles and their followers, the prophet goes on to enlarge on the *greatness of this divine favor*. "Behold," he says, "darkness shall cover the earth, and a mist the people; but the Lord shall arise upon thee, and His glory shall be seen upon thee." Behold, he exclaims, all around darkness reigns, the darkness of heathenism and idolatry. All have in the darkness of sin and error abandoned the way of salvation, and hasten to their eternal destruction. But the Sun of justice and truth shall arise and shine over you, and you shall see the glory of God, that is, Jesus Christ, who is the glory of the Eternal Father, acknowledge and confess Him, and join Him as His chosen followers. Behold the greatness of this privilege conferred on the apostles. In the world there are so many great, wise, rich, and powerful men; but, in preference to all these, God has chosen poor, lowly fishermen to communicate His Spirit to them, to make them princes and rulers of His kingdom. "Behold, darkness shall cover the

earth, and a mist the people; but the Lord shall arise upon thee, and His glory shall be seen upon thee." Beloved brethren, would it not be a great privilege, an extraordinary favor, if, while the whole surrounding country is encompassed with dense darkness, the sun arose in all his glory over our city, and we alone beheld the glory of the heavens and basked in the serenest light? Similar, but incomparably greater, was the privilege and favor conferred by God on the apostles, who, while the whole world was buried in the profoundest gloom of ignorance, had a perfect knowledge of the true God, and walked in the rays of the Sun of justice.

But, as I have said, this favor was not destined for the apostles alone; through them it was to be communicated to all the nations of the earth.

II. THE VOCATION OF THE NATIONS.

All that appertains to the vocation of the heathen nations through the ministry of the apostles—the mission of the apostles to the nations, their marvellous success, the order in which they were to perform their task—is contained in the remaining portion of the epistle of to-day.

1. With regard to the *mission* of the apostles the prophet says: "The Gentiles shall walk in thy light, and kings in the brightness of thy rising," viz., the nations shall walk in the light of the apostles, and kings in the splendor with which they are enlightened; for we must not forget that by the city of Jerusalem the prophet understands the primitive Church of Christ, and chiefly the apostles, who mainly constituted it. Accordingly, the God-given mission of the apostles was to impart to others that light and grace which they themselves had received. They were destined

not only to be enlightened themselves, but to shed their light upon all nations. As a crystal which is illuminated by the rays of the sun not only becomes luminous itself like the sun, but also enlightens the surrounding objects, so the apostles were called to illumine others with the light wherewith they themselves were enlightened. Kings and nations were destined to walk in their light. That was the mission of the apostles to the nations, to reflect upon them the light of the Sun of justice.

2. That they were, also, destined *successfully to accomplish* this task, the prophet, likewise, expressly informs us, when he says: " Lift up thy eyes round about, and see ; all these are gathered together, they are come to thee ; thy sons shall come from afar, and thy daughters shall rise up at thy side. Then shalt thou see, and abound, and thy heart shall wonder and be enlarged, when the multitude of the sea shall be converted to thee, and the strength of the Gentiles come to thee. . . . " And have not these prophetic words been literally fulfilled ? Is not the propagation of the Church over the whole world a conspicuous fact?

But why does the prophet, after stating that " the nations shall walk in the light " of the Church, add these words: " And kings in the brightness of thy rising." Are these words not superfluous? Do not the kings also belong to the nations? Certainly ; but the prophet wished also to intimate the order in which the apostles were to fulfil their mission.

3. And what is this *order?* Almighty God in His infinite wisdom wished that first the poor and simple people, and then, in the second place, the rich and great and powerful of this world should be illumined by the light of faith. And why did He wish this ? For the following very important reasons :

a. In order that the conversion of the world might not be attributed to the influence of kings, or of the rich and powerful of this world, or to any natural causes, but only to the supernatural *power of God.* It was to become patent to all that faith is a divine gift, and that the kingdom of Satan was destroyed, not by the power of men, but by the omnipotence of God.

b. It was the intention of God that the first Christians, who were to be the foundation of the Church, should be conspicuous for their *heroic virtues.* But, if kings and princes and the powerful of the earth had first embraced Christianity, their subjects would not have had occasion to practise this heroism; for then they would not have had to make any great sacrifice to become Christians. They would have had to suffer no reproaches, nor persecution; much less would they have been called upon to shed their blood for their faith. In short, they would not have been tested in the furnace of tribulation and proved as good and faithful Christians. If, then, the first Christians have given such a marvellous proof of their constancy, this is owing chiefly to the fact that not the great and powerful of this world, but the poor, simple and lowly were first called to Christianity.

c. Moreover, by this order God wished to administer to us a practical lesson that *we should not envy the rich* and powerful of this world on account of their wealth, honors, and dignities. For, by the very fact that He called the poor and lowly—fishermen, shepherds, workmen—before the rich and mighty of the world, He proved to evidence that not those who are first in the eyes of the world are, in like manner, first in His eyes; but that, on the contrary, in many instances those who are first among men are the last with God.

d. The fourth and last reason is because the poor and lowly are, as a rule, *better disposed* to receive the good seed of the word of God, and, therefore, yield more abundant fruit than the great ones of the world. For the heart of the rich man, as our blessed Lord Himself says (Matt. xiii. 22), often resembles a field which is overgrown with thorns and thistles. For the rest, since the end of the Gospel of Jesus Christ is none other than to detach men from the goods of this world and to unite them with God, it is manifest that the object of the Gospel is more easily obtained with the poor and humble than with the rich and powerful.

However, although the latter are hard to convert to God, yet the Gospel of Christ has the power to convert even them. We have a sure proof of this fact in the instance of the Magi from the East, who were not only wise men, as their name indicates, but also, according to ancient tradition, powerful and wealthy kings. Yet, notwithstanding all their wealth, power, and greatness, they did not disdain to seek the new-born Child in the crib, to bow to Him in adoration and offer their costly gifts to Him, and thus by their example to show the way of salvation and perfection to all men. If, then, beloved brethren, we would seek the divine Child with an upright and simple heart, we have only to do as they did.

First of all we must leave our country and our friends as they did, that is, we must strip ourselves of the immoderate attachment to places, persons, and objects. We must, secondly, like them, pay no attention to the talk of men, but follow the light of the star, i. e., the teaching of our holy faith. Listen not, beloved brethren, to the advice of those who speak only the language of flesh and blood; but listen to the voice of God in your hearts, and the voice of the Church, who instructs you by the lips of her priests. Listen, not to the voice of Herod, but to the voice of the angel. Moreover, be not scandalized at the poverty and lowliness of the crib, but admire the abyss of God's love and condescension, who, though infinitely rich, became poor to enrich us. Lastly, come not to the crib of your Infant Saviour empty-handed, but like the royal sages of the East, bring the costliest gifts you can procure—gold, frankincense, and myrrh—the gold of the love of God, the incense of prayer, and the myrrh of mortification and self-denial. Almighty God, who has in His liberality given Himself entirely for us, wishes to have nothing less than our whole heart and our whole being in turn. Having made this oblation, we shall hear the voice of the angel, admonishing us not to return to Herod; and we shall return, like those holy sages, another way to our country—the sure way that leads to eternal life. Amen.

Feast of the Most Holy Name of Jesus.

SANCTITY AND POWER OF THE HOLY NAME.

"In the name of Jesus every knee should bow of those that are in heaven, on earth, and under the earth."—Phil. ii. 10.

TO-DAY we celebrate the feast of the most Holy Name of Jesus. Our blessed Saviour received His most adorable name on the day of the Circumcision, which is commemorated on New Year's day; but, as on that festival the mystery of the circumcision forms the chief object of the Church's veneration, and the Holy Name is, as it were, thrown into the background, the Church has set apart a special day in honor of the adorable Name of Jesus. It is the second Sunday after Epiphany, which falls on to-day. As may be seen from the Office and Mass of the feast, the intention of the Church is to promote in the faithful the devotion to the Holy Name; and it is my duty on the present occasion to contribute my part towards the same end. For this purpose I wish to put before you two causes which are well fitted to inspire us with a great devotion to the Holy Name of Jesus.

The Name of Jesus is, in the first place, most holy, and consequently it is our duty to honor it; the Name of Jesus is, in the second place, most powerful, and therefore we should confidently invoke it. But the devotion to the Holy Name, like every other devotion, consists in honor and invocation. It will, therefore, be my object to show you—

1. *The sanctity of the Holy Name;*
2. *The power of the Holy Name.*

Feast of the Most Holy Name of Jesus.

I. THE SANCTITY OF THE HOLY NAME.

The Name of Jesus is holy particularly in three respects, in its origin, in the person of Him that bears it, and in its signification.

1. *Origin.* The author of this adorable name is God Himself. For it was God who chose it for His only-begotten Son; and it was also God that caused it to be announced as the name of the coming Saviour. Our blessed Lord has received His name, therefore, not as other children do, from His parents or His friends; no, not even from an angel, but from God Himself, His eternal Father. With the Incarnation of His Son the heavenly Father had decreed from all eternity that His name should be called Jesus, according to the words of Ecclesiasticus (xv. 6), who says that among other gifts the Eternal Wisdom should cause Him to inherit an everlasting name.

But Almighty God Himself not only chose this Holy Name as the most suitable for the Word made flesh, He also *prefigured and foretold* it in the Old Testament as one of the grand facts connected with the work of our Redemption. He so ordained in His providence that two of those who, in a most especial way, were figures of the coming Saviour, bore that name, Josue, or Jesus, the Son of Nun, who led the chosen people into the promised land; and Jesus, the son of Josedec, who led back the people from the captivity of Babylon. To these two leaders, who were conspicuous types of the Messias, He disposed that the name of Jesus should be given. And when the fulness of time had come, He caused this Holy Name to be revealed, not by the mouth of man, but by an angel of the highest rank, by the archangel St. Gabriel. How holy is, therefore, the origin of this most adorable Name, which God has not only decreed from all eternity, but also prefigured in time, and announced to man by the lips of one of the highest of His heavenly spirits!

2. But the Name of Jesus has further been sanctified by the infinite *holiness of Him that bears it*. For, what makes a name venerable and holy above all other things is the reverence, love, and gratitude due to the person of the bearer. Therefore we hold in veneration the names of those who have attained to high honors and have distinguished themselves by great virtues and noble deeds; hence children venerate the names of their parents; hence the world celebrates the names of its prominent men; and for the same reason we Catholics honor the names of the saints. But what are our parents, what are the great personages of history, what are even the saints of God, if we compare them with our Divine Saviour, who as man is the greatest and holiest of all men, who as God is the author of all greatness and holiness? Is not, therefore, the Name of Jesus infinitely holier and more venerable than all other names, a name which is above every name?

3. The Name of Jesus is also infinitely holy in its *signification*. What an infinite treasure of significance is included in this Holy Name! This adorable Name comprises all that the Son of God has done to merit to be so called. For we must not forget, beloved brethren, that Jesus Christ, according to the teaching of the Apostle, has merited this name. "He hath debased Himself," says the Apostle, "He hath humbled himself, becoming obedient unto death, even to the death of the cross. For which cause God also hath exalted Him, and given Him a name which is above all names" (Phil. ii. 7, 8, 9). What was, then, the price at which Jesus Christ purchased His most adorable Name?

The title of Creator cost Him but one word: "*Fiat*, let it be made;" and the whole universe from its nothingness sprang into existence. The name of Creator therefore, great as it is, expresses but this one act of His all-powerful will. But the Holy Name of Jesus cost Him sacrifices which in number, greatness, and significance surpass all understanding. To make this Name of Jesus, or Saviour and Redeemer (for this is the meaning of the word), a truth, not a mere title, to merit this Holy Name, the Son of God had to submit Himself to an infinite humiliation. He had to become man; the infinite Creator had to put on the finite nature of His creature; for, had He not become man, He could not have suffered for us, He could not have satisfied the infinite justice of God for us, He could not have become our Redeemer. He had to submit to a life of privations, toils, and sorrows. Else He could not have been our leader, our example, nor, consequently, our Redeemer. Finally, He had to consummate His sacrifice by laying down His life amid the most bitter torments, by the most cruel death. For without passing through the gates of death He could not have opened for us the gates of heaven. The Holy Name which He bears has, therefore, cost Him the self-abasement of His Incarnation, the self-abnegation of His life on earth, the pangs and sufferings of His passion and death. All this was necessary, according to the divine dispensation, to realize the meaning of the Holy Name. The Holy Name contains, therefore, summarized in one word, all the mysteries of the life, passion, and death of our Divine Lord. The adorable Name of Jesus, therefore, is in itself, as it were, a whole Gospel. Can we say more of the sanctity of this Holy Name? How true are, then, the words of the Prince of the Apostles, when he says of this Holy Name: " Neither is there salvation in any other. For there is no other name under heaven given to men, whereby we must be saved " (Acts iv. 12).

Therefore, beloved brethren, honor the Holy Name of Jesus, which in its origin, in its bearer, and in its import is of such infinite sanctity. Honor it with your hearts and with your lips, taking the greatest care not to pronounce it thoughtlessly or rashly, but always with the greatest reverence. But honor this adorable Name also in your actions, by doing all things in the Name of Jesus. In the Name of Jesus arise from sleep and begin the day; in the Name of Jesus perform your daily actions; in the Name of Jesus retire to rest. This is what the Apostle admonishes us to do, when he says: " All whatsoever you do in word or in work, all things do ye in the Name of the Lord Jesus Christ" (Col. iii. 17).

But to the Holy Name of Jesus we owe, not only honor and reverence, but also great confidence; for it is not only the holiest, but also the most powerful of all names

II. POWER OF THE HOLY NAME.

If the Name of Jesus is so holy, as you have just seen, it cannot but be, at the same time, most powerful. For all that is holy has a powerful efficacy with Almighty God. Prayer is holy; and therefore it is all-powerful with God. The sacraments are holy; hence the wonderful graces which they effect in the soul. And how many miracles has God not worked at the intervention of the name of His holy Mother and of the saints, at the sign of the cross, or even at the sprinkling of a little holy water? What must not, accordingly, be the power of the most Holy Name of Jesus! But the efficacy which is inherent in this adorable Name is best manifested in the *effects* which it has produced and still continues to produce.

1. In the *past* this Holy Name has worked the greatest

of all miracles, *the conversion of the world* from heathenism to Christianity. This complex miracle comprises two subordinate miracles, each of which again is made up of numberless miracles.

The first of these two great miracles is the conversion of the world *from paganism*, the destruction of the realm of darkness, the extermination of idolatry. The apostles went forth on their mission without patronage or influence, without money or means, without human learning or knowledge, without forces or arms, equipped only with the most Holy Name of Jesus. And behold, the prince of this world is thrust from his throne; the spirits of darkness are driven in fear and trembling from their strongholds; the oracles of the heathen soothsayers are hushed; the altars and idols of the gods, which covered the whole earth, crumble to dust, the realm of darkness is demolished to its very foundations!

But the second miracle is greater than the first—the conversion of the world *to Christianity*, that is, the building up of the kingdom of God on the ruins of the kingdom of Satan. It was in the Name of Jesus that the deep-seated and degrading principles of paganism were uprooted and the saving maxims of the Christian doctrine implanted. It was in the Name of Jesus that the churches and altars of the true God were set up on the ruins of the temples and idols of the false pagan deities. It was in the Name of Jesus that the virtues of humility, voluntary poverty, and chastity took the place of pride, avarice, and licentiousness. It was in the Name of Jesus that thousands upon thousands of generous Christians renounced the world with all its attractions, to devote their lives to perpetual penance and mortification within the walls of the cloister or in the recesses of the desert. It was in the Name of Jesus that millions of brave martyrs, of both sexes and of every age and condition, have not only fearlessly but even joyously undergone the most unheard-of torments, and poured forth their blood as a testimony of the faith that was in them. Are these not most marvellous results achieved by the most Holy Name of Jesus? And do not these effects produced by the Holy Name give evidence of its wonderful power and efficacy?

2. No less wonderful, however, are the effects produced by the Holy Name *in our own days*. I might describe to you the wonderful works which are performed among the heathen nations in the Name of Jesus; how thousands are brought out of the darkness of error, ignorance, and sin, and brought into the admirable light of the Gospel, to true Christian enlightenment and virtue, by the power of the Holy Name. But time does not permit me to enlarge on this subject. I shall, therefore, confine myself to the effects which this Holy Name produces in the hearts of those Christians who with firm confidence take refuge to it.

On these it bestows all the gifts and graces they stand in need of, according to their various circumstances; to the weak it gives courage and confidence in the face of the terrible and just judgments of God, lovingly reminding them of the infinite gentleness and mercy of their Redeemer. It reminds them of the goodness and meekness of Jesus Christ; that meekness which never repulsed the contrite sinner; that meekness which the Prophet describes, when he says: "He shall not contend, nor cry out, neither shall any man hear His voice in the streets. The bruised reed He shall not break, and smoking flax He shall not extinguish" (Matt. xii. 19, 20). The Name of Jesus leads the sinner to conversion and reconciliation with God, according to the words of the angel: "Thou shalt call His name Jesus; for He shall save His people from their sins" (Matt. i. 21). To the penitent, finally, it gives strength and perseverance; for all the gifts of grace, and among them the grace of perseverance, are included in this adorable Name, since our blessed Lord Himself says: " Amen, amen, I say to you: if you ask the Father anything in My name, He will give it you" (John xvi. 23). Or have you not tested the power of this Holy Name by your own experience? If not, it is a sure sign that you have never had recourse to it with confidence.

Make it, then, a constant practice, beloved brethren, from this day forward in all your necessities to have recourse to the most Holy Name of Jesus. When evil thoughts and desires awake in your hearts; when you are tempted to anger, to revenge, to impurity, to blasphemy, to despair, or to any other sin, be it what it may, call upon the Holy Name of Jesus, and you are sure to overcome the temptation, however violent it may be. If you are weighed down by sorrow and affliction, if you are straitened by doubts and anxieties, call upon the Holy Name of Jesus, and you will gain courage, comfort, and relief in all your sufferings. If you have need of any special grace, again call upon the Name of Jesus, and you will obtain what you ask for. But, above all, call upon the Name of Jesus if you have the misfortune to fall into grievous sin; for, however grievous and numerous your sins may be, you will find forgiveness, if with firm confidence and perseverance you have recourse to the Holy Name of Jesus. Thousands of poor unfortunate sinners have, according to the testimony of St. Bernard, found salvation in the Name of Jesus. Nay, if Judas himself, the betrayer of our Divine Lord, had taken refuge to the Holy Name of Jesus, he would have certainly found forgiveness. Let the most Holy

Name of Jesus, therefore, be always in your hearts, always on your lips; then will this adorable Name be your strength and consolation on your death-bed; it will be the last utterance of your mortal breath, and a sure pledge of everlasting happiness. Amen.

Feast of the Purification of the Blessed Virgin.

THE SELF-SACRIFICE OF THE MOTHER OF GOD.

"And after the days of her purification according to the law of Moses were accomplished they carried Him to Jerusalem, to present Him to the Lord."—Luke ii. 22.

THE feast of to-day, which occupies a prominent place among the festivals of the Blessed Virgin Mary, very commonly receives but a superficial consideration. In considering it we are but too likely to confine ourselves to the external circumstances, to attend only to the outward ceremony by which the Mother of God, according to the prescription of the law, submitted herself to the rite of legal purification, and presented her divine Son as her first-born in the temple. That is all very good and edifying; but it is not enough; there is still more to be considered. We must further enter into the spirit of the occasion, and particularly consider the *self-sacrifice* which our blessed Lady has shown in the observance of this law.

Now, self-sacrifice manifests itself, above all, in the actual sacrifices which one makes; and the greater our sacrifices are, the more self-denial and humiliation they cost us, the greater our self-sacrifice is shown to be. But the Virgin-Mother of God, by the observance of this law, made two sacrifices of unparalleled self-abnegation—one sacrifice on the part of her virginity, and another on the part of her motherhood. In order, therefore, to bring home to you the greatness of the self-sacrifice displayed by our holy Mother on this occasion, I shall try to make you understand the greatness of her twofold sacrifice—

1. *Her sacrifice as Virgin;*
2. *Her sacrifice as Mother.*

I. HER SACRIFICE AS VIRGIN.

The sacrifice which the Mother of God, in her capacity as Virgin, made in the mystery under consideration consisted in this, that, although a spotless virgin, *she submitted to the law of purification.* The observance of this law, which entailed no great sacrifice in the case of other women, was for her the most humiliating, the most heroic which a virgin could be called upon to make. For, by the observance of this law she placed herself externally on the same level with other women, and thus before the eyes of the world she apparently renounced that prerogative which was dearest to her immaculate heart—the prerogative of her virginity.

1. Now, let us briefly consider *what a sacrifice* this humiliation must needs have cost her. In order to understand the import of this sacrifice we must bear in mind that there is no honor to which a maiden clings with such tenacity as to that of her virginity. So deeply is this sense of honor rooted in the heart of every young woman that, unless she has lost all human sentiment, she would rather part with life itself than with the reputation of her virginal purity. Nay, even those who have not blushed to sacrifice their innocence in the most shameful way will cling to the last to their good reputation, have recourse to all expedients, make all possible sacrifices, and even endanger their very lives, to conceal their ignominy. But if persons who have sunk so low, who have thrown away the greatest ornament of womanhood, who have sur-

rendered their innocence and even their natural modesty and delicacy, are still so much concerned for their honor, how dear must the honor of womanhood be to those who have preserved unsullied and unseared the spotless lily of their innocence, and have forfeited nothing of their original delicacy! To these an unblemished name and the honor of their virginity are worth more than a thousand lives.

This being the case, what a heroic sacrifice did the Immaculate Virgin make to God by externally renouncing here on earth her peerless virginity—she who was the Virgin of virgins; she who esteemed the prerogative of her virginity so highly that she secured it by a perpetual vow of chastity; she who shrank even from the divine Motherhood in consideration of her virginal purity, and refused to accept the highest dignity which God could confer, until she was assured that by divine intervention she would become the Mother of God without ceasing to be a virgin; she whose virginity was confirmed and augmented by conceiving in her most chaste womb and giving birth to the Eternal Word—what an unspeakable sacrifice, I say, must it not have been for her to renounce, to all appearances, this transcendent dignity of her undefiled virginity! Oh, how keenly must not this most modest and angelic virgin have felt the humiliation, there in the midst of sinful women, for whom this rite was instituted, before the gaze of men, publicly, in the temple, to stand like a poor sinner with her divine Child in her arms, while in truth she had been raised to the dignity of the Mother of God and the Queen of heaven and earth, of angels and of men! How humiliating must it not have been for her thus to acknowledge herself subject to a weakness and imperfection from which she actually shrank more than from death itself, and to forfeit the honor of a prerogative that was dearer to her than all else besides! Beloved brethren, was that not the greatest sacrifice of which as a virgin she was capable?

But, to fathom the greatness of this sacrifice, we must further consider that this humiliation on the part of the Mother of God was *entirely voluntary;* for she could have withdrawn herself from this self-abasement, if she chose, without violating any duty towards God or towards the law. She might have exempted herself altogether from the rite of purification, without making herself guilty of any violation of the law, because the law of purification, as is manifest from its tenor, did not concern her who had conceived and given birth in a miraculous way, by the intervention of the Holy Ghost; and though she might consider herself bound, according to the example of her divine Son, who submitted to the law of circumcision, to comply with this law, which had no reference to her, yet she might have eschewed the humiliation by revealing to the by-standers the mystery which the divine Omnipotence had operated in her favor. And why should she not reveal the mystery, which could no longer be concealed; which had already been revealed to the Jews by the voices of angels, and to the heathens by a miraculous star; and which, even on this occasion, was manifested by the Spirit to the aged Simeon and the prophetess Anna? But to this expedient she was unwilling to have recourse. And *why?*

Here, beloved brethren, let us admire the heroic *humility* of the Mother of God. However anxious she was to preserve the honor of her virginity, yet this eagerness could not prevail over her humility. As before the birth of her divine Child she preferred to leave her beloved and holy spouse St. Joseph in the greatest anxiety rather than to reveal to him her dignity as

Mother of God, so now she suppresses this favor in the deepest silence. Rather will she undergo any humiliation than reveal the divine favors that have been conferred upon her, and as on the day of the Annunciation she was prepared to renounce the infinite dignity of the divine Motherhood, if this were necessary to preserve her virginity, so now she decides rather to renounce the honor of her virginity before the world than to forfeit even the least degree of her humility. From humility she prefers to be looked upon as an ordinary mother rather than as the miraculous Virgin-Mother of God. What a wonderful sacrifice of self-denial, beloved brethren! Yet, great as is this sacrifice which she made as a virgin, still greater is that which she made as a mother.

II. HER SACRIFICE AS MOTHER.

Now, in what did this her sacrifice as mother consist? It consisted in *the presentation* of her Son in the temple. This offering of her divine Son had for the Blessed Virgin a special significance. It was a ratification, as far as she was concerned, of the offering of the Eternal Father, whereby He gave His only-begotten Son for the redemption of mankind. By presenting her divine Son in the temple, therefore, she gave her free consent to the eternal decree of the heavenly Father; and in this solemn ratification consisted her sacrifice as mother, which was a renewal of the total sacrifice which she made when, expressing her consent to become the Mother of God, she spoke: " Behold the handmaid of the Lord ; be it done to me according to thy word " (Luke i. 38). In order to form, if possible, an idea of this second sacrifice of the Mother of God, we shall briefly consider it, first, in itself, and secondly, in its circumstances.

1. *In itself.* Here we must take two things into consideration: the tender love of Mary to Jesus, her Child, and the consequences which her offering involves for her divine Son. For it is evident that the sacrifice was great and difficult for her in proportion to the greatness and intensity of her love to her Son, on the one hand, and the painful effects which her offering entailed on Him, on the other hand.

But who can conceive the *love* which the Mother of God cherished for her Son? That love surpassed that of all earthly mothers taken together, that of all the angels and saints of God. For Jesus was not only her Son; He was her only-begotten Son—and what a Son! How worthy of her motherly love! He was not merely her only Son; He was also her God and her all. Her love to Jesus, her Son, therefore, combined the most perfect motherly love, the most perfect love of God, and therefore far surpassed all created love of men and angels. Such was her love to her divine Son; and this love manifestly made her offering most painful, particularly as she well knew that it involved the most painful consequences for her Son.

And what were the *consequences* of this offering? They were the bitter passion and the cruel and ignominious death of her beloved Son. And these sufferings were by no means unknown to her, who was the Queen of prophets. She well knew that, by giving her consent to the decree of the heavenly Father, she delivered Him up, not so much into the hands of God, His Father, as into the hands of His executioners. What a terrible sacrifice was it for her, then, to give her consent by this offering of her divine Son! What an unspeakable anguish must have seized her most tender heart at the very thought of this approaching sacrifice! Every thought of this offering was a sword of grief that transfixed her loving heart. But who can describe the anguish of her heart when that solemn moment approaches, and she enters the temple with the divine Babe in her arms, as if to sign His sentence of death with her own hand? But, despite all this, because such was the will of God, and because our salvation was at stake, she generously gave her consent. What a bitter sacrifice! But what makes the sacrifice still greater are the circumstances which accompany it.

2. *In its circumstances.* The first circumstance which strikes us in this sacrifice, and which makes it more heroic, is the *freedom* with which it was made. For, as the Mother of God was exempt from the law of purification, so she was also free to omit the presentation of her divine Son in the temple, because this law was binding neither on her nor on her Son.

Another circumstance was that *only with her consent*, as she well knew, the sufferings of her divine Son were to take place; for without her consent the heavenly Father would not have allowed Him to suffer the death of a criminal. And why? Because, as St. Thomas well reasons on the point, in the first place, if Almighty God would, against her will, destine her innocent Son to such an ignominious death, He would thereby, in a certain sense, violate the right which the divine Motherhood conferred upon her in regard to Jesus, her Son; which would be contrary to His eternal decree. Besides, as the Angelic Doctor further remarks, the divine justice required that the sacrifice of the passion and death of Our Lord should be in every respect a free one, which it could hardly be called if it took place without the consent of His holy Mother. Finally, he says, it is not at all likely that God, who asked her consent to become the Mother of

His Son, would without her consent deliver her Son up to the death of the cross. The Blessed Virgin, therefore, gave her consent to the passion and death of her Son, although she knew that by withholding it she might have rescued Him from His sufferings. But does this circumstance not show the heroic character of the sacrifice of the Mother of God in the clearest light? Does this circumstance not make the surrender of the Son, whom she loved so intensely, doubly difficult for her? O Christian mothers, consult the feelings of your own hearts, and then say if this sacrifice of the Mother of God was not the most heroic of sacrifices.

A further circumstance which added to the bitterness of this sacrifice was the *tender age* of her Child. Scarcely had she given birth to Him, when she was called upon to sign the warrant of His death. What bitter pangs of grief must not this have caused her! Who does not know the tenderness of a mother's love to her new-born child? Who is not familiar with the anxiety with which she watches over its welfare? This same tenderness and anxiety, which God has implanted in the heart of every mother, the Mother of God also cherished towards her divine Infant, but in an infinitely higher degree. What grief and anguish, then, must not have overwhelmed her heart at this dread sacrifice, when she cast her eyes upon this tender Babe whom she pressed to her bosom, and whom she knew to be foredoomed to such terrible torments! Were not the words of the aged Simeon then realized upon her? Did not a sword of grief transfix her heart?

Lastly, by this surrender of her Son she consigned herself to a *life-long martyrdom*. For what else than a continual martyrdom was henceforth to be the life of this afflicted Mother, before whose soul the terrible ordeal of her Son's passion and death, the whole dreary way of the cross, was always pictured in all its awful detail?

How great, then, was the sacrifice which our blessed Lady as Mother of God offered for us in this mystery! And how justly, therefore, do the Fathers of the Church give her the title of the " mediatrix and restorer of the human race"! Does St. Bonaventure, then, exaggerate when, alluding to the words of our blessed Lord to Nicodemus (John iii. 16), he exclaims with joy and gratitude to the Mother of God: " So *Mary* loved the world that she gave her only-begotten Son for its Redemption "?

Beloved brethren, this wonderful self-sacrifice which we have considered in our holy Mother Mary is well calculated to make us, her children, blush for shame. For, while by her voluntary sacrifices for us she shows so much concern for our salvation, we ourselves are often so little concerned for our spiritual welfare that we can hardly determine ourselves to make the comparatively small sacrifices which are absolutely necessary for our salvation, and which we are in duty bound to make. How neglectful are we often in regard to our most important duties; in regard to prayer, the reception of the sacraments, the assisting at divine service! And how many there are who seek vain excuses, to relieve themselves of those Christian duties which are disagreeable to them: for instance, the fasts of the Church, the duty of giving alms, the obligation of avoiding the occasion of sin! And how great is the neglect of some parents in the fulfilment of their duties towards their children! And are not all those duties of the highest importance for our salvation? Have we not, therefore, great reason to blush for shame when we compare our own reckless neglect with the heroic self-sacrifice of our holy Mother? Let us, then, endeavor in future to conform ourselves to her example, and thus to do honor to our glorious Mother.

Yet the chief fruit of our meditation on this holy mystery, it seems to me, should be a tender love for, and an unshaken confidence in the Mother of God. For what can be more suitable to awake our love and confidence than the consideration of the unheard-of sacrifices which she made to God for our sake? Do these sacrifices not give us a clear insight into her loving heart? Do they not reveal to us the full glow of her motherly love towards us? Let us, therefore, beloved brethren, love our good Mother Mary with our whole heart, and cherish in our hearts a child-like and unwavering confidence in her; and she will not suffer that these her sacrifices have been made for us in vain. She will be our protection in all dangers, and will not rest until she has secured our salvation—the eternal union with her divine Son in His heavenly kingdom. Amen.

Feast of St. Joseph.

ST. JOSEPH'S HOLINESS.

"He made him master of his house, and ruler of all his possessions."
—Ps. civ. 21.

TO-DAY, on the feast of the glorious patriarch St. Joseph, spouse of the Blessed Virgin, Mother of God, foster-father of Jesus Christ, and patron and protector of the universal Church, it will be my endeavor to show you the consummate *holiness* of this most highly privileged of God's saints, excepting His own immaculate Mother. The sanctity of St. Joseph must be measured by the intimate relation in which he stood to Mary, his spotless virgin-spouse, and to Jesus, his divine foster-child. And from this twofold relation I do not hesitate to pronounce him, next to the Mother of God, the highest, the holiest, and I may add, the most powerful of God's saints. I shall, therefore, endeavor to show you the extraordinary sanctity of St. Joseph—

1. *As the spouse of the Blessed Virgin Mary;*
2. *As the foster-father of Jesus, the Son of God.*

I. ST. JOSEPH THE SPOUSE OF THE BLESSED VIRGIN.

St. Joseph was in reality the true spouse, or, as the words of Holy Scripture (Matt. i. 20; Luke i. 27) seem to convey, the true husband of Mary. It would seem, therefore, that a true marriage existed between them. The circumstance that they mutually renounced certain rights connected with the married state, and led a life of perpetual virginity, as is clearly intimated in the Gospel (Luke i. 37), was no bar to their union, but only rendered it the more holy, intimate, and pure. Their union was, therefore, the closest that could exist, a union of heart with heart, a union of purest and holiest love. And St. Joseph, as the husband, was the head of this holy union, and was divinely constituted in authority over the Mother of God.

1. As this holy union was ordained by God Himself, it was He who chose St. Joseph in preference to all men to be the spouse of His holy Mother. This choice of the Divine Wisdom must certainly have been a wise and happy one. Now, when is a choice for marriage said to be a wise and happy one? Above all, when there is a *likeness*, particularly a likeness of character and sentiment, between the parties; for else the first and most necessary condition of a happy union is lacking—the inward sympathy of the heart. Likeness of character and sentiment, therefore, existed in reality between these holy souls; and, since God chose St. Joseph in preference to all others, we may with good reason conclude that St. Joseph of all men had the greatest inward likeness to the Mother of God, and was, therefore, next to her, the holiest in sentiment and character. But internal sanctity, or holiness of sentiment, displays itself also in the external life and actions of man. Hence it follows that St. Joseph was not only internally the holiest of men, but that his life was the holiest, that he excelled all in holiness, his own blessed spouse always excepted. This consideration leads St. Bernardine of Siena to remark that, as Mary, the *virgo singularis*, the peerless virgin, has no equal among women, so St. Joseph, her spouse, has no equal among men. We may, therefore, justly apply to St. Joseph, the spouse of the Blessed Virgin, the words which Ecclesiasticus (xlix. 17) writes of Joseph of Egypt— "that no man was born on earth like Joseph." Such

was his sanctity even before his union with the holy Mother of God. Such sanctity was required to prepare him for that holy union. To what a height of sanctity must he, then, have arisen during this union!

2. This holy union could not but have proved most fruitful in holiness to St. Joseph, if for no other reason, because of the continual *conversation with the Blessed Virgin.* You all know what powerful influence for good or evil social intercourse exercises on man, especially the familiar and intimate intercourse with his nearest friends, who possess all his love and confidence. It has been truly said: tell me with whom you associate, and I will tell you what you are. A man is little more and little less than his surroundings. Judge, then, for yourselves, beloved brethren, what chastening, what sanctifying effect this continued and familiar converse with the Mother of God, who was of such inconceivable holiness, and whom he loved so tenderly and esteemed so highly, had on the life and actions of St. Joseph. If one visit of the Blessed Virgin had hallowed and filled with blessings the house of Zachary and Elizabeth, and sanctified the infant John the Baptist in the womb of his mother; if, according to ancient tradition, the very look of this holy Virgin filled the most immoral men with a love of virtue and holiness; nay, if, according to the testimony of the Apostle St. Paul (I. Cor. vii. 14), a pagan husband is sanctified by a believing wife; what fruits of sanctity must not a life of some twenty or thirty years, spent in the most familiar and intimate converse with the Virgin of virgins, have brought forth in the soul of St. Joseph, who had been already so richly endowed by God with piety and holiness, and whose heart was so susceptible of all good influences! Who can fathom the holiness of this great saint?

3. But a still more powerful factor in the sanctity of St. Joseph was *the great love* which the Mother of God cherished for him. His holy spouse loved him as a great saint and as a husband with a much more tender and intense love than that with which she loves all those who are but her children. And as her love was a true and active love, which consisted not in mere sentiment and words, there is no doubt that, next to the glory of God, she had no greater concern at heart than the welfare of her holy spouse. Hence she knew no greater desire than to see him raised to the highest degree of spiritual perfection and sanctity. This being the case, she did all in her power to assist him to this exalted grade of sanctity. And who shall doubt that she had the power to advance him on the way of sanctity? For, in the first place, we all know what power a good and holy wife—and such certainly was the Blessed Virgin—exercises over the heart of a husband, especially over the susceptible heart of such a noble husband as Joseph was; and, secondly—what was the most powerful agency—because all her wishes and desires were inspired by the Holy Ghost and accompanied with an infallible divine grace, which insured their fulfilment. Therefore St. Joseph received abundant and efficacious graces to ascend to that exalted degree of sanctity to which his holy spouse desired him to attain. Hence we must conclude that the Mother of God by her special, tender, and active love to St. Joseph, her spouse, has actually enabled him to attain to a degree of sanctity that knows no parallel on earth or in heaven. Such is our great saint as the spouse of the Mother of God.

II. ST. JOSEPH THE FOSTER-FATHER OF JESUS.

1. As the foster-father of Jesus Christ, the Son of God, St. Joseph stood in closer *relation to the fountain*

of all holiness than all the other saints, the Mother of God alone excepted. And this circumstance alone justifies us in saying that he attained to an unparalleled degree of sanctity. For, as St. Thomas teaches, every being partakes of the perfection of its original source or principle in proportion as it is more closely united with it. Thus the light is more brilliant the nearer it is to the sun; the heat is greater the nearer we approach to the fire; the water is purer the closer we come to the source. But, if this is the case, how incomparable must be the perfections of St. Joseph, who stood in such close proximity to the source of all sanctity. For, if we except His own holy Mother, who ever enjoyed such familiar intercourse with the Son of God as His foster-father, St. Joseph? Who bore Him oftener in his arms? Who pressed Him oftener to his bosom? Who had a greater right to call Him his own than St. Joseph?

Since, therefore, St. Joseph was so closely united with Jesus, the source of all sanctity, must we not say that he had a greater share in His infinite sanctity than any other—always excepting His holy Mother? Are we not justified, with so many learned and holy divines, in calling St. Joseph *the greatest* of all the saints? Hear how Father Francis Suarez, who enjoys the highest reputation for learning, thoroughness, and piety, expresses himself on this point. " I consider it no rash or improbable opinion, he says, but a pious and well-founded one, that St. Joseph surpasses all other saints in grace and glory. But to those who would oppose to this opinion the words of Our Lord, who says: Amen, I say to you that there hath not risen among them that are born of women a greater than John the Baptist " (Matt. xi. 11) —to them we would answer that our blessed Lord here speaks of St. John as the greatest of all prophets, not as the greatest of all saints; for so we read in St. Luke (vii. 28), who thus gives the words of our blessed Lord: " Among those that are born of women there is not a greater prophet than John the Baptist." And, in fact, when we consider the incomparable dignity of St. Joseph; when we reflect that the heavenly Father has appointed him as lord over His house, and ruler and director of the Holy Family; that He has made him the head of that privileged household in which He incorporated His own beloved Son, which was to be the perpetual model and ideal of every future household; when we remember the intimate relation in which he stood to Jesus Christ, the eternal and substantial sanctity; we cannot withhold our judgment that St. Joseph, next to the Mother of God, is the greatest of God's saints.

2. St. Joseph, however, not only stood in the closest relation to Jesus Christ, the source of all sanctity, but he was also destined by his position *to make the Son of God his debtor* by favors of the highest order, which he was to bestow on Him. Almighty God had destined St. Joseph to be the foster-father, protector, and preserver of His only-begotten Son. But what sanctity does not this choice suppose in Joseph! How high in the estimation of God must not that man have stood to whom He entrusted such an office—the care and providence for the life and person of His divine Son! Must he not, as guardian and ruler of the Saviour of the world, have possessed all virtues in the highest degree? Must he not, in the capacity of foster-father of Jesus, have also practised all virtues—self-abnegation, prudence, love to the divine Child—in the highest and most perfect degree, in order to make himself worthy of this sublime trust? And with what perfection did he discharge this office! With what

zeal and self-devotion did he not provide for the life and comfort of the divine Child! Judge, then, beloved brethren, if St. Joseph does not stand in the highest esteem with God, if he does not, after the Mother of God, occupy the highest place in the hierarchy of God's saints.

3. Nay, more, to St. Joseph belongs quite a *special place outside the ordinary ranks of the saints*, which is peculiar to him alone. Of the good works of the other saints God will say in the judgment: "Amen, I say to you, as long as you did it to one of these My least brethren, you did it to Me" (Matt. xxv. 40). But not so shall He address St. Joseph. To this saint, who rescued Him from the snares of Herod, who fled with Him into Egypt and brought Him back safe to Nazareth, who on that dreary journey appeased His hunger and quenched His thirst, who so often bore Him in his arms, who so long and lovingly provided for all His wants—to him, I say, the Judge of the living and the dead will address other words. He will thank St. Joseph for the kind services rendered to Him, not in the person of His brethren, but in His own person. If, then, what our blessed Lord says is true, that "he that receiveth a prophet in the name of a prophet shall receive the reward of a prophet; and he that receiveth a just man in the name of a just man shall receive the reward of a just man" (Matt. x. 41), what must be the reward of St. Joseph, who received in his hospitality, and under his care and protection, not a prophet, not a just man, but God Himself in the person of His divine and co-eternal Son? His will be, not the reward of a prophet, or of a just man, but the reward of God, that is, a reward that is in keeping, as far as may be, with the infinite greatness and dignity of his divine guest.

Now, if we take all we have said to show the pre-eminent holiness of St. Joseph together—his intimate relation to the Mother of God as her divinely-appointed spouse, and to the Son of God as His chosen guardian and foster-father, and the numberless graces and prerogatives connected with his exalted office—must we not of necessity conclude that Almighty God has raised him to a degree of sanctity and glory that far transcends that of any other of God's saints, the Mother of God alone excepted? It was this consideration that induced the Church to declare him her supreme and universal patron. But as the guardian and patron of the entire Church he is the patron saint of every one of us, who have the great happiness to be the children of the Church. Let us, then, to-day renew our devotion to St. Joseph; let us henceforth honor and love him, next to his immaculate spouse, and have confident recourse to him in all our spiritual and even temporal wants; and, as he was once the guide and protector of the divine Child, so he will be our guardian and patron, direct us through the many dangers that threaten us, and lead us safe to the goal of our pilgrimage, to the land of everlasting bliss. Amen.

Feast of the Annunciation.

GENEROSITY OF THE MOTHER OF GOD.

"How shall this be done, because I know not man?"—Luke i. 34.

AMONG all the feasts of the Blessed Virgin Mary there is hardly one which invites us more eloquently to pay her honor than that of to-day. For it has been instituted as a perpetual memorial of the divine message which has distinguished her above all the daughters of man. But what made this occasion so glorious for her was no less the heroic generosity of soul which she displayed on receiving this message than the incomparable dignity which it announced to her.

It is on the *generosity* displayed by the Mother of God in this mystery that I intend to dwell in the present discourse. This generous disinterestedness was manifested by her both in the initial renunciation and in the final acceptance of the unspeakable dignity of the divine Motherhood offered her by the angel. I shall, therefore, endeavor to show you her generosity (1) in *refusing*, (2) in *accepting* the dignity of Mother of God.

I. HER REFUSAL.

The refusal of the prerogative of divine Motherhood, to which I here refer, was made *in favor of her virginity*, which the Blessed Virgin would have chosen in preference to the dignity of Mother of God, if it were necessary to renounce one of the two. This is the only possible explanation of the answer she gave the angel: "How shall this be done, because I know not man?"

By these words she manifestly gave to understand that she hesitated to accept the dignity offered her, because she feared the violation of her virginal purity. Thus several of the holy Fathers explain this passage, among others St. Ambrose, St. Augustine, and St. Bernard; and they add that our blessed Lady would consider the loss of her virginity a greater evil than her exclusion from the privilege of the divine Motherhood. And St. Gregory Nyssen says in express terms that she preferred her virginal integrity to the prerogative which God extended to her; and that, if the dignity of divine Motherhood were incompatible with her virginity, she would have chosen to decline the highest of all honors rather than forfeit the latter. These are his words: " The angel announces her maternity, but she insists on her virginity, and judges that inviolate purity is preferable to the dignity that is tendered her.

1. This supposed, I maintain that this renunciation on the part of the Blessed Virgin was an act of the *most heroic self-sacrifice*, which gives evidence of an incomparable generosity. We shall easily realize the truth of this assertion, if we only consider the greatness of the prerogatives contained in the divine Motherhood. And the first thing that strikes us here is the marvellous dignity and honor of this singular distinction. This distinction is so great that it is impossible to give even a remote idea of it. Even the holy Fathers of the Church dared not venture to give an adequate description of this unspeakable honor, doubtlessly convinced of the impossibilty of describing it, and thinking that silence is more eloquent than speech on a subject which so far transcends our power of conception and expression. Nay, the Mother of God herself was nnable to find utterance for the greatness of the dignity conferred upon her. All that she was able

to do was to express her wonderment at the marvellous things the Almighty had done to her. "He that is mighty," she says, "hath done great things to me." It were vain for me, then, to attempt to describe to you the greatness of a dignity that baffles all description. All that I can say of this prerogative is that it is most intimately connected with the infinite greatness of God Himself, that it is, in a certain true sense, infinite, and therefore far surpasses human understanding. What an heroic act of self-sacrifice, then, on the part of our blessed Lady to decline the acceptance of this transcendent dignity!

Perhaps some one may think the Blessed Virgin declined this honor because she did not realize the privileges connected with it. But, apart from the knowledge of the Messias which she drew from constant prayer and the reading of the Sacred Books, the angel expressed himself so clearly that there was no mistaking of his meaning. Nor did he fail to propose the most powerful motives to induce her to its acceptance. "Fear not," he says, "for thou hast found grace with God. Behold, thou shalt conceive in thy womb, and shalt bring forth a Son, and thou shalt call His name Jesus. He shall be great and shall be called the Son of the Most High; and the Lord God shall give unto Him the throne of David; and He shall reign in the house of Jacob forever, and of His kingdom there shall be no end" (Luke i. 31-33). Can we, then, suppose that Mary was not sufficiently instructed on the dignity and importance of the motherhood to which she was divinely appointed? Yet all the prerogatives implied in this highest of all honors could not lessen her preference for the virginity which she had consecrated to God. Therefore she hesitated to give her consent, and her first impulse was to ask;

How can that be done, because I know not man?

2. And how could her virginity make up for the dignity of the divine Motherhood? This virtue, beloved brethren, could in this life procure her nothing but *self-denial and contempt:* self-denial, because by the profession of virginity she condemned herself to a life of retirement and obscurity; of contempt, because, her virginity being unknown to the world, she exposed herself, in the eyes of men, to the reproach of sterility, which was looked upon by the Jews not only as a disgrace, but as a curse and a divine chastisement. In the next life, it is true, her virginity gave her a right to a glorious crown, the crown of virgins, but not the right to the peerless crown of the Mother of God. When, therefore, she declined the distinction of divine Motherhood in favor of her virginity she did so purely from love and esteem for this holy virtue. But such a disinterested love of virtue, not for the sake of its advantages, but for its own sake and for God's sake, implies the noblest and most heroic self-denial and, consequently, the highest degree of generosity that can be imagined.

We must, therefore, conclude that the Blessed Virgin on this occasion, by renouncing the dignity offered her, gave proof of the greatest and most admirable generosity. But no less marvellous was the generosity shown by her subsequently in accepting the honor proffered her.

II. HER ACCEPTANCE.

1. It is an act of generosity purely for God's sake to resolve one's self to a step which one foresees to be connected with the most painful consequences; and the more painful the consequences are the more heroic is the generosity displayed. Let us apply this principle to

that momentous step upon which our blessed Lady resolved when she finally accepted the proffered dignity of the divine Motherhood, and we shall at once see what wonderful generosity she displayed.

a. She submitted to this call purely *to please God.* For by the fact that she previously declined the dignity of Mother of God she sufficiently manifested that she did not accept it for its own sake nor for the sake of the prerogatives connected with it, but solely for God's sake.

b. She accepted this dignity although she fully realized the *painful consequences* which it entailed. For, on the one hand, she knew very well that by accepting the dignity held out to her by the angel, she was to become the Mother of the Redeemer; and, on the other hand, as the holy Fathers assure us, she was well acquainted with the sufferings which the Saviour was to undergo. And apart from all private revelations which God may have granted her, how could she be unacquainted with those sufferings, since they are most minutely described in the books of the Old Testament, with which she was familiar? Did she not know that He was to be wounded for our iniquities and bruised for our sins; that the chastisement of our peace was upon Him, and that by His bruises we should be healed? Did she not know that His hands and feet were to be transfixed, and that all His bones were to be numbered; that from the crown of His head to the sole of His foot there should be no soundness in Him; that He should be a worm and no man, the reproach of men and the outcast of the people; a man of sorrows and acquainted with infirmity? (Ps. xxi; Is. liii.) Must she not have clearly foreseen, therefore, the terrible anguish which was in store for the Mother of the Redeemer, that is, for herself, in case she accepted this dignity? Must not even then the sword of grief have transfixed her immaculate heart? And, if this was the case, must we not acknowledge that in the acceptance of the dignity of divine Motherhood she has given proof of the most heroic generosity?

2. It might be objected, perhaps, that our conclusion is true only in the supposition that our blessed Lady at the moment of her consent actually reflected on the disagreeable consequences of her maternity. But is this supposition well grounded? Must we not, on the contrary, suppose that at that moment, for her so glorious, her mind was so engrossed with the greatness of the honor tendered her that, for the time being, she altogether forgot the painful consequences it involved?

No, beloved brethren; our supposition is well founded. She *actually thought of the disagreeable feature* of the honor conferred upon her. For Almighty God evidently wished that her acceptance should be altogether free, and therefore, that it should be obtained with a full knowledge of all its consequences and with perfect deliberation on her part. Therefore it is beyond all doubt that God revealed to her at that moment the long series of sufferings which her acceptance entailed. And this supposition is the more likely also for this reason, because it was the will of God that the work of Redemption should, also on her part, begin with an heroic act of self-devotion. This same supposition is confirmed also by the answer which she gave to the angel: "Behold the handmaid of the Lord, be it done to me according to thy word." This answer implies not so much an acceptation of a proffered favor as the humble and voluntary submission to a disagreeable and repugnant duty imposed upon her against her will. In fact, if she had not actually reflected upon the disagreeable consequences of the divine Motherhood, but on its joys and honors, she would doubtless have given a very different answer. She would have given expression to her gratitude, and to the sense of her unworthiness of such an infinite dignity. But, instead of any such protestations, she answers: "Behold the handmaid," the humble servant, "of the Lord: be it done to me according to thy word." So spoke our blessed Lord in His agony in the Garden of Olives: "Not My will, but Thine be done." This is the language of one who in obedience submits himself with repugnance to some great sacrifice. Nay, beloved brethren, so great was this sacrifice on the part of the Blessed Virgin, that no other human sacrifice can be brought in comparison with it. Only the sacrifice made by her divine Son in Gethsemani surpassed it in bitterness. Justly, then, has the Church given her the title of Queen of Martyrs. By this very act of self-sacrifice she more than merited this glorious title. Who, then, will further say that she gave her consent without a full knowledge of all the long martyrdom of sufferings which the divine Motherhood involved?

Our holy Mother Mary, therefore, both in her first refusal and her subsequent acceptance of the dignity of the divine Motherhood, gave evidence of the most heroic self-denial and the most marvellous generosity. And this, beloved brethren, is the clearest proof that God has chosen her as the fittest of all women to be the Mother of His only-begotten Son. Or, has there ever been any other among women capable of such wondrous self-sacrifice and generosity?

And this His own so highly favored Mother Almighty God in His infinite love has given us as our Mother. Have we not just cause to be proud of such a Mother, and to glory in the happiness of being her children? Rejoice, then, beloved brethren, rejoice from your heart, that God has given you such a Mother; but at the same time endeavor, as becomes good children, to do honor and give joy to your heavenly Mother. Choose her, then, to-day as your model and pattern, and take care to imitate her particularly in that virtue which above all others is dear to her—in the virtue of holy purity. If you cultivate this angelic virtue, each according to his state in life, you shall give joy to the spotless heart of your dear Mother; you shall be worthy children of such a Mother; and you shall secure the powerful protection of the Queen of Heaven. She shall be your support in the trials and temptations of this life, your consolation in death, your advocate before the judgment-seat of God, and shall receive you into the number of her glorious children in heaven. Amen.

Good Friday.

THE PASSION OF OUR LORD.

"O all ye that pass by the way, attend, and see if there be any sorrow like to My sorrow."—Lament. i. 12.

THE sufferings of Our Lord Jesus Christ, which in the mystery of to-day have attained their height and consummation on Calvary, are calculated to fill our hearts with a holy sorrow and sadness. For He who on the cross yields up His spirit in death is not only the most innocent, the most amiable, and the fairest among the children of men (Ps. xliv. 3); He is also our God, our Creator, our good Lord and Master, our loving Father, to whom we owe all that we possess, and whatever we are in soul and body. If even those who had crucified Him returned from Mount Calvary with drooping heads, remorsefully beating their breasts, how much more should we, who are endowed with more humane sentiments, return from the consideration of this direful ordeal with heads bent in sorrow and hearts filled with sadness, beating our breasts in penitence, in view of the suffering we have caused our Divine Saviour by our sins! However, it is not only grief and compassion we should carry with us from this scene of suffering, but also an intense hatred of sin, an ardent love and deep sense of gratitude towards our Divine Lord. For it was sin which caused Him all His sufferings, and it was His infinite love to us which moved Him to cast Himself into this sea of bitterness. Let us, then, beloved brethren, that we may take home with us these precious fruits of the

The Passion of Our Lord. 89

bitter passion of our Divine Master, approach this ocean of sorrows and taste of its bitterness, in accordance with the invitation of Our Lord through the mouth of His prophet: "O all ye that pass by the way, attend, and see if there be any sorrow like to My sorrow." Let us endeavor to fathom the depth of this sea, and we shall easily convince ourselves—

1. *That no one has ever suffered under such painful circumstances;*
2. *That no one has ever suffered such grievous torments.*

O sweet Jesus, who hast to-day upon the cross consummated the work of our Redemption, enlighten our understanding that we may realize the extent of Thy sufferings and the greatness of Thy love, and move our hearts that they may be filled with compassion, thankfulness, and love to our dying Redeemer!

I. CIRCUMSTANCES OF HIS SUFFERINGS.

1. The first circumstance which rendered the passion of Our Lord most painful was its *extent*, which comprised His whole person. He suffered at the same time the most unspeakable torments in His soul as well as in His body, so that He may justly be called the "Man of Sorrows" (Is. liii. 3).

His *soul* was a prey to the most dreadful sufferings of every description: fear and heaviness, sorrow and desolation, horror and anguish, tormented and oppressed His soul at the same time. In the Garden of Gethsemani His sacred soul was so overpowered with sufferings that drops of bloody sweat issued from the pores of His body, and death itself was imminent. "He began to fear, and to be heavy; and He saith to them: My soul is sorrowful even unto death" (Mark xiv. 33, 34), "And His sweat became as drops of *blood* trickling down upon the ground" (Luke xxii. 44).

And, if we contemplate His *body*, we find no limb, no spot, which had not its torture. His pallid face is disfigured with dust and clotted blood, livid and swollen with the blows dealt Him by the ministers. His lips are parched with thirst and His palate is tormented by the bitterness of the gall that was given Him to drink. On His head is pressed the crown of sharp thorns, and His tender hands and feet are pierced with rough nails. His sinews are stretched to their utmost tension; His shoulders are weighed down by the heavy weight of the cross. The cruel scourging had spared neither His loins, nor His breast, nor any part of His body. His whole body is, as it were, one livid and bleeding wound. "We have seen Him, and there was no sightliness" (Is. liii. 2). If we consider, moreover, how perfect and tender His sacred body was, how great His sensibility for pain, since as Redeemer He was destined to suffer, and had, therefore, assumed a most sensitive and passible body, we may easily perceive that His sufferings far surpassed anything ever endured by man.

2. A second no less painful circumstance was the *duration* of His sufferings. You must not think, beloved brethren, that the sufferings of our blessed Lord were confined merely to the days of His passion. These days, spent in the hands of His torturers, were only the consummation of the pangs and sorrows of three and thirty years. From the first instant of His existence as man the terrible ordeal of His passion was continually before the eyes of His mind, according to the words of the Psalmist: "My sorrow is continually before Me" (Ps. xxxvii. 18). And this picture of His sorrows stood before His soul in all its dreadful detail. He saw and felt every scourge, and every wound,

and every insult. He saw and felt the crown of thorns piercing its sharp points into His sacred temples; He saw His face buffeted and disfigured; He heard every reproach and blasphemy that was launched against Him while He hung on the cross; in short, He saw and heard and felt in all its pungent bitterness every pang of His coming passion. Therefore St. John the Evangelist says of Him that He knew all things that were to come upon Him (John xviii. 4). And this intuition of His coming passion was infinitely more painful to Him than is the expectation of coming evils to us. For we have always some hopes of escaping impending ills, or, at least, of shortening or alleviating them; but this was not the case with Jesus, who foresaw every detail of His sufferings, and, after once freely embracing them, could not and would not forego a single circumstance of the bitter ordeal. Oh, now I am not astonished at what an ancient tradition tells of our dear Lord—that He was never seen to laugh or smile, but that, according to the words of the Psalmist, " He walked sorrowful all the day long " (Ps. xxxvii. 7); and that " His life was wasted with grief, and His years in sighs " (Ps. xxx. 11).

And yet I have thus far said nothing of the sadness which the thought of the numberless *evils of future times* produced in His soul; for He saw all the sins of the whole world to the end of time; He saw the persecutions of His beloved spouse, the Church; He saw the tortures to be endured by His followers, His holy martyrs; He saw the fruitlessness of His passion for so many millions, and the final reprobation of so many souls; all this sad picture was constantly delineated in clear outline before His sorrowing soul. Beloved brethren, if the death of Lazarus brought tears to His eyes, what a deluge of sorrow must not the sight of all those evils have brought upon His tender and compassionate heart? Truly, our blessed Lord has borne not only His own suffering but the suffering of the whole world! "Surely, He hath borne our infirmities, and carried our sorrows" (Is. liii. 4). Where, then, is the sorrow to be compared with His sorrow?

3. A further most painful circumstance of His sufferings was that *all classes of the people conspired* against Him. We have never heard of any other human being who was persecuted by all classes. Different individuals and different classes have often different interests at stake. They are also different in their views and desires. Hence it comes that persecuted parties always find some to sympathize with them and to extend their protection to them. In this regard our Divine Lord is a solitary exception. All without exception conspired against Him: Jews and Gentiles, rulers and people, priesthood and laity, judges and soldiers, rich and poor. Therefore He says Himself by the mouth of the Psalmist: "Many calves have surrounded Me; fat bulls have besieged Me. Many dogs have encompassed Me; and the council of the malignant hath besieged Me" (Ps. xxi. 13, 17).

But what rendered this fact the more ungrateful and the more painful to our dear Lord was that He was the *benefactor of all*. He could, in truth, say with holy Job that He was "an eye to the blind, a foot to the lame, the father of the poor" (Job xxix. 15, 16); He was the guide and the way to the erring, the defence and protection of the helpless. What a deep wound must not such ingratitude have inflicted upon His noble heart! How truly, then, is it not said of Him by the Royal Prophet: "They are multiplied above the hairs of my head, who hate me without cause" (Ps. lxviii. 5)!

4. The fulness of bitterness is contained in the ingratitude of *Judas, His betrayer.* If there was one on whom He had conferred the most signal favors, it was this traitor. Having chosen him from the millions, and having received him into His most intimate confidence, for three long years He bestowed all care and diligence on the training of his heart and mind. He had worked numberless miracles before his eyes, and given to the traitor himself the power of working even greater miracles. He had made the laws of nature, and even the evil spirits themselves, subject to him. He had raised him to the highest dignity on earth, the dignity of an apostle. And what a grand prospect did He open to him! In His glorious kingdom He had prepared a throne for him, and in this world he was destined to be an object of veneration to all Christendom. But all this love and liberality did not suffice to move the heart of this perverse traitor. At last his Lord and Master, lowly bent before him, washes his feet and wipes them with a towel with which He had begirt Himself. Will this not move him to better sentiments? Oh, no, beloved brethren; despite all this, he betrays his Master! He betrays Him in the most ignominious way! He betrays Him for thirty vile pieces of silver! Oh, what a wound did this black ingratitude inflict on the Sacred Heart of Jesus!

Where, then, beloved brethren, can we find in the records of history a human being who suffered so much and under such aggravating circumstances as our dear Lord and Saviour Jesus Christ—who suffered at the same time in body and soul; whose inward suffering was an uninterrupted, life-long martyrdom; who, although the benefactor of all mankind, was persecuted by all classes and conditions, and betrayed even by His own bosom friend? No, beloved brethren; under such a series of painful circumstances no other ever suffered but the Son of God. Nor did any one ever suffer similar outrages.

II. NATURE OF HIS SUFFERINGS.

All classes, as we have seen, had conspired against our blessed Lord; all actively contributed to His sufferings. In considering the nature of His sufferings we shall reduce them to two chief heads—what He suffered from those in authority; and what He suffered from His executioners.

1. *What He suffered from those in authority.* It is the consummation of injustice, beloved brethren, if wrong is inflicted by those who are set up for the maintenance and administration of justice. And this was the case in the condemnation and execution of our Divine Lord.

a. After the High Priests had already resolved upon His death they caused Him to be taken prisoner. An *arrest* so unjust and shameful has never taken place in the history of man. To be arrested as a criminal is in itself a most humiliating and painful thing. For from the moment one is put under arrest he is lawfully looked upon as a suspect, as one who is under the suspicion and charge of wrong-doing. Therefore the arrest of a man who is under no suspicion is, and has always been, considered an injustice and an outrage. And the more groundless the arrest is, the greater is the outrage. But if such a seizure is, moreover, executed in an unseemly way, and if the person arrested is a man of good character, his treatment becomes a most crying outrage.

Judged by these principles of justice and equity, I say that the seizure of Our Lord was the greatest outrage ever inflicted on man. For, in the first place, it was altogether *groundless.* On our blessed Lord there not only rested no suspicion, but not even the shadow of a suspicion. It was only a few days before that the people of Jerusalem had gone forth to meet Him, and led Him in triumph into the city. What else than the firm conviction regarding His sanctity could have induced the people to go forth in a body with palm-branches in their hands to meet Him, to spread their garments on the streets before Him, and to greet Him as the Messias, the Saviour of the world, with the words: "Hosanna to the Son of David; blessed is He that cometh in the name of the Lord! Hosanna in the highest!" (Matt. xxi. 9.) Nay, even after His arrest, no charge could be brought against Him, though His enemies spared neither pains nor money; for the hired witnesses contradicted one another. His seizure was, therefore, a most flagrant injustice.

And if we further consider the *manner* of this shameful arrest, we find no terms to characterize its injustice. If the mob which was sent to the Garden of Olives to seize Our Lord had fallen, not upon an innocent and unsuspected man, but on a convicted robber or murderer, could they have treated him with greater harshness? Their mission gave them the right, at most, to lay hold of Him and convey Him before the tribunal. Why, then, drag Him through the streets, like a lamb that is led to the slaughter? Why strike Him with their fists and clubs like a stubborn animal? Why drag Him through the dirt and tread Him under foot? Is that the right and the task of the servants of justice? Is that not rather the work of the executioner? Do not right and justice demand that even the greatest criminal should first be heard and be allowed to defend himself, and only then, if he is found guilty, be sentenced and punished? With what right, then, has this procedure of equity been inverted in the case of our Divine Saviour? Why is He first punished, and then sentenced?

And *who is this divine prisoner* who is thus unjustly treated? It is the Son of God, the Creator of heaven and earth, the Saviour and Redeemer, whose mission was already universally acknowledged by the people. Can there be anything more shameful and unjust than this treatment of our Divine Lord?

b. But no less unjust and ignominious was His treatment *before the tribunals.* What is granted to the greatest criminals was denied Him. Even the most ruthless felon is allowed to defend himself. To Jesus Christ, the Son of God, is denied this right. He is interrogated concerning His disciples and His teaching. But, scarcely had He opened His divine lips and answered in the most peaceful and becoming terms, when one of the ministers raises his sacrilegious hand and deals a heavy blow upon His face. This was the freedom of defence accorded Him. He was questioned, but not allowed to answer. But, if they will not hear Him, why do they question Him? And if they question Him, why not listen to His answer? If He speaks, they strike Him; and if He is silent, as before Herod, He is mocked and scoffed at as a fool. Has ever a man been so unjustly treated? Was there ever a trial in which the accused was allowed neither to speak nor to be silent?

c. Still more outrageous, however, is the *condemnation* of Our Lord. This fact stands unparalleled in the history of the world. 'Tis true, many have been, in the course of time, condemned unjustly; but they were first, though falsely, convicted and declared guilty. To condemn an innocent man is such a flagrant violation of all right and justice that even the most demoralized human being shrinks from the very thought of it. If, then, there was question of putting a guiltless man to

The Passion of Our Lord.

death, people tried, at least, by false evidence to convict him of a crime in order to have him condemned with some show of justice. But in the case of our blessed Lord this design miscarried. His sanctity was so manifest and universally acknowledged, that it was impossible to cast even the shadow of an imputation on His character. Since, therefore, His death had with fiendish malice been resolved upon from the outset, His enemies, putting aside all sentiments of right and justice, condemned Him even without the pretence of guilt. Hear the sentence of Pilate, pronounced in explicit terms and, as the Gospel tells us, from the seat of justice: " I find no cause of death in Him " (Luke xxiii. 22). The only reasonable and natural sequence to be expected from these words would be: Therefore loose Him from His chains and let Him go. But no, the consequence drawn by the shameless and cowardly judge was: " I will chastise Him, therefore, and let Him go." And when the Jews insisted that He should be crucified, Pilate answered: " Take Him you, and crucify Him, for I find no cause in Him " (John xix. 6). Therefore, because He is innocent, chastise Him; because there is no cause of death in Him, let Him be handed over to the executioners and crucified. And priests and people ratified this sentence pronounced on Him who had been plainly declared guiltless. What a fiendish hate against the sacred person, what a diabolical contempt for the innocent life of Jesus Christ!

But this is not all, beloved brethren; for Christ is not only condemned as innocent; but, *because He is innocent, He is submitted to other torments* more dreadful than death itself. For had He been found guilty, He would have been condemned according to law to some definite punishment. But, as He had been convicted of no crime, they considered themselves free to chastise and torment Him without measure, without restraint, and without any law—free to bring to bear upon Him the scourges, the crown of thorns, the cross, the gall and vinegar; in short, all manner of reproach, ignominy, and ill-treatment. Thus He was abandoned to the caprice of the mob, and to the fury of His bitter enemies and executioners, who thirsted for His blood—to be abused, racked, and tortured at pleasure. Was ever such a sentence pronounced on any other, I will not say, innocent man, but even on the most ruthless criminal? On the innocent Lamb of God alone in the history of man were such caprice, fury, and cruelty brought to bear! "Jesus he [Pilate] delivered up to their will" (Luke xxiii. 25).

2. *What He suffered from the executioners.* As soon as our blessed Lord was delivered up into the power of the executioners, they fell upon Him with diabolic fury, rent His clothes from His sacred body, and *scourged* Him with the most savage cruelty. The impious judge had determined neither the number of the scourges nor the duration of the torture, but left all to the caprice of His enemies. He delivered Jesus up to their will. Thus it happened, according to the private revelations granted by God to some of His saints, that the executioners relieved one another at their unhallowed work, so that renewed strength and fury were brought to bear on our dear Lord, until He sank all but lifeless under the cruel scourges. Portions of His adorable flesh were torn from His sacred body, until the very bones were laid bare. At length His body is but one bleeding wound. But the fury of His enemies is not yet satisfied. They continue to heap wound upon wound, according to the words of the Psalmist: "They have added to the grief of My wounds" (Ps. lxviii. 27).

His head was the only part of Our Lord's body which was yet free from wounds. The cruel monsters noticed this and soon devised in their fury a means to torture this seat of divine wisdom. They remembered that He was a king, and He must receive kingly honors. They plaited a *crown of sharp thorns* and pressed it upon the sacred brow and temples of the King of kings. Now they took a soldier's purple cloak and cast it over His shoulders, and put a reed into His hand as a sceptre, and bent the knee before Him as before a mock-king. They then blindfolded Him; and crowding close around Him, one spat in His face, another struck Him on the cheek, a third plucked out His beard, as if He were a fool and a criminal at the same time.

At length, weary of their devilish sport, they fetch the *cross*, the final instrument of Our Saviour's death. But instead of concealing it from His view, a regard of delicacy which was had even for the basest felon, it is exposed to His agonizing gaze, and then laid upon His lacerated shoulder. Thus laden with the heavy cross, surrounded by a countless multitude of men, amid the scoffs, and insults, and ill-treatment of a furious mob, He is led forth through the streets of Jerusalem to the hill of Calvary. Arrived here, faint and exhausted as He is, they again tear His garments from His wounded limbs, stretch Him naked upon the cross, and fasten His hands and feet with rough nails to the tree of shame. At length they rear the cross with its bleeding Victim, and expose the King of heaven and earth in His agony between earth and sky, a thief and robber on either side, to the reproach and ridicule of the infuriate mob. I forego to describe His agony. Let what I have said suffice.

But let me ask you once more, beloved brethren, in the name of our dying Lord, with the words of the prophet: "O all ye that pass by the way, attend, and see if there be a sorrow like to My sorrow"! Has ever a human being suffered such ill-treatment, such tortures as Jesus Christ, our Saviour and Redeemer? What love, what thankfulness do we owe Him, that He has undergone such dreadful torments for our sake! What would have become of us if our Divine Saviour had not intervened between us and the divine justice. But, if the heavenly Father has exacted such a satisfaction from His only-begotten Son for our sins, what a terrible evil must sin be; and what a terrible chastisement does it not merit in the life to come! Should not this consideration fill our hearts with shame, and confusion, and sorrow? Oh, how could we degrade ourselves so low as so often and so long to harbor in our hearts sin, that dreadful enemy which crucified our Lord and Saviour! How could we have been so ungrateful as to choose the degrading pleasure of sinful thought or action in preference to Jesus Christ, who has thus in unspeakable torments laid down His life for us! Oh, alas! for the ingratitude and insensibility of our hearts, that can be restrained from sin neither by the prayers, nor by the sighs, nor by the sorrows of our dying Lord! O Jesus, our Redeemer, how couldst Thou resolve Thyself to die for so hard-hearted, so ungrateful, so unfaithful a people!

Yet, we return thanks, thanks without end, to Thy never-failing, invincible love! It has at length triumphed over our hard hearts! It has opened our eyes to tears, and our hearts to sorrow. Yea, O sweet Jesus, we are heartily sorry for, and detest with all the intensity of our souls, our past ingratitude and unfaithfulness. We are firmly resolved in all future time to avoid sin, and flee the occasion of sin, as the greatest evil. Thou, O Jesus, shalt henceforth be the object of our love. In Thy love, O Jesus, shall we live ; in Thy love shall we, with Thy assistance, persevere to the end; in Thy love may we breathe our last breath, and yield forth our souls into Thy loving embrace! Amen.

Easter Sunday.

THE RESURRECTION OF OUR LORD.

"**Be not affrighted**; He is risen; He is not here."—Mark xvi. 6.

THE Resurrection of our Divine Saviour, which was announced by the angel to the holy women with the words I have just cited, had a twofold influence upon them. It, first of all, strengthened them in their faith in the Divinity of Our Lord; and, in the second place, it filled their hearts with love for His sacred Humanity. This we see as well from the joyous fervor with which they discharged the message the angel gave them, as also from the fact that, from this moment, they gave their hearts entirely to the service of their Saviour, lived for Him alone, and walked with unfaltering steps on the path of sanctity to the summit of perfection. These very same effects the Resurrection of Our Lord should produce in all of us. Hence I consider it my duty to-day to contribute what little I can towards this end. For this purpose, therefore, I shall endeavor to show you that the glorious *Resurrection* of our crucified Lord from the dead is *the most powerful motive—*

1. *Of our belief in the Divinity of Jesus Christ;*
2. *Of our love to His sacred Humanity.*

I. THE MOTIVE OF OUR BELIEF.

The Resurrection of Our Lord is the chief motive of our faith in the Divinity of Jesus Christ for this reason, because it is the clearest and most incontrovertible evidence of His Godhead, and is therefore the fittest motive to induce us to believe, or to strengthen our belief, in this great truth of our religion. Now, why is the fact of the Resurrection the chief evidence of the Godhead of Jesus Christ?

1. The Resurrection of Christ is the one great fact on which all other arguments for His Godhead depend. All evidence for His Divinity stands or falls with the fact of the Resurrection. Christ Himself, as we see from Holy Scripture, *constantly appeals to this one miracle*, leaving all His other numerous miracles out of the question. On this one miracle, therefore, according to Christ's own teaching, rests the evidence of His Godhead and His divine mission. And justly so; for, if He were not God, He could not arise from the dead; if He were not God, neither could God raise Him from the dead; because, in that case, God, the all-holy and all-truthful, would invincibly lead the world into error, confirming by a miracle of miracles the most enormous falsehood.

But *if He had not arisen from the dead* He would by His own words have annihilated the faith in His Godhead, frustrated all His miracles, and reduced Christianity to a mere fable. For thus He would have prophesied what would not have come to pass and would have stamped upon Himself the seal of a false prophet. Therefore St. Paul says: "If Christ be not risen again, then is our preaching vain, and your faith is also vain" (I. Cor. xv. 14). But now, since He is arisen, the heavenly Father has impressed upon Him the seal of truthfulness; now all men who have eyes to see and ears to hear must confess that Jesus Christ, crucified and arisen from the dead, is the true messenger of God; therefore, that all His words are truth, also the words: "I and the Father are one" (John x. 30); consequently, that He is true God.

2. The Resurrection is also *in itself*, abstracting from the fact that Christ appeals to it in particular, the chief evidence of His Godhead; for it is of its own nature the most convincing argument. Why? Because it is not only a miracle, but *the greatest of all miracles*. The greatest of all miracles, says St. Augustine, is the raising of one who is dead to life; but of all the miracles of resuscitation the most marvellous is the raising of one's self to life. For evidently only the man who is at the same time God can raise himself to life. Only a God-man can in truth say: " I lay it [My life] down of Myself, and I have power to lay it down; and I have power to take it up again " (John x. 18). The Resurrection of Jesus Christ is, therefore, of its very nature, the clearest and most convincing evidence of His Divinity.

3. Besides, the Resurrection is the *most manifest* and best established of all the miracles worked by our Divine Lord. And this extraordinary certainty it owes, by a special disposition of divine Providence, to a circumstance which was intended and well calculated to effect the contrary—namely, to the hatred of the Scribes and Pharisees against the person of Jesus Christ. Their implacable hatred against Him induced them to have recourse to a measure which shows beyond all doubt that the bitterest enemies of Our Lord considered His Resurrection as the decisive proof of His Divinity, but which, at the same time, placed the fact of the Resurrection beyond the possibility of a doubt. This measure consisted in placing a strong guard at the grave of Our Lord, lest, as they declared to Pilate, the body should be removed secretly and the last error should be worse than the first, that is, lest the people might believe in His Resurrection, and thus be invincibly led to acknowledge Him as the promised Messias,

as the Son of God. This step evidently shows what importance the enemies of Christ attached to His Resurrection, namely, that he who believed in His Resurrection must of necessity believe in His Godhead.

But by this measure, at the same time, the fact of the Resurrection *is placed beyond the shadow of a doubt*. For thus it becomes absolutely impossible to explain the disappearance of Christ's body otherwise than by His Resurrection. If the Scribes and Pharisees had omitted this precaution, they might with some show of probability have said that the disciples of Our Lord had secretly removed the body. But can they do so now? True, in their embarrassment they take refuge to this pretext; but who does not now see their absurdity? How could the apostles take away the body, while the guard is stationed at the grave? And if, as the Jews pretended, the guard was asleep, who was witness of the deed? Was it the sleeping soldiers? Must we not, therefore, admire the wisdom of Jesus Christ, who has availed Himself of His most bitter enemies to give the most convincing evidence of His Resurrection, and thus to strengthen us in the belief in His Godhead!

4. It is, finally, the Resurrection of Jesus Christ that of all His miracles *contributed most towards the propagation of the faith* in His Godhead, which is the foundation of Christianity. It was the Resurrection of Jesus Christ which the apostles first of all preached to the nations. This was the constant and almost only theme of their preaching; and it was this marvellous mystery which gave such efficacy and power to their preaching, as we read in the Acts of the Apostles: " With great power did the apostles give testimony of the Resurrection of Jesus Christ Our Lord ; and great grace was in them all" (Acts iv. 33). In fact, as the sacred writer

records, so great was the power of this argument that the hearers could not resist its force, and Jews and gentiles entered by thousands into the bosom of the infant Church. The Resurrection is, therefore, the chief evidence of the Godhead of Jesus Christ and the main-stay of our Christian faith.

But some one may say to me: Why go to such trouble to prove the Divinity of our blessed Lord, which we all believe? Beloved brethren, I am well aware of that; I know very well that you all without exception firmly believe in the Divinity of Jesus Christ. But what is an incomprehensible mystery to me is the *life* which, despite their faith in Jesus Christ, so many Christians lead. For if you believe in the Godhead of Jesus Christ, you believe also that God died for us on the cross, you believe that it was sin that nailed Him to the cross, and that, consequently, sin is the greatest evil, a deicide, the taking of the life of God. How can this conviction be reconciled with the lives of many amongst you, who have little or no detestation of sin, who seek the occasion of sin, daily offend God grievously, and live in the state of sin from year to year?

If you believe in Jesus Christ as the Son of God, you believe also in the *Church* which He founded—a divine institution established for our salvation, in which alone we can be saved—you believe that her commandments are the commandments of Christ, whose representative on earth she is; that these commandments are, consequently, divine and bind you in conscience to obedience. How can this belief, again, be reconciled with the behavior of some amongst you—for instance, with the conduct of parents who give their consent to mixed marriages on the part of their children; of young people who without cause absent themselves from Mass on Sundays and holy-days of obligation ; of all those who recklessly transgress the commandments of the Church? The only explanation of this sad fact is that the faith of such people is a dead faith ; and to enliven this faith was the object I had in view, and may Almighty God grant that my words may have the desired effect! But let us proceed further, and see how the Resurrection of Our Lord is the strongest motive to impel us to the love of the sacred Humanity of Jesus Christ.

II. THE MOTIVE OF OUR LOVE.

Love, my dear brethren, demands love in return. Now, the glorious Resurrection of Our Lord is not only a mystery of divine Omnipotence, but also *a mystery of infinite love.* This may seem to you at first sight a strange assertion, as the Resurrection, this stupendous miracle which has been worked in favor of the Humanity of Our Lord, would seem, if viewed superficially, to have no bearing on His infinite love. Yet this is so far from being the case that my assertion is well grounded and most undoubtedly true. For, under whatever aspect we consider the mystery of the Resurrection—whether in regard to its purpose, its circumstances, or its effects—we find that the infinite love of Jesus Christ is prominently manifested in it, nay, that in this mystery all the other mysteries of His love find their completion and perfection.

1. Let us consider, first, the *purpose* of the Resurrection. Its purpose is our salvation ; for, as truly as Jesus Christ by His Resurrection entered into His glory, so truly did He arise for our sanctification. And this truth is clearly laid down by the Apostle when he says that Jesus Christ, the Son of God, " was delivered up for our sins, and rose again for our justi-

fication" (Rom. iv. 25). He is arisen, as St. Augustine remarks, to awake in us a firm confidence in His sacred Person, and to enkindle in our hearts the fire of His love, which had consumed sin. Therefore the well-known words of Our Lord, "God so loved the world, as to give His only-begotten Son" (John iii. 16), refer no less to His Resurrection than to His Incarnation and death on the cross. For in the Resurrection the heavenly Father gives His only-begotten Son in a new and glorious manner for our salvation as our glorified saviour, shepherd, and teacher.

God gave Him as our *saviour*, because in the Resurrection it was that He sealed the work of our Redemption. For if Christ had not arisen from the dead, as we have seen, the work of our Redemption would remain ineffectual, without evidence, without stability, without authority. It might be compared to a document without a seal, which has no legal value. Had Christ not arisen from the dead, therefore, we might well exclaim with the Apostle: "The scandal of the cross is, therefore, made void" (Gal. v. 11). "Then Christ died in vain" (Ibid. ii. 21). It was, therefore, in this glorious mystery that Jesus Christ as Saviour consummated His work of infinite love, the work of our Redemption.

God gave Him as our *shepherd*. Did our blessed Lord not on this occasion manifest Himself particularly in the capacity of Good Shepherd? Did He not take care forthwith to gather His dispersed sheep and bring them back to the fold? Did He not take care to bring back to the salutary pasture of faith and hope those that had strayed into the desert of doubt and despair, as we see in the case of the incredulous St. Thomas, and of the two disciples with whom He journeyed to Emmaus? And was it not on this occasion that He secured for His flock to the end of time the visible and permanent good shepherd in the person of St. Peter and his successors, the supreme rulers of His Church? Where, then, has the Good Shepherd shown greater love to His sheep than in His Resurrection?

Finally, in the Resurrection God gave Him as our *teacher*. This St. Luke expressly tells us in the Acts (i. 3). Our Divine Lord devoted the forty days He remained on earth after His Resurrection to the instruction of the apostles in the mysteries of our religion, in order to introduce them into its fundamental truths, and thus enable them to instruct the world. For the doctrines which He reveals and explains to them during this period, as we learn from Holy Scripture, form the pith and substance of the Christian revelation.

From all this we see that the end of the Resurrection is our salvation, that Christ has arisen for our sanctification, and that the mystery of His glorious Resurrection is, consequently, if considered in its purpose, a grand manifestation of the infinite love of Jesus Christ to us, His children.

2. But the Resurrection of Our Lord is also in its *circumstances* the most striking manifestation of His love towards us. We shall consider but one circumstance, which is perhaps the most conspicuous in the glorious Resurrection of the Son of God—the fact that He retained the *marks of the wounds* on His glorious body. Why did He retain them? For many reasons, which were all prompted by His love for us, answers St. Augustine; reasons which cannot but make a deep impression on a faithful Christian's heart.

First of all, He retained the marks of the sacred wounds to show us that *He would not forget us* in His glory, but that He would fulfil what He had foretold by the mouth of His Prophet: "Behold, I have graven thee in My hands" (Is. xlix. 16). Behold these wounds, He says to each and every one of us; they shall forever remind Me of thee, and plead for thee! "Can a woman forget her infant, so as not to have pity on the son of her womb? And if she should forget, yet will not I forget thee. Behold, I have graven thee in My hands" (Ibid. 15, 16). How, then, could I forget My children!

Secondly, He retained the impress of the wounds to satisfy the justice of God, and *to plead* continually with the heavenly Father in our behalf. Truly has St. John said: "If any man sin, we have an advocate with the Father, Jesus Christ, the just" (I. John ii. 1). We can say to Him, in the words of the Royal Prophet: "My lots are in Thy hands" (Ps. xxx. 16). Yea, O sweetest Jesus, my lot is in Thy loving hands; it is not necessary that Thou shouldst speak for me; only lift Thy wounded hands to Thy heavenly Father, and Thou shalt obtain for me what Thou wilt.

Thirdly, our blessed Lord retained the marks of the wounds as a *memorial of His sufferings*, to keep the memory of His passion ever fresh in our minds, that we might always remember it with love and gratitude; that we might live as crucified with Christ; that we might deny our sinful inclinations and withstand the allurements of the world and the assaults of the evil spirit. For nothing is more suited, says St. Chrysostom, to secure for us this victory than the sight of a God who appears crucified on the throne of His glory. Thus we see that the Resurrection, considered in its circumstances, is eminently a **mystery of love.**

3. Finally, it is also a mystery of love in regard to its *effects*, or its eternal duration. For Jesus Christ, aris-

en from the dead, lives, and lives eternally, to gladden our hearts and fill them with love forever. In His glory He continually displays the most amiable object before the eyes of our souls; an object which is well fitted to inflame our hearts with love to His sacred Person— His glorious Humanity, radiant in the divine light of His Godhead. Is there anything in this world which might be compared with the glorious Humanity of Jesus Christ, which is the eternal delight of the saints? Does not this infinite glory continually admonish us to despise the things of earth and seek that which is heavenly, that which is represented to us by the glorious Humanity of Jesus Christ?

The Resurrection is, therefore, pre-eminently a mystery of love—of active, intense, permanent love, which extends beyond the grave and reaches into eternity. Does not such love demand our love in turn? Must not such love prevail upon us to lead a life that is pleasing to Jesus' loving Heart? Let us, then, to-day, on the glorious feast of His Resurrection, make the generous resolve to overcome ourselves, to conform ourselves with Jesus Christ in this life, that we may contemplate and love His glorious Humanity forever in heaven. Amen.

Easter Monday.

OUR OWN RESURRECTION.

"We shall all indeed rise again, but we shall not all be changed."
—I. Cor. xv. 51.

HAVING in yesterday's discourse considered the bearing of Christ's glorious Resurrection on His Godhead and Manhood—how it is the most powerful motive of faith in His Divinity and love towards His sacred Humanity—we shall to-day proceed to consider its relation to our own resurrection; to our future bodily resurrection at the end of time, as well as to our present spiritual resurrection to a new supernatural life. For we cannot hope for a glorious resurrection of the body unless we have first spiritually risen from the grave of sin; and unless we appear before the judgment-seat of God at our death with our souls arrayed in new life, that is, in sanctifying grace, our bodies shall not be glorified, according to the words of my text: "We shall all indeed arise, but we shall not all be changed."

What, then, is the bearing of Christ's glorious Resurrection upon *our own bodily and spiritual resurrection?* The answer to this twofold question will form the subject of the present discourse. The two points, therefore, which will occupy your attention are—

1. *Christ's Resurrection and our bodily resurrection;*
2. *Christ's Resurrection and our spiritual resurrection.*

1. CHRIST'S RESURRECTION AND OUR BODILY RESURRECTION.

The glorious Resurrection of Jesus Christ bears a twofold relation to our future bodily resurrection. It is at the same time the pledge and the pattern of our resuscitation from the dead.

1. *The pledge.* Christ's triumph over death and the grave leaves no room to doubt our future resurrection. For from this glorious fact it is manifest that Jesus Christ, the risen Saviour, is both able and willing to raise us to life again.

a. He is *able* to raise us; for, if He could raise Himself to life again, it is evident that He can also raise us. And the reason of this power lies in His Divinity, which is manifested in His own Resurrection; for only a Godman has power thus to lay down His life and take it up again (John x. 18). If, then, Christ raised Himself to life again, He is truly God, and can also raise us to life. Or, should He who first called us forth from our nothingness into existence not be able to resuscitate our bodies from the dust, and restore to them the soul which He first breathed into them? If, therefore, Christ Himself arose from the dead, He can also rebuild this tenement of ours, and again pour into it this same lifegiving soul.

b. But neither does the Resurrection of Jesus Christ leave any room for doubt that He is *willing* actually to raise us from the dead; at least, in the supposition that we abide in His love, that is, die as living members of His mystic body. For the head and the members naturally belong together; and where the head is there should be the members. Since, therefore, Christ, who is the head, is risen from the dead, must He not naturally desire to have us, the members, united with Him, and, consequently, be willing, and even eager, to raise us to life again, that, as the head lives, so also the members may live? Justly, then, does the Apostle say: " Now, if Christ be preached that He arose again from the dead, how do some among you say, that there is no resurrection of the dead?" (I. Cor. xv. 12.) The Resurrection of our blessed Lord is, therefore, in truth a sure pledge of our future resuscitation from the dead. But it is likewise, as I have said—

2. *The pattern* of our future resurrection. Is it not a general law of the divine art and workmanship of God, in the supernatural as well as in the natural order, that the members should be proportioned and similar to the head? This being the case, Christ will not only raise us again to life, but He will raise us in a condition altogether conformable to His own, that is, in a transfigured spiritual and glorious state, according to the words of the Apostle, who says that He " will reform the body of our lowness, made like to the body of His glory " (Phil. iii. 21). If, therefore, you wish to know the future condition of our bodies in the resurrection, I answer that, like the transfigured body of Christ, they shall possess the four glorious attributes of impassibility, brightness, agility, and spirituality.

Our bodies shall be endowed with the gift of *impassibility*, or incorruptibility, whereby they shall forever be exempted from decay, from suffering, and from death, according to the words of the Apostle, who assures us that, being sown in corruption, they shall rise in incorruption (I. Cor. xv. 42). Like Christ, once arisen we shall die no more; death shall have no more power over us (Rom. vi. 9). This corruptible body of ours shall put on incorruption; this perishable frame shall put on immortality; then shall death be swallowed up in victory (I. Cor. xv. 53, 54).

They shall be arrayed in *brightness* and glory. Then shall they shine like the stars of the firmament, star differing from star in glory (Ibid. 41). Being sown in dishonor, they shall rise in glory (Ibid. 43).

They shall be gifted with such *agility*, or suppleness,

as to be exempted from the laws of time and space, so as to be able to move at pleasure, through the spaces, with the quickness of thought, from one end of the universe to the other. Being sown in weakness, they shall rise in power (Ibid. 43).

And like the glorious body of Our Lord, which no barrier could preclude from the object of His desire, as when He entered into the supper-room and stood in the midst of His apostles, while the doors were shut, so our awakened bodies on the last day shall possess the property of *spirituality*, or penetrability, so that no obstacle can bar them from the place or object of their affection. Sown as natural bodies, they shall rise as spiritual bodies (Ibid. 44).

The Resurrection of Christ is, therefore, not only the pledge, but also the pattern of our glorious resurrection, provided we only conform ourselves with Him in this life. If we take part in His sufferings, that is, if we deny ourselves in this life and follow Him faithfully, we shall also have a full share in His glory. But in order to do this, we must first arise spiritually with Him to a new life; for it is only this spiritual resurrection, on our part, and this newness of life, that can give us the surety of a glorious resurrection with Christ on the last day. But for this spiritual resurrection Jesus Christ in His glorious Resurrection again offers us a true model.

II. CHRIST'S RESURRECTION AND OUR SPIRITUAL RESURRECTION.

That the glorious Resurrection of Jesus Christ is the model of our own spiritual resurrection is clearly testified by the words of the Apostle St. Paul, where he says: "We are buried together with Him by baptism into death; that as Christ is risen from the dead by the glory of the Father, so we may also walk in newness of life" (Rom. vi. 4). As the Resurrection of Our Lord, therefore, was a true and permanent one, so also *our spiritual resurrection* should be true and permanent.

1. *True.* The Resurrection of Christ was therefore a true one, because, after it had taken place, there was, on the one hand, no longer any vestige of His death, and, on the other hand, He gave the most unmistakable manifestations of life.

a. No vestige of death remained. The heavy stone with which the grave was secured was rolled away; the grave lay open and empty; the winding-sheets lay folded within; the guards had fled; the grave was deserted.

So also, beloved brethren, in *our* spiritual resurrection no traces of death must be left. The heavy weight of sin that pressed upon our conscience must be removed. The grave of our souls, which was shut and sealed, must be opened by a sincere and sorrowful confession of our sins. The guards that kept watch at the gates of our souls to prevent our spiritual resurrection, that is, the enemies that held us in their power, must be dispersed and put to flight by the absolution of the priest. The shrouds that held our limbs and our souls entangled in their folds, viz., our passions, our evil inclinations, and sinful habits, must be loosed and cast aside. Finally, the grave must be empty and deserted, that is, the proximate occasion of sin, that foul dungeon in which our souls were so long imprisoned, must be abandoned; in short, we must walk in the fulness of life, that it may be said of us, as the angels said to the holy women at the grave: "Why seek ye the living with the dead? He is not here, but is risen" (Luke xxiv. 5, 6).

b. After His Resurrection, Christ gave *unmistakable signs of life.* St. Luke, in the Acts of the Apostles, tells us that " He showed Himself alive after His passion, by many proofs, for forty days appearing to them [His apostles and disciples], and speaking of the kingdom of God " (Acts i. 3). He therefore showed Himself, showed Himself frequently, in various places, and to different persons; but He manifested Himself in the newness of His glory, always working for the kingdom of God, and interested for the salvation of souls.

Thus, *we* too, beloved brethren, if we would arise with Christ to a new life, must give clear proofs of spiritual life. We must prove our supernatural life by supernatural works—by a thorough internal change of disposition; by a newness of life altogether different from the past; by the earnest, faithful, and conscientious discharge of those various duties towards God, our neighbors, and ourselves, which we have thus far but too sadly neglected. But in order that we may be an exact copy of our risen Saviour, our spiritual resurrection must, likewise, be—

2. *Permanent.* " Now, if we be dead with Christ," says St. Paul, " we believe that we shall live also together with Christ; knowing that Christ, rising again from the dead, dieth now no more; death shall no more have dominion over Him. So do you also reckon that you are dead to sin, but alive unto God in Christ Jesus Our Lord " (Rom. vi. 8-11). With these words the Apostle evidently proposes the glorious Resurrection of Christ as the model of our spiritual resurrection, and insists particularly on the permanence of the Resurrection of Our Lord. As Christ Our Lord, therefore, arose from the dead to die no more, so we should arise from the grave of sin to new spiritual life to die no more; in other words, our spirit-

ual resurrection should be a permanent one. And, in fact, what will it avail us to have risen from spiritual death, if we die again, if we fall again into the same grave, if we again relapse into our former sinful condition, and in this state be called before God's awful tribunal? Thus our last state shall be worse than the first.

But *how* can we make our spiritual resurrection a permanent one? I answer: we must employ those means that are especially adapted to secure for us the grace of perseverance. Therefore we must—

a. Frequently and seriously *reflect* on the malice and pernicious effects of the relapse into sin. We must often think that it is the vilest and most shameful ingratitude, after we have regained sanctifying grace, the friendship of God, the right of inheritance and freedom of His children, to throw away those precious gifts and to cast ourselves again into the grave of corruption and sin. We must bear in mind that sin is the greatest perfidy on our part, after we have made so many good resolutions and given so many promises of amendment and perseverance; that it is the most outrageous mockery of God, after so many sighs and tears of penance, again to return to our evil ways.

b. We must carefully *avoid* those occasions which have given rise to our sins, and which sad experience has shown us to be connected with danger to our salvation; convinced that, if we seek the danger, we cannot avoid the sin, but are sure to relapse, and return again to the grave from whence we have arisen.

c. We must assiduously *resort* to the means of preserving our spiritual life and vigor, viz., prayer, devotion to the Blessed Virgin and to the Sacred Heart of Jesus. But, above all, beloved brethren, do not neglect to draw the invigorating waters of eternal life from the fountains of salvation, that is, from the holy Sacraments of Penance and the Eucharist. Thus cleansed, and sanctified, and strengthened in the Blood of Jesus Christ, you will triumph over the death and grave of sin, and, being once risen with Christ, you shall die no more.

Therefore, to conclude, I say with the Apostle, "if you be risen with Christ, seek the things that are above; mind the things that are above, not the things that are upon the earth" (Col. iii. 1, 2). Let your thoughts, and aims, and desires be heavenward bent, directed to God, towards the securing of the salvation of your souls. If you have once spiritually arisen with Christ, continue to make a good use of the means of salvation, and you will certainly persevere in the supernatural life to which by the mercy of God you have been raised; and when the last dread trumpet shall sound to awake the dead to judgment, it will be for you, not a signal of terror, but of joy, summoning you to a glorious resurrection, to be united with Christ, your head, in the infinite glory of His Resurrection forever. Amen.

Feast of the Ascension.

ON HEAVEN.

"And the Lord Jesus, after He had spoken to them, was taken up into heaven, and sitteth on the right hand of God.—Mark xvi. 19.

TO-DAY we commemorate the glorious Ascension of our blessed Lord into heaven, there to take up His permanent abode at the right hand of His heavenly Father. This mystery forcibly reminds us that not this earth, but heaven is our true home. For, if Christ is our head, and we His members; and if where the head is, there should be also the members, it is manifest that our resting-place is not on earth, but in heaven. This being the case, our thoughts, desires, and intentions should be directed towards heaven; we should seek our happiness, not in this vale of misery, but in our heavenly home. And that is what I would exhort you to in the present discourse. For this end I will put before you two motives which are well suited to induce us to seek the things that are above, not the things of this world. The first is the nothingness and insufficiency of the goods of earth; the second is the infinite worth and fulness of the treasures of heaven. Being once fully convinced of these two truths, we cannot but conceive an inward contempt of the things of this world, and a high esteem and intense longing for the infinite riches of the heavenly kingdom; and both will be equally efficacious to make us seek our bliss, not in this world, but in the world to come. It will be my endeavor, therefore, as far as lies in my power, to make you understand—

1. *The nothingness of the goods of earth;*
2. *The infinite value of the goods of heaven.*

May our Divine Lord shed a ray of His glorious light upon us, that we may learn to despise what is earthly and love and seek what is heavenly!

I. THE NOTHINGNESS OF THE GOODS OF EARTH.

The goods of this world are vile and altogether unfit to make us truly happy. That only can make us truly happy which can completely satisfy our inborn longing for happiness. Until this inward longing is gratified, we can have no rest. This natural craving of our hearts for absolute bliss must needs be appeased. Now, I maintain that no earthly good can satisfy this craving, or hunger and thirst, for happiness. The goods of this world are partly inward, or such as pertain to the well-being of our person—for instance, knowledge, which is the treasure of the mind, and health, which constitutes the good of the body—partly outward, or such as are accessory to our person. And both are equally inadequate to produce perfect happiness.

1. First, with regard to the *internal goods*, though they are by far the noblest and best we can enjoy in this life, yet they fail to make us truly happy. For, let a man enjoy the most perfect health, yet he will have much to suffer from the many ills and calamities with which even the happiest in this life are familiar—toils, hardships, cares, reverses, death itself, and the numberless evils which either press upon him or threaten him in the distance. Again, however deeply a man may have drunk at the fountain of knowledge, yet his mental store is small, and almost vanishes when contrasted with the countless things he does not know. Our knowledge here on earth is only piece-work, and

cannot, therefore, satiate our yearning and make us truly happy.

2. How much less, then, are the *external goods* of this life capable of satisfying our longing for happiness, if those inward goods, which are much more perfect, fall so far short of this effect. All outward goods may be reduced to three distinct classes: riches, honor and its accompanying influence, and sensual enjoyments.

a. Among all external goods there is none that exerts a more powerful influence on man than *riches;* yet they cannot make us truly happy. For how could that good make us happy which is unable to appease the craving of our hearts, but only enhances our thirst for possession? How could that make us truly happy which deprives the body of its rest and the soul of its peace; which by its increase only adds to those cares and anxieties which are the thorns and thistles that stifle the growth of true internal happiness?

Let us examine only one of those properties of riches a little more closely. I said that riches, *far from satisfying, only increase* our thirst for earthly possessions. Does not experience bear out this statement? Do you remember, my dear friend, how, when you came to this country, you had no further ambition than to secure a comfortable home? You thought, that if you had once a house that you could call yours, be it ever so humble, your happiness would be complete. With much toil and patience you gained the object of your desire. No king was happier than you, when you took possession of your new home. That was a little realm in which you were lord, and reigned supreme. Your satisfaction was great and at the same time pure and laudable. But soon your eye fell on the house of your neighbor, which was much larger, and finer, and more comfortable than your own. Then you thought:

Oh, if I possessed such a residence! All your joy was gone. You had no rest, until you had realized your desire. But then the old furniture was no longer to your taste; a new and costly set had to be procured. Were you then satisfied? Perhaps for the moment; but you soon grew impatient of your dependence on others. You had as yet no business of your own; you worked only for others. Again you could find no rest in your present situation. The thought of establishing a business of your own haunted you day and night. Why should I work for others? I have been long enough a slave, you thought to yourself. I have sufficient capital; so I shall sell out and set up on my own account. You did so; you sacrificed the comforts of your new home and threw your whole heart, and soul, and the last farthing of your money into your business. Your business throve, as I suppose. Your fortune gradually accumulated. But were you then satisfied with your progress? Did not your desires increase with your fortune? The more you had the more you desired. And has not your craving for money continued to increase to this day? Thus you see, beloved brethren, that riches do not satisfy the craving of man for wealth, but rather stimulate and intensify it.

b. Are the *honors, dignities,* and *power,* which this world can bestow, of more avail to secure true happiness? Such is the dream of the proud and ambitious. But with what cares and anxieties are these goods not fraught! To what criticism, and hatred, and envy, and jealousy, and suspicion do they not expose their possessors! And how often does it not happen that those much coveted earthly distinctions make their owners the object of ridicule and contempt, by exposing their faults and weaknesses to the public gaze?

For, as he who stands on an eminence is thereby not rendered better, or better-looking, but only more exposed to view, that he may be seen by all as he really is, so he who is placed in a position of honor, dignity, and influence is not thereby rendered wiser or better, but only exhibited to the gaze of all with whatever good or evil qualities he possesses. Therefore it by no means seldom happens that one who in his private capacity was looked upon as prudent, honest, and sincere was, after being promoted to a high position, discovered or at least unjustly stamped as a fool, a knave, or a cheat. And the higher the dignity and the greater the power man attains to on this earth, the farther is he removed from true happiness. Ask the minister in the cabinet or the monarch on his throne, and he can only give the answer of Solomon, who had tasted the sweets of all earthly goods and honors: " vanity of vanities; and all is vanity!" Do we not see kings and emperors trembling on their thrones? All their power, and all their wealth and magnificence cannot secure them a tranquil night's sleep, or an hour of true happiness. Such is the inefficacy of worldly honors and their attendant dignity and power.

c. And what shall I say of the *sensual enjoyments* of this world? It goes without saying, beloved brethren, that these cannot make us truly happy, as they only impede those functions in which our true happiness consists. They clog the activity of the understanding, weaken the will, obscure the light of reason, blunt the acuteness of the mind, ruin the health of the body, and produce only loathing, grief and remorse. Where there is question of true happiness, therefore, sensual enjoyments cannot be taken into account.

3. From what I have so far said, we must manifestly conclude that the goods of this world, taken singly or

in separate classes, cannot make us truly happy. But may they not be more efficacious if *taken together?* This I deny; though we possessed them all, in all their fulness, not only what is vile and contemptible amongst them, but also what is prized highest, what is noblest and most sublime in this world. And why? For the simple reason that one attribute is always wanting to them, without which they can impossibly fill the measure of our happiness—they are *perishable*. Whatever attractions they may have, whatever enjoyments they may afford, they are fleeting, they are transitory, they may soon decay; and therefore their possession is always connected with fear and anxiety. But where there are fear and anxiety there cannot possibly be true happiness.

Do not these considerations, few and brief as I have been obliged to make them, amply show the nothingness of the goods of this world? Those who seek their happiness on earth, therefore, only lose time and labor, seeking bliss where it is not to be found. And yet, how many there are who thus labor in vain! How many there are, even among well instructed Christians and Catholics, who should know better, and yet allow themselves to be carried away by the current of this material age, and to be ruled by the perverse spirit of this world! Are there not amongst us many who seem to have no higher aspiration than to hoard up money and accumulate wealth? Are there not such whose only thought, from morning till night and from day to day, is to become rich? If the loss of their precious time were the only damage they bring upon themselves, it were an incalculable loss, it is true; yet it might be borne or repaired to some extent. But that is not all. For, besides forfeiting the peace of their souls, which is the only good in this world that deserves the name, if they continue on the course of their worldliness, they shall also infallibly suffer the loss of their eternal happiness. For the eternal happiness to which we are called consists in the beatific vision of God face to face, to which only those can attain who despise the goods of this life, at least so far as not to neglect those of heaven, which alone can make us truly happy.

II. INFINITE VALUE OF THE GOODS OF HEAVEN.

The true and perfect happiness of man consists in the *vision of God face to face*. For what is it that constitutes the infinite happiness of God Himself? It is nothing else than the contemplation of Himself. If the aspect of a beautiful object—of charming natural scenery, of the starry firmament—can give us such delight, what rapture, what unspeakable delight, must not the intuition of the infinite beauty and perfection of God awake in the soul that has been admitted into His blissful presence! As this intuition forms the infinite bliss of God Himself, so it will render us infinitely happy. Happiness, as I have said before, consists in the perfect possession of all goods. But the contemplation of God face to face puts the blessed in the perfect possession of all goods, so that their yearning for happiness is perfectly satisfied. For, notwithstanding the simplicity and spirituality of this beatific vision, it comprises all that the heart of man can desire; nay, infinitely more than we can realize in this present life, according to the words of the Apostle: "Eye hath not seen, nor ear heard, neither hath it entered into the heart of man, what things God hath prepared for them that love Him" (I. Cor. ii. 9). It affords infinite riches, boundless power, inconceivable dignity and honor, and unspeakable delight.

1. And, first of all, as to the *riches* of heaven, suffice

it to say that the blessed will possess God Himself, the infinite riches. God, who is all in all, will be their possession, their home, their food, their drink, their raiment. His riches will be theirs, His glory will be theirs, His joys will be theirs, He Himself will be theirs. What, then, can be wanting to the fulness of their possession, if they possess the Infinite Good Itself? Will not the boundless treasure of God's riches satisfy every desire and appease every yearning of their hearts, so that they will rest in the abundance of every possession? Is this not the fulness which Almighty God Himself promises to His faithful servants: "Good measure, and pressed down, and running over, shall be given unto your bosom"? (Luke vi. 38.) Again, our blessed Lord says of the good and faithful servant: "Amen, I say to you, He shall place Him over all His goods" (Matt. xxiv. 47). What words, then, can express the fulness of the treasures which the all-faithful, and all-possessing, and all-bountiful God here promises to His faithful servants? Only he can conceive the riches of the blessed who can fathom the endless treasures of God; for "He will place them over all His goods."

2. What must, accordingly, be the *power* of the blessed in heaven! They are not only secure from every grief or harm, but in a certain sense almighty. For we call him almighty who can accomplish whatever he desires, and whose will nothing can thwart. And this is literally true of the blessed in heaven. For their will is so perfectly united with the will of the All-powerful that they will nothing but what God wills; that God's will is their will; that God's greater pleasure is their greater desire and delight. Hence all their wishes are accomplished, and nothing takes place but what they wish. But is not this perfect harmony with the will of God, in a certain true sense,

omnipotence? Therefore the Psalmist exclaims in his astonishment: "The saints shall rejoice in glory, they shall be joyful in their beds. The high praises of God shall be in their mouth; and two-edged swords in their hands; to execute vengeance upon the nations, chastisements among the people; to bind their kings with fetters, and their nobles with manacles of iron; to execute upon them the judgment that is written; this glory is to all His saints" (Ps. cxlix. 5–9).

3. Yet their *honor and dignity* are no less than their power. Or can there be any greater honor, any greater glory, than to be seated around the throne of the Son of God as His friends, as the members of His household; nay, as kings and princes to sit upon the throne of the King of kings, as He promised His faithful followers with the words: "To him that shall overcome, I will grant to sit with Me in My throne; as I also have overcome and am set down with My Father in His throne"! (Apoc. iii. 21.) Will not the blessed, when promoted to this sublimest of dignities, forget their former toils and struggles and suffering for Christ's sake, when God with His own almighty hand shall place upon their brow the crown of victory, and, in the presence of all the heavenly hosts, conduct them to the throne of their glory? Then shall they understand the meaning of the words of the Apostle: "The sufferings of this time are not worthy to be compared with the glory to come, that shall be revealed in us" (Rom. viii. 18).

4. The joys, finally, of the saints are such that they defy all description. No human mind can conceive them, nor words depict them; not even the words of him who was rapt to the third heaven. Joy is always proportioned to the object that produces it; and as the object of the delight of the saints is God Him-

self, the infinite greatness and goodness, contemplated face to face, satisfying to the full every faculty of the soul, their joy and delight must be infinite and, therefore, surpass all human understanding and expression. Nay, as the vision of God consists in the most intimate union of the human soul with its Creator, so that the blessed contemplator becomes, as it were, one soul and one spirit with God, the infinite joy and bliss of God becomes the joy and bliss of His saints. The infinite delight of God Himself is therefore the delight of His saints. If, then, all the joys and pleasures of all men who ever lived were united in one human breast, it would be as a tiny drop compared with that ocean of delights in which the blessed in heaven are immerged.

Oh, what joy and delight it will be to contemplate without ceasing that face from which sun, moon, and stars, and the whole universe have borrowed their beauty! What joy and delight, to possess the Supreme Good, which is the sum and substance of all goods; to be able to call our own that infinite world of perfection, which is in itself a thousand worlds! If the queen of Saba, after seeing the glory, and listening to the words, of the wise Solomon, enraptured, exclaimed: " Blessed are thy men, and blessed are thy servants, who stand before thee always, and hear thy wisdom " (III. Kings x. 8), what unspeakable delight must it not be always to stand in the presence of, and listen to the words of, the true Solomon, the eternal and uncreated Wisdom! What delight to contemplate as it is the inscrutable mystery of the Most Holy Trinity, and to see in God all things for the knowledge of which the mind of man may crave! For what can be hidden to him who beholds the mirror in which all things are reflected? Then the human mind shall rest in the possession of all knowledge. Then all the desires of the human will shall be gratified in the possession of all good. Then shall we sing that canticle of praise, which, though ever sung, is always new, being the constant expression of never-fading joy. For, as the glorious bodies of the blessed shall neither perish nor grow old, so their joy, and delight, and glory shall never wane nor fade, but ever remain unchanged in their original purity and freshness.

How dreadful would be our misfortune, then, beloved brethren, if for the vile and perishable goods of this earth we should lose this infinite and endless treasure of everlasting happiness! Let us, therefore, to-day, that our divine Master has given us in His Ascension a glimpse of the glory of His heavenly kingdom, make the firm purpose to combat the immoderate attachment to the things of this earth, and to set our whole heart on the treasures of heaven. Let us resolve henceforth to manage our temporal affairs, not for the gratification of our passions—of our avarice, ambition, and sensuality—but as the discharge of a duty that has been imposed upon us by God, that the things of this world may be for us a stepping-stone to things eternal. Thus our hearts shall be free, and we shall walk without faltering to the goal of glory which Our Lord has ascended to prepare for us in His heavenly kingdom. Amen.

Whitsunday.

MISSION OF THE HOLY GHOST.

"But the Paraclete, the Holy Ghost, whom the Father will send in My name, He will teach you all things, and will bring all things to your mind, whatsoever I shall have said to you."—John xiv. 26.

THE mission of the Holy Ghost, referred to in the words cited, which took place on the day of Pentecost, after Our Lord's Ascension, is the chief object of to-day's celebration. This feast commemorates the day on which the promulgation of the New Law was inaugurated by the apostles in Jerusalem. But this inauguration, as you know, is the work of the Holy Ghost, the fruit of His mission. For it was the Holy Ghost who inspired and transformed the apostles and fitted them for the great work which they had been called to fulfil. Therefore I have chosen *the mission of the Holy Ghost* for the subject of my discourse, with a view to contribute to the renewal of your devotion to the Third Person of the Adorable Trinity. But as the sending of the Holy Ghost upon the apostles on the feast of Pentecost can hardly be sufficiently understood without first having a clear idea of the mission of the Holy Ghost in general, I must first premise a few truths, that will give you the necessary insight into this mystery. I shall, therefore, treat—

1. *Of the mission of the Holy Ghost in general;*
2. *Of His special mission on the feast of Pentecost.*

I. MISSION OF THE HOLY GHOST IN GENERAL.

What, then, are we to understand by the mission of the Holy Ghost in general? In order to answer this question thoroughly we must understand two things: viz., *by whom* and *to whom* He is sent. For, a messenger, or one who is sent, must be sent by another to a third party. This belongs to the nature of a true mission, such as we believe that of the Holy Ghost to be.

1. To the first question I answer that the Holy Ghost is *sent by the Father and the Son*. For Christ says: "I will ask the Father, and He shall give you another Paraclete, that He may abide with you forever, the Spirit of truth" (John xiv. 16-17); and again He says: "It is expedient to you that I go; for if I go not, the Paraclete will not come to you; but if I go, I will send Him to you" (Ibid. xvi. 7). From these two passages it is manifest that the Holy Ghost is sent, and that He is sent by the Son as well as by the Father. However, though this truth is certain beyond all doubt, it is not so easy to explain *how* one Divine Person can send another, who is equal to Him in all things. Nay, this difficulty is so great that it led the followers of the heretic Arius to deny the Divinity of the Holy Ghost. For, they argued, the Holy Ghost is sent by the Father and the Son, as is evident from the Scriptures; but the person sent is always less than the person who sends. Thus the servant is sent by his master, the soldier by his officer. Therefore, they concluded, the Holy Ghost, who is sent, must be less than the Father and the Son, by whom He is sent.

Yet no truth is more clearly contained in Holy Scripture than the *Godhead of the Holy Ghost*. Numerous are the passages of Holy Writ in which this truth is unmistakably laid down or hinted at. And, first of all, is it not peculiar to God alone to be everywhere present? Now, the Psalmist says: "Whither shall I go from Thy Spirit; or whither shall I flee from Thy face?" (Ps. cxxxviii. 7.) Again, is it not peculiar to God alone to fill all places with His presence? But the Wise Man says: "The Spirit of the Lord hath filled the whole world" (Wis. i. 7). Is it not peculiar to God alone to know all things? And the Apostle says: "The Spirit searcheth all things, yea, the deep things of God" (I. Cor. ii. 10). Is it not peculiar to God alone to do all things, and to dispense the gifts of grace? But the same Apostle says: "All these things one and the same Spirit worketh, dividing to every one according as He will" (Ibid. xii. 11). Is it not peculiar to God alone to create? Now, what does the Royal Prophet say of the Spirit? "Thou shalt send forth Thy Spirit, and they shall be created; and thou shalt renew the face of the earth" (Ps. ciii. 30). Is it not, in fine, peculiar to God alone to have a temple for His dwelling-place? And again, the Apostle says: "Know you not that your members are the temple of the Holy Ghost, who is in you? Glorify and bear God in your body" (I. Cor. vi. 19-20). And who was it that spoke through the mouth of the prophets? Was it not God? For we read in the canticle of Zachary: "Blessed be the Lord God of Israel; for He hath visited and wrought the redemption of His people; . . . as He spoke by the mouth of His holy prophets, who are from the beginning" (Luke i. 68-70). But St. Peter assures us that it was God the Holy Ghost who spoke through the prophets; "for," he says, "prophecy came not by the will of man at any time; but the holy men of God spoke, inspired by the Holy Ghost" (II. Pet. i. 21). Finally, St. Peter in the Acts of the Apostles expressly teaches the Divinity of the Holy Ghost, when he says to Ananias: "Why hath Satan tempted thy heart, that thou shouldst lie to the Holy Ghost? . . . Thou hast not lied to men but to God" (Acts v. 3-4).

The Holy Ghost is, therefore, true God, equal to the Father and the Son. He is sent, then, not as an inferior but as an equal both by the Father and the Son.

How, then, are we to understand His mission? Beloved brethren, a mission or sending may take place in two ways: first, by command; and, secondly, by production. In the first manner the servant is sent by his master, the embassador by his sovereign or government; in the second way the rays of light and heat are sent by the sun, sweet odor is diffused by the flower. In the first case the person sent is an inferior; for only an inferior can receive a command, and only a superior can give such. But not so in the second case; for the light and heat of the sun, the sweet scent of the flower, are nothing foreign to the nature of the sources from which they are sent; and if the sun or the flower were something simple and indivisible, as is the nature of God, it would communicate not a part, but the whole of its nature. It is, therefore, in the second manner, that is, *by production*, that both the Son and the Holy Ghost are sent; the Son of the Father alone, by generation, the Holy Ghost of the Father and the Son as the mutual act of their infinite love. There is this difference, however, as I have said, between production in God and in His creatures, that God, being simple and indivisible, communicates His entire nature, while the creatures communicate their nature only in part. Thus the Holy Ghost is said to be sent, to be produced, or to proceed from the Father and the Son, as from one source or principle.

2. Let us now proceed to answer the second question: *To whom*, or *where* is the Holy Ghost sent? We say that a Divine Person has been sent, or comes to a certain person or place, when He begins to dwell or to operate with that person, or in that place, in a

new and special manner. For, as God is everywhere present, we cannot say that a Divine Person comes, or is sent, where He did not exist before; but only that He exists or operates there in a new and special way, in which He did not exist or operate before. Thus the Son and the Holy Ghost were in the world from the beginning. Therefore St. John says of the Son of God: "He was in the world, and the world knew Him not" (John i. 10). But He was not present from the beginning as man; and therefore He is said to be sent by the Father, that is, to have assumed a new mode of existence on earth: "And the Word was made flesh and dwelt amongst us" (Ibid. 14).

The mission of the Holy Ghost takes place in a *similar way*. He is said to be sent to us when He begins to dwell in us in a new manner, or when He begins to operate in us with His grace, and sanctify us in a new way. And what is this new manner in which the Holy Ghost dwells and operates in us? There are many and various ways—as many and as various as are the graces, gifts, and virtues which He communicates to the soul. If, for instance, an infidel or heretic is converted to the true faith, the Holy Ghost is sent to him with the gift of faith; He is present in his soul in a new way, operating through faith. If a sinner who has not lost the faith does penance, and is reconciled with God, the Holy Ghost is sent to him. For, though He operated in his soul already through the gift of faith, yet He now takes up His abode with him anew, and operates within him by sanctifying grace and the various supernatural virtues and gifts which He communicates to the sanctified soul.

This being the case, since the Holy Ghost comes into our hearts and transforms them; since He infuses salutary sorrow into our souls and gives us the grace of true repentance; since He continues to dwell in our hearts as in His temple, after they are once cleansed from sin; since He enlightens and inspires us, and urges us on to the practice of Christian virtue; since He is the true comforter, who confers upon us true peace and happiness, and smoothes our path to everlasting life; should we not love Him with our whole heart and our whole soul? Should we not often enter in the spirit of faith into our own hearts, which are His dwelling place, and there adore and honor Him? But still stronger motives of honor and devotion to the Third Person of the Blessed Trinity we shall find in —

II. HIS SPECIAL MISSION ON THE FEAST OF PENTECOST.

In order now to make you understand the wonderful mission of the Holy Ghost on the feast of Pentecost, which forms the chief object of to-day's feast, I may confine myself to what is peculiar to this great mystery, namely, the *manner* in which the Holy Ghost is here sent by the Father and the Son, and the *gifts* which He bestowed on the apostles on this occasion.

1. The *manner was new* and extraordinary. For He did not descend in the form of a dove, as He did on Our Lord at His baptism (John i. 32); not in a gentle breath, as on the occasion on which Jesus Christ conferred their highest spiritual authority on the apostles (Ibid. xx. 22); not at the preaching of the Gospel, as He descended on Cornelius, the centurion (Acts x. 14); nor, finally, in stillness and seclusion, as He once descended on the Mother of God (Luke i. 35). But, while the apostles were assembled in the upper room of the house, in fervent prayer and anxious expectation of the Comforter that had been promised them, "suddenly there came a sound from heaven as of a mighty wind

coming; and it filled the whole house where they were sitting. And there appeared to them parted tongues as it were of fire; and it sat upon every one of them, and they were all filled with the Holy Ghost; and they began to speak with divers tongues, according as the Holy Ghost gave them to speak" (Acts ii. 2-4).

But this manner of sending the Holy Ghost was not only new and unwonted; it was also highly *befitting*, and suited to the purpose of His mission. For by the various signs which accompanied this communication of the Holy Ghost were symbolized the various gifts which He bestowed on the apostles—the gift of wisdom, the gift of love, the gift of tongues, the gift of miracles. And who does not see in this wonderful fire which descended on the apostles the emblem of wisdom and of love? And do not the parted tongues clearly signify the gift of speaking various languages, which the apostles displayed on their first appearance as the preachers of the New Law? And what else is the signification of that mighty sound of winds coming from heaven than the wonderful power which they were to exert over the elements of nature, the power of working miracles; and, above all, that miracle of miracles, the conversion of the nations by their preaching? This commotion of the elements, at the same time, signifies the wonderful power of the Holy Ghost which was to reside with them, to confound and vanquish their enemies, and fill all men with holy awe and admiration of the power which God had given to men.

2. The *gifts* which the Holy Ghost communicated to the apostles on the feast of Pentecost were the best adapted to their vocation. Their vocation was to announce the Gospel of Christ to all nations, and to become the ideals and models of the preachers of God's word that were to come after them.

For this end, poor and ignorant fishermen as they were, they needed, in the first place, the *gift of wisdom*. Before appearing as teachers of others they themselves had to be instructed in the mysteries of the kingdom of God. And this was the work of the Holy Ghost, who was to teach them all truth, and practically to introduce them into the teachings of Christ, which so far they had been unable to understand.

No less necessary for them was the *gift of love*. For what would all their wisdom avail them, if they did not possess this virtue, so indispensable to the apostles of Christ? What is the fruit of the preaching of the Gospel if it enlightens the understanding without inflaming the heart? Now, it is love, and not wisdom, that inflames the heart; it is love that edifies; without it knowledge only puffeth up (I. Cor. viii. 1).

They further needed the *gift of tongues* and powerful eloquence. Their mission was to all people, of all tribes and tongues. But what would their wisdom and zeal profit them, if their words could not reach the minds and hearts of their hearers? This difficulty was remedied by the gift of tongues, in virtue of which, while they preached, they were understood by all as speaking in their own tongue. But it was necessary also that they should speak as having power, that they should convince and move their hearers. And therefore the Holy Ghost added to the gift of languages that of extraordinary eloquence, so that only the obdurate could withstand the power of their words.

Finally, it was befitting, if not necessary, that they should possess the *gift of miracles*. They were sent to preach a new religion, to enforce a new law—a religion and a law which were repugnant to human nature, and most particularly to a depraved and sensual generation. Miracles were, therefore, morally necessary to commend the truths which they preached, to impress upon their doctrine a divine seal, which no one could contest or gainsay. For miracles are the arguments of God Himself, which He is wont to use to accredit His special messengers here one earth. And without this divine approval their preachings would be vain.

Thus you see, beloved brethren, that the Holy Ghost equipped the apostles with all gifts requisite for their divine vocation. But the Holy Spirit is at all times ready to do the same in favor of all of us. How comes it, then, that the apostles received so largely, while we often obtain but a small share of the gifts of the Holy Ghost? One reason is, because the apostles had a much higher and more arduous vocation than we have, and therefore had need of a greater fulness of the gifts of the Spirit than we. But another reason is, that we have not the same intense longing for those supernatural gifts which the apostles had, and that we do not pray for them fervently, and dispose our hearts to receive them. In short, we have not sufficient devotion to the Holy Ghost.

And, in fact, how little are we accustomed to think of the Third Person of the Adorable Trinity! How seldom do we invoke the Holy Ghost! How seldom do we thank Him for the countless favors which He bestows on us! Numberless, indeed, are His benefits to us. For, as the works of omnipotence are attributed to the Father, the works of wisdom to the Son, so the works of love are attributed to the Holy Ghost, who is the Spirit of love. From Him proceed, therefore, all graces which we receive. It is He who sustains us in temptation and preserves us from sin; it is He who gives us the strength to overcome ourselves, to perform our duties faithfully, and to advance in perfection and holiness. In short, it is He who continually guides us on the way to our eternal salvation. How grateful and tender, then, should be our love to the Holy Spirit! Does not our own highest interest, as well as the duty of gratitude, demand that we should love and honor the Holy Ghost?

Let us, then, to-day, on this glorious feast of His manifestation, be renewed in our devotion to the Holy Ghost; let us henceforth carefully avoid all that could grieve this Spirit of love, and especially all impurity, whether in thought, word, or deed—this sin which most of all defiles His sacred temple—and let us invoke Him in all our necessities. Thus He will continue to dwell in our hearts, adorn them with His virtues and gifts in this life, and, in union with the Father and the Son, will be the source and the object of our eternal happiness. Amen.

Whitmonday.

BAPTISM.

"And he commanded them to be baptized in the name of the Lord Jesus Christ."—Acts. x. 48.

By the communication of the Holy Ghost, which was the subject of yesterday's discourse, the apostles, as we have seen, were fully equipped for the great mission which Christ had confided to them—the foundation of His Church among all nations. Therefore the descent of the Holy Ghost coincides in time with the establishment of the Church, so that the feast of Pentecost may properly be called the birth-day of the Church of Christ. Now, the gate by which we enter the Church is Baptism. Therefore St. Peter, as we read in to-day's epistle, commanded that even those who had already received the Holy Ghost should be baptized. "And he commanded them to be baptized in the name of the Lord Jesus Christ." For this reason I have taken Baptism for the subject of the present discourse; and I was the more eager to discuss this matter before you, because I am well aware that we are but too apt to lose sight of the blessings as well as the responsibilities attaching to this holy Sacrament. The blessings connected with the Sacrament of Baptism consist chiefly in the dignity which it confers upon us; but in order, as far as possible, to realize this dignity, it will be necessary, first, briefly to consider the nature of Baptism. We shall, therefore, ask ourselves, and answer, as briefly and fully as possible, the following three questions—

1. *What is Baptism?*
2. *What dignity does it confer upon us?*
3. *What duties does it impose upon us?*

I. NATURE OF BAPTISM.

What is Baptism? It may be described as a remedy for a very grievous and universal spiritual disease of the soul—a disease with which the whole human race is affected. This disease, as you all know, is *original sin*.

1. It is an undeniable fact, beloved brethren, that we are all born into this world under the curse of sin, *in a fallen state*. Even natural reason itself enables us to conjecture this. For, although, strictly speaking, God could have originally created us such as we now are, with all our moral weakness, depravity, and inclination to sin, yet it is not at all likely that He, who is so infinitely good and merciful, would have thus called into existence the masterpiece of all His works, the king of His visible creation, with such an inborn aversion to good and propensity to evil, as every reflecting human being experiences within his heart. Hence it is that reason itself emphatically confirms what Holy Scripture and Tradition expressly teach—that we are now in a fallen state; that we enter this world under the curse of sin, and are, therefore, a proscribed race; that we have all sinned in our first parent, Adam.

The *objections* often raised by unbelievers against this teaching commonly flow from a wrong conception of original sin. For original sin is falsely imagined by some to be similar to those sins which we ourselves personally commit. But this is an altogether erroneous notion; for original sin is not a sinful act of ours, as are our own personal sins; but it is a sinful state or condition, that is, a state of enmity or disfavor with God, which renders it impossible for us to gain our last end, and save our souls. Now, while it were not conceivable how we could have sinned in another by action, it is not at all difficult to understand how we contracted this state of guilt or disfavor with God through our first parent. For, if a father of a family, for instance, fails in business, he fails not only to himself personally, but also to his whole family and to all his heirs; and his descendants may, even centuries later, say with truth that they suffer a loss in or through him. Thus it is with original sin. It is not a sinful act of ours, but a sinful condition, that is, a state of disfavor with God, in which we are conceived and born into this world on account of the disobedience of our first parent, and which of itself makes salvation impossible for us. This disability we have contracted, therefore, through no fault of ours, but only as the descendants and heirs of our common father.

2. Having described to you the nature of the universal disease under which we labor, I shall now briefly show you *how God has remedied it*, and raised mankind again to His favor and friendship. For this end He sent a second Adam, more perfect than the first, His only-begotten Son made man, to be the father of all men according to the spirit, as the first Adam was the father of all according to the flesh, that in Him we might regain what we had lost in the first Adam. By the very fact of the Incarnation He gave us power to become His kindred, His heirs, and His children, and partakers of all His satisfactions and merits. Now, it is by Baptism that we are actually incorporated in the household of Jesus Christ, the second Adam; that we become His kindred and His heirs. "For," says the Apostle, "in *one* spirit were we all baptized into *one* body" (I. Cor. xii. 13); and that one body is the mystic body of Jesus Christ. Picture to yourselves, beloved brethren, one countless family, united by the grace and cemented by the blood of Jesus Christ, composed of three classes of members—the glorious in heaven, the militant on

earth, and the suffering in purgatory; picture to yourselves, if you can, this great body, so united, enlivened by the supernatural vital principle of sanctifying grace, with Christ triumphant in His glory in heaven as its Head, and you have a true idea of the Church as the mystic body of Jesus Christ. Now, it is Baptism that makes us living members of the Church, members of Christ's mystic body. How great, then, must be the dignity to which the holy Sacrament of Baptism elevates us!

II. DIGNITY CONFERRED ON US IN BAPTISM.

The dignity to which Baptism has raised us is incomparably great both in itself and on account of the rights and privileges attached to it.

1. Great is this dignity *in itself*. For, since Baptism makes us members of Christ's body, that is, His brothers and joint-heirs, it makes us, at the same time, children of the heavenly Father, and living temples of the Holy Ghost. Do not the members live the self-same life as the head? Do not we, then, as Christians, as members of Christ, live the life of Jesus Christ, our Head? And if we live the life of Jesus Christ, does not the Holy Ghost, who is His life and the breath of His love, live and work within us? Are we, then, not truly the temples of the Holy Ghost? Baptism, therefore, really raises us to the dignity of the children of God the Father, the brothers and joint-heirs of God the Son, and the sacred temples of God the Holy Ghost.

Hence our dignity as Christians is no despicable one, no merely human one; it is a supernatural and truly *divine* dignity, according to the words of Holy Scripture: "I have said: you are Gods, and all of you the sons of the Most High" (Ps. lxxxi. 6). The Christian, therefore, how poor, how lowly, how miserable, how despised soever he may be, is raised to a dignity infinitely above that of all kings, princes, and potentates of this world. Therefore St. Leo the Great in this connection exclaims: "Acknowledge, O Christian, acknowledge thy dignity, and having become partaker of the divine nature, beware of returning to an unworthy life, to thy former lowness! Remember of what body and of what head thou art a member; and forget not that thou art freed from the powers of darkness, and transferred into the light and kingdom of God!" Is there, then, my dear brethren, a dignity on earth to be compared with the dignity of the Christian, the dignity to which we have been raised by the holy Sacrament of Baptism?

2. But what still enhances this dignity are the *rights and privileges* connected with it. Baptism, in the first place, gives us a right to *sanctifying grace*. For, by making us members of Jesus Christ, it gives us a claim to the life that is in Him, to the supernatural and divine life of in-dwelling grace. Now, sanctifying grace is, as I have shown you on another occasion, the most precious treasure a man can possess on this earth.

But Baptism gives us a right to partake, not only of the grace but also of the *glory* of Jesus Christ. For the members of the body have a just claim not only to the life of the head, but also to the living union with it. Where the head is, there should be the members, as the partakers of its life, its functions, and its well-being. Where Christ the Head is, therefore, where Christ lives and reigns in His glory, there also the Christian shall once be, shall once live and reign for all eternity —there he shall eternally reside in the mansions of the blessed, be eternally free from all evils, eternally enjoy all goods, in union with Jesus Christ, his Head.

The dignity to which Baptism has raised us, therefore, infinitely surpasses all earthly greatness, both in itself and in the rights and privileges connected with it. So great is this dignity that it transcends all human conception and baffles all efforts at description. But the higher this dignity is to which Baptism has raised us, the greater are the responsibilities and duties it imposes upon us.

III. DUTIES IMPOSED ON US IN BAPTISM.

By Baptism, beloved brethren, we become members of Christ's mystical body. Baptism, therefore, requires of us, first of all, to *renounce Satan*, the adversary of Christ; and all His *pomps*, that is, the world with all its sinful allurements, and all the occasions of sin; all his *works*, that is, sin itself in all its various forms. For a member of Christ cannot at the same time be a servant and a slave of Satan, His arch-adversary. But servants and slaves of Satan are manifestly all those who do not renounce Satan, and the vanities of this world, and the works of darkness.

By Baptism we have been made members of Jesus Christ. By Baptism, therefore, we have taken upon ourselves the obligation to *believe* in the teaching of Jesus Christ—to believe in the Triune God: the Father, whose children we have become; the Son, whose brothers and sisters we have been rendered; and the Holy Ghost, whose living temples we have been made in the waters of regeneration.

By Baptism we have been made members of Jesus Christ. Baptism, therefore, obliges us to aim at Christian perfection and *holiness* of life. For, as is the head so should be the members. Consequently the life of the Christian should be a real copy of the life of Jesus Christ—a perfect, a holy, a Christ-like life.

By Baptism we have been made members of Jesus

Christ, the founder of the Church, who said to her:
He that heareth you, heareth Me, and he that despiseth
you despiseth Me; and if any one doth not hear the
Church, let him be to you as a heathen and a publican.
Hence Baptism obliges us also to *hear the Church;* to
love, honor, and obey her; for the Church of Christ is
the living and visible representative of Christ, our
Head, here upon earth.

These are, briefly stated, the obligations imposed upon us in Baptism. They are, as you see, the duties contained in the promises made by us through our godparents at our Baptism, commonly called the *baptismal vows.* Hence you see that the Church requires nothing arbitrary of us, but only the fulfilment of those obligations which every Christian contracts by the very fact of his Baptism and by his reception into the bosom of the Church. These obligations we have not only solemnly promised in the person of our sponsors at Baptism, but also personally ratified, when we came to the use of reason, at our First Communion and Confirmation.

But have you been *always faithful* to these promises? Have you not at any time bartered your souls to Satan for a miserable mess of sensual enjoyment? Have you not served the world and its vanities—its honors, riches, and pleasures? Have you not allowed yourselves to be allured by the pomps of Satan, to be enticed into the occasion of sin? And instead of the works of Christ, the works of your salvation, have you not often done the works of Satan, which you had renounced— the works of pride, of injustice, of intemperance, of impurity? And have you never refused the due reverence, love, and obedience to your holy mother, the Church? Would that it were so! Would that you had never deserted the banner of Jesus Christ, to whom you have vowed allegiance, and followed the standard of Satan, His adversary! O beloved brethren, is this the gratitude we owe to the infinite love and mercy of the bountiful and generous heart of Our Saviour for having given us, in preference to so many millions, the grace of Baptism, and conferred upon us the inestimable dignity of the children of God and the heirs of His kingdom?

Let us, then, dear brethren, bewail our former disloyalty to Jesus Christ, and promise our dear Saviour henceforth faithfully and conscientiously to keep our baptismal vows; and let us rest assured that our merciful Lord will, in the infinite love of His Sacred Heart, pardon our past transgressions and, despite all our excesses, lead us to that never-ending happiness to which He has called us, and of which He has given us an earnest in the Sacrament of Regeneration. Amen.

Feast of the Most Holy Trinity.

BELIEF IN THE MYSTERY OF THE TRINITY.

"In the name of the Father, and of the Son, and of the Holy Ghost."—Matt. xxviii. 19.

THESE words, beloved brethren, express the mystery of mysteries which forms the object of to-day's celebration—the mystery of the Most Holy and Adorable Trinity. It is on this mystery that I would address you to-day. But as the mystery of one God in three Persons is the most unfathomable of all mysteries which God has been pleased to reveal to us, I thought it more advisable, instead of explaining its contents to you, to put another question, the answer to which will, perhaps, be more useful, and no less instructive to you: viz., *why Almighty God revealed to us this inscrutable mystery.* I answer: He did so for three reasons, one of which has reference to Himself, the second to us personally, and the third to our neighbor; for *the belief in the Most Holy Trinity is—*

1. *The greatest homage paid to God;*
2. *The firmest ground of our hope;*
3. *A most effectual means of promoting charity.*

I. THE GREATEST HOMAGE PAID TO GOD.

The belief in the mystery of the Most Holy Trinity is the greatest homage which faith enables man to pay to his Creator. For our homage towards God is the greater, the more we thereby glorify Him and humble ourselves before Him. But by the belief in the Holy Trinity we give the greatest glory to God, and, at the same time, exercise the profoundest self-humiliation.

1. *We give the greatest glory to God.* For we cannot pay a higher tribute of praise and glory to God than by professing our belief that He is absolutely incomprehensible. Why? Because we thereby form and express the highest conception of God's greatness, namely, that He is great beyond all conception and expression. And, indeed, to believe that God is incomprehensible is nothing else than to say: O my God, I do not comprehend Thee, and I am altogether unable to comprehend Thee. Though I should strain all the forces and faculties of my soul to the utmost; though I possessed all the intelligence of Thy angels and saints; though I were endowed with all the gifts of grace and glory, and beheld Thee face to face, as do Thy blessed in heaven: yet I could not fully comprehend Thee, and my conception of Thee were still as far from the reality as the finite is from the infinite. For, if I could comprehend Thee, Thou wert not what Thou art, Thou wert not infinite, Thou wert not God; if I could comprehend Thee, I would not be what I am, I would not be finite, I would not be Thy creature; I would be equal to Thee, who alone canst comprehend Thyself.

Now, let me ask you, beloved brethren, is that not *the grandest profession of faith* in God's greatness of which man is capable? Is not His incomprehensibleness the grandest of God's divine attributes, the attribute which is peculiar to Him as God? Is not God, then, glorified most of all by the acknowledgment and profession of our faith in this attribute? And in what mystery do we profess our faith most of all in this attribute? In the mystery of the Holy and Undivided Trinity, because this mystery represents God most of all as the Incomprehensible. All we understand of this mystery is that we understand nothing of it. There is no other article of faith, therefore, the belief in which so glorifies God as the mystery of the Adorable Trinity.

2. The belief in the mystery of the Most Holy Trinity implies the *profoundest self-abasement* before God on our part. When we elicit and profess our faith in this mystery, we sacrifice to God the noblest part of our being, our understanding.

a. Here we submit our understanding to a truth of which *we have no direct knowledge*, of which we had not the slightest notion, until God revealed it to us. This is not the case, to the same extent, with other revealed truths. For without any revelation we might easily come to the knowledge, for instance, that God exists, that He is good and holy, that He governs the world, etc. A glance at His works in the universe, as the Apostle teaches us, is sufficient to convince us of these truths. But that in God there is one nature and three Persons, the Father, the Son, and the Holy Ghost; that the Son is born of the Father before all ages by the infinite knowledge which the Father has of Himself; that the Holy Ghost proceeds from the Father and the Son by Their mutual love; while the Father Himself proceeds from none; that these three Divine Persons are co-eternal and equal in all things; these are truths of which no trace is to be found in creation, truths of which we should never form the slightest conjecture, had not God revealed them to us.

b. Here we submit our understanding to a mystery for whose truth the human mind *cannot find the slightest reason*, even after it has been revealed. It is not thus with other mysteries, for instance, the mystery of the Incarnation. After this mystery has been once revealed, we can find some plausible reasons why God in His goodness and mercy has accomplished it. We can easily see that it is the best and most perfect way of atonement for our sins; that it is highly in keeping with the divine attributes and with God's loving providence towards us, His creatures. But when there is question of the Most Holy Trinity; of three distinct Persons in one undivided nature and substance; when it is asked why the Father is not greater than the Son, and how the Holy Ghost is the mutual love of the Father and the Son; the mind of man stands before a mystery whose depths are under every aspect unfathomable.

c. Finally, we here submit our understanding to a mystery which, at first sight, even *seems to us to involve a contradiction.* For we believe that the three Persons, who are one in substance, are yet really distinct from one another, so that the Son is not the Father, nor the Holy Ghost the Father nor the Son; that each of the three Divine Persons is true God, and yet that there is but one God. Does that not, at first sight, seem a contradiction in terms, though it is not such in reality? And yet we believe it, believe it firmly and without hesitation; and we are, with God's grace, if called upon to do so, ready to die for our belief. Is that not the noblest sacrifice we can make to God, the completest submission and surrender of the understanding?

The belief in the inscrutable mystery of the Holy Trinity, therefore, not only renders God the highest tribute of honor and glory, but implies, at the same time, the profoundest humiliation of self, the noblest and most generous sacrifice which man is capable of offering to his sovereign Lord and Creator. But this belief is for ourselves, at the same time—

II. THE FIRMEST GROUND OF OUR HOPE.

It is the unshaken foundation of our hope for the reason that we ultimately owe to this belief whatever entitles us to an unlimited confidence in the goodness, bounty, and faithfulness of God—our justification, the infallible promises of God, and all the means of sanctification and salvation.

1. And, first of all, what is the ground upon which our justification, our adoption as the children of God and heirs of heaven, rests? Is it not *faith?* Does not the Council of Trent (Sess. 6, cap. 8, de justif.), in accordance with the doctrine of the Apostle St. Paul, teach us that faith in God's Revelation is the beginning, the root, the foundation, of our justification? But among the first and most important truths of Revelation, which every Christian is bound not only implicitly to believe, but also to know, is the mystery of the Most Adorable Trinity. The belief in this mystery, therefore, above all others, may be said to form the ultimate ground of our justification.

2. Besides, it is by faith, and particularly by the submission of the understanding to this greatest of all mysteries, that, like Abraham, we receive the re-assuring *promises of God.* "Abraham believed God," says the Scripture, "and it was reputed to him unto justice" (Gen. xv. 6). Therefore God promised to bless him and to give him issue in his old age from which the Saviour of the world was to be born. "Because thou hast done this thing," says the Lord to him, that is, because thou hast submitted thy judgment in faith and obedience to My word, "and hast not spared thy only-begotten son for My sake, I will bless thee and multiply thy seed" (Ibid. xvi. 17). Abraham's faith, therefore, was to him the source of all his blessings, the ground on which he received the promise of God. And does not God speak to us in like manner? Because thou hast done this, He seems to say to us, because thou hast believed My word, and hast not spared that

which is nearest and dearest to thee, thy own judgment, but hast sacrificed it for My sake, submitting it to a mystery which so far surpasses thy understanding, therefore I will bless thee, and enrich thy soul with My graces, and multiply thy merits as the stars of heaven and the sands on the sea-shore. May not our confidence rest firm on such a promise?

3. It is, in the third place, through our belief in the mystery of the Most Holy Trinity that we are made partakers of the *means of grace* which Christ has treasured up in His Church. For it is in the name of the Blessed Trinity, the Father, the Son, and the Holy Ghost, that the sacraments are administered to us, that the holy sacrifice of the Mass is offered, that the word of God is preached to us, that the various blessings of the Church are dispensed to us. And this is done, as St. Augustine remarks, in order that we may understand that in the religion of Jesus Christ there is no grace, no justification, no salvation except through the faith in the mystery of the Most Holy Trinity. It is, therefore, by our belief in this mystery that we secure to ourselves the means of grace and salvation.

Hence you see, beloved brethren, that it is through our belief in the mystery of the Holy Trinity that we ultimately receive whatever inspires us in this life with an unbounded and unshaken confidence in God; that the belief in this august mystery is, consequently, the firm foundation of our hope. For the rest, this truth is confirmed by the teaching of the Church; for by the mouth of the priest, who assists the dying, she invokes the mercy of God for the departing soul with these touching words: "Though Thy servant has been a sinner, yet he did not deny the Father, and the Son, and the Holy Ghost, but believed in Them." By the very fact, therefore, that the Church, in the last

moment, on which depends our eternal lot, insists on
our belief in the Holy Trinity as the most eloquent
plea to induce Almighty God to extend His mercy to
us, she shows clearly that she considers it the most
efficacious motive before God, the surest pledge of
salvation and, consequently, the firmest foundation of
our hope. But, besides being the solid basis of our
confidence in God, and, as we have seen, the greatest
homage we can pay to Him on earth—the belief in this
adorable mystery is, moreover—

III. A MOST EFFECTUAL MEANS OF PROMOTING CHARITY.

The belief in the Holy Trinity is a most powerful
means of promoting charity to our neighbor for two
reasons: first, because it offers us the strongest motive;
and, secondly, because it holds out to us the grandest
model of charity towards others.

1. It offers us the *most powerful motive*. This was
manifestly the opinion of St. Paul, as we may conclude
from his epistle to the Ephesians. For after earnestly
recommending to them the virtue of charity, he finds
no stronger motive to urge them to its practice than
their belief in the Holy Trinity. He exhorts them to
be careful to keep the unity of the spirit in the bond
of peace—one body, and one spirit, as they are called
in one hope of their vocation—one Lord, one faith,
one baptism; one God and Father of all (Eph. iv. 1-5).
The Apostle's argument comes to this: As we all have
one and the same God, one and the same faith, one
and the same baptism, so we all form but one body,
which is the Church of God. Is it not meet, therefore,
that we should all have one and the same spirit? We
are all united in our faith in one and the same God;
should we not, therefore, be one in every other respect?
We acknowledge in this one and the same God the Fa-

ther, whose children we are; the Son, whose brothers and sisters we are; the Holy Ghost, the life-giver, who is the principle of our supernatural life, and whose living temples we are. Since, therefore, the belief in one God in three Persons unites us so intimately with each other, were it not in the highest degree unbecoming if our hearts were divided by hatred and strife? Thus St. Chrysostom understands the argument of the Apostle. It is, he says, as if the Apostle said to the Ephesians: What astonishes me is that, while we are one in a belief which involves such difficulty as that of one God in three Persons, we should daily quarrel about trifles, and fall into enmity with one another.

2. Our belief in the Most Holy Trinity, in the second place, holds up to us the most perfect *model* of charity to our neighbor. The love which the Divine Persons of the Blessed Trinity cherish for one another is a pattern of that Christian charity which we should entertain one towards another. And who is it that holds up this model to us? It is Jesus Christ Himself, the eternal and infinite Wisdom. "Holy Father," He says, addressing His heavenly Father, "keep them in Thy name, whom Thou hast given Me; that they may be one as We also are" (John xvii. 11). But, you will say, how is this possible? The Father and the Son are the same nature and substance. What love can thus unite us? Hear the answer of St. Augustine. What Christ would give us to understand here, says the holy Doctor, is this: that we should be perfectly one as far as our hearts and wills are concerned, that by grace and by the imitation of the Holy Trinity we should endeavor to be what the three Divine Persons are by the necessity of Their being. As with the three Divine Persons all things are in common, and as They have no conflicting interests, so our love should be also regardless of

self, and seek and desire the same thing, the good of all. O beloved brethren, if this disinterested love reigned in the hearts of all, how different would be the aspect of the world! There would be no more dishonesty, no more oppression, no more cruelty, no more discord in families, no more quarrels among neighbors. In short, the world would be changed into a Paradise, a perfect image of heaven; Christians would be a true copy of the Holy Trinity, the ideal which Christ holds up to our imitation. Then might we, in truth, say with the Royal Prophet, in the joy of our hearts: " Behold how good and how pleasant it is for brethren to dwell together in unity!" (Ps. cxxxii. 1.)

These, beloved brethren, are the reasons why God was pleased to reveal to us the mystery of the Most Holy Trinity—to exalt our faith to the highest degree of divine homage, to lay the firmest foundation for our hope, and to offer the strongest motive and the most perfect model for our love towards our neighbors. Should this consideration not inspire us with the deepest affection for this holy mystery, and impel us to utilize it for our salvation, according to the intentions which the all-wise and all-bountiful God had in revealing it to us? With what reverence and devotion should we not, therefore, pronounce the holy names of the Divine Persons, especially when we make the Sign of the Cross! With what confidence should we not invoke the Holy Trinity, the Father, the Son, and the Holy Ghost, in temptation or other affliction! And how earnestly should we not endeavor, according to the example of the three Divine Persons, to foster union and charity among ourselves! Do this, beloved brethren, and the Holy and Undivided Trinity will be your protection in life, your comfort in death, and your exceeding great reward in heaven. Amen.

Feast of Corpus Christi.

THE REAL PRESENCE.

"He hath made a remembrance of His wonderful works, being a merciful and gracious Lord; He hath given food to them that fear Him."—Ps. cx. 4, 5.

THE celebration of to-day, beloved brethren, is entirely directed to the honor of Our Lord's presence in the Most Holy Sacrament of the Altar. It is a solemn profession of faith in the real presence of Jesus Christ. For those who do not possess this faith the solemnity of to-day has no signification; it is but a vain display, a meaningless pageant. The livelier our faith in this mystery is, on the other hand, the more eagerly and joyously shall we take part in this sacred festivity, and the greater advantage shall we derive from it. Therefore I thought that it would be quite in keeping with the object of this feast, and not without profit for your spiritual advantage, if to-day I should endeavor to strengthen your faith in the real presence of Jesus Christ in this adorable Sacrament. I propose, therefore, to show you, as briefly as possible, that this grand truth of our holy faith rests on the clearest evidence of Holy Scripture and Tradition, and that the objections which unbelievers raise against it are utterly without force. My discourse will accordingly consist of the following three parts—

1. *The evidence of Holy Scripture;*
2. *The evidence of Tradition;*
3. *The futility of the objections.*

I. THE EVIDENCE OF HOLY SCRIPTURE.

1. Our belief in the real presence of Jesus Christ in the Most Holy Sacrament of the Altar rests, first of all,

on the *promise of Our Lord* recorded by St. John in the sixth chapter of his Gospel. After our blessed Lord had miraculously fed several thousands of men in the desert with a few loaves and fishes, He took occasion from this material food to direct their minds to a higher spiritual, heavenly food, which He would give them for the supernatural life of their souls. " I am the living bread," He says, " which came down from heaven. If any man eat of this bread, he shall live forever; and the bread that I will give is My flesh for the life of the world." Now, the Jews, on hearing this, began to dispute among themselves, saying: " How can this man give us His flesh to eat?" (John vi. 51-53.) From this fact it is manifest that the Jews understood those words in their literal sense, and were convinced that Christ spoke of His real flesh and blood.

And, in fact, Christ *wished so to be understood.* For, if He wished to be understood otherwise, He would surely have corrected their misunderstanding. If He had not meant His real flesh and blood, as a teacher he was bound to explain His meaning, when misunderstood. In that case He would have said: My dear friends, you misconceive My meaning; it is not My true flesh and blood that I will give you to eat and to drink, but only bread and wine as the figure or symbol of My true body and blood. But instead of thus correcting them, He plainly shows them that He wishes to be understood as speaking of His true flesh and blood, and emphatically confirms what He had just said, adding: " Amen, Amen I say unto you: except you eat the flesh of the Son of man, and drink His blood, you shall not have life in you. ... For My flesh is meat indeed, and My blood is drink indeed " (Ibid. 54, 56).

But the Jews persisted in their unbelief; nay, many even of *His disciples murmured,* and said : " This saying is hard, and who can hear it?" And they withdrew, we are told, and walked with Him no more (Ibid. 61, 67). And how does Christ behave towards them? Does He retract, or explain, as He was bound to do, if misunderstood? No; He allows them to go. Nay, He even puts the faith of His apostles to the test, saying to the twelve: "Will you also go?" (Ibid. 68.) Now, I ask, beloved brethren, would Christ permit His disciples to abandon Him, if there was question only of a misunderstanding of His meaning? Is it not evident that He, the Good Shepherd, who goes over hill and dale to seek the lost sheep, would on this occasion have taken the trouble to remove a simple misconception rather than allow His sheep to abandon Him? Since, therefore, Our Lord gave no explanation, but, on the contrary, exacted from His apostles themselves a profession of faith in His words as understood, that is, in their literal meaning, it is beyond all doubt that His words were understood aright; and that, consequently, what He promised to give was His true flesh to eat and His true blood to drink.

2. The doctrine of the real presence of Jesus Christ rests, moreover, on the well-known words which describe the *institution* of the Most Holy Sacrament. They are to be found substantially the same in three of the Gospels and in the First Epistle of St. Paul to the Corinthians (Matt. xxvi., Mark xiv., Luke xxii., I. Cor. xi.). "And whilst they were at supper, Jesus took bread, and blessed, and broke, and gave His disciples; and said: Take ye, and eat, this is My body. And taking the chalice, He gave thanks, and gave to them, saying: Drink ye all of this. For this is My blood of the New Testament, which shall be shed for many unto the remission of sins" (Matt. xxvi. 26–28). That these words

are to be taken in their literal signification may be concluded from the fact that they are manifestly the fulfilment of the promise which Christ gave in the sixth chapter of St. John, to give His true flesh to eat, and His true blood to drink. He promised them His real flesh and blood. It is, therefore, His real flesh and blood that He gives them. But, independently of the promise of Christ, these words can be taken in none other than their literal signification. Why?

a. A man's words, whoever he be, *cannot be distorted* from their literal signification at pleasure; much less may the words of Holy Scripture, and, above all, the words spoken by the divine lips of the God-man, Jesus Christ, be thus arbitrarily treated. When, therefore, Christ Our Lord says: This *is* My body; this *is* My blood, who, then, can without presumption modify His words and say to Him: Thou meanest, doubtless: This *signifies* My body, My blood. Would any ordinary speaker allow his words to be thus distorted? And who would have the hardihood so to distort the words of any reputable public speaker?

b. Besides, to whom were these words directed? They were immediately addressed to *His disciples*, in whose memory the recent promise was still fresh. If, then, our blessed Lord was always careful to speak in the clearest terms, not in figures and parables, to His own disciples, must He not in this point of doctrine, which had lately created such misgiving in the minds of His followers, have used the most explicit and unmistakable language? These words are, moreover, addressed to His *apostles*, the messengers who are destined by Him to preach and dispense this same holy mystery to all people: " Do this for a commemoration of Me." Must He not, then, according to the most ordinary rules of common prudence, deliver this message to His ambassadors in the clearest and most definite terms possible?

c. Again, what is the matter in question here? There is question of *a law* to be observed for all future time: " Do this for a commemoration of Me." But the first quality of a law requires that it be clearly and distinctly expressed. Must not the lawgiver, therefore, above all, abstain from the use of figurative and otherwise ambiguous language, and use words in their proper and literal signification? There is question of *a sacrament* of Christ's Church. But must not the nature of a sacrament be clearly brought out, that the faithful may know exactly what it is they receive in it, and how they are to prepare themselves for its reception? And is this precaution not most necessary in the case of this Sacrament, the misconception of which would lead to the most disastrous consequences, even to the most abominable idolatry? Could, then, Our Lord use ambiguous and misleading expressions in so momentous a case? Again, there is question of *the last will* of Christ to His Church. Are bequests to be made in doubtful terms? Could our blessed Lord in His last loving testament to His Church leave His children in doubt whether He left them His true body and blood, or only a figure and remembrance of the same? There is question, finally, of *a memorial of His love*, which Christ left to His spouse, the Church. Is this memorial of His love and of His wonderful works only a small wafer of bread? Do, then, all our worship, all our devotion, all our gratitude, all our love cluster around a paltry piece of unleavened bread? Is it thus Christ has loved us? Is this the memorial of His love, whose delight it is to be with the children of men?

3. The real presence of the body and blood of Jesus

Christ may be inferred also from those passages of Holy Writ which refer to the *reception* of the Most Holy Sacrament. To be brief, I shall only call your attention to one passage, in which the Apostle St. Paul speaks of the unworthy reception of the Holy Eucharist. "Whosoever," he says, "shall eat this bread, or drink the chalice of the Lord unworthily, shall be guilty of the body and of the blood of the Lord. He that eateth and drinketh unworthily, eateth and drinketh judgment to himself, not discerning the body of the Lord" (I. Cor. xi. 27, 29). According to these words the unworthy reception of this Holy Sacrament is, to say the very least, possible; and, if actually perpetrated, it is a most grievous sin. For to be guilty of the body and blood of Jesus Christ signifies as much as to be guilty of taking away the life, of shedding the blood, of Jesus Christ. And what does it mean to eat judgment to one's self, unless to deserve judgment, that is, eternal condemnation? But if the true body and true blood of Christ were not really present in this Sacrament, such an unworthy reception were impossible. For, surely no one, though he were the greatest sinner, could be guilty of the body and blood of the Lord, if he received only mere bread and wine. Therefore, either Jesus Christ is really and truly present in the Blessed Sacrament, or the words of the Apostle have no meaning whatever. The doctrine of the real presence of Jesus Christ in the Holy Eucharist is consequently the clear and unmistakable teaching of Holy Scripture. But it is no less evidently the teaching of Tradition.

II. EVIDENCE OF TRADITION.

1. It is an incontrovertible fact, beloved brethren, that the Church has *at all times* held and believed the doctrine of the Real Presence. Volumes would be

unable to contain the testimonies of Tradition on this point. Time permits me to bring forward only a few evidences. As early as the *first century* St. Ignatius, the Martyr, a disciple of the apostles, wrote concerning certain heretics of his time: "They abstain from the Holy Eucharist, and from prayer, because they do not believe the Eucharist is the flesh of Our Saviour Jesus Christ, that flesh which suffered for our sins." Hence follows manifestly that the orthodox Christians, or Catholics, believed the contrary, namely, that the Holy Eucharist was really the flesh of Jesus Christ, that suffered for us; for, if it was heretical to deny the real presence of the body of Christ, it was Catholic doctrine that Christ was really present. About the middle of the *second century* St. Justin Martyr, in a defence of the Christians addressed to the Emperor Antoninus, writes concerning the Holy Eucharist: "We receive it not as common bread and ordinary drink, but as the flesh and blood of Jesus, the Son of God made man, as we have been taught." No less explicit is the teaching of St. Irenæus and of Tertullian, who lived but a short time after St. Justin. In the *fourth century* St. Cyril of Jerusalem says in one of his Catechetical Instructions: "Since the Lord Himself said of the bread [of the Holy Eucharist]: This is My body; who will, then, dare to call it into question? And since He, in like manner, assures us, saying: This is My blood; who, then, could have any further misgiving, and think that it is not His blood?" It were an easy matter, did time permit, to continue the chain of evidence to our own day. It is an undeniable fact, then, that the Church in all ages believed and taught the doctrine of the real presence of Jesus Christ in the Most Holy Sacrament of the Altar.

2. Very true, say our adversaries; it cannot be de-

nied that the Church has at all times believed and taught this doctrine; but *may not the Church have erred in this matter?* No, beloved brethren; though we had no evidence of the infallibility of the Church; nay, though the Church were not infallible, yet it is most certain that Almighty God could not permit her to err in this point. For, had God permitted an error in this matter, for more than 1800 years all the Church's children would have been practising the most abominable idolatry, adoring a morsel of bread and a chalice of wine instead of Jesus Christ, the Son of God. And who would be responsible for such an error and such dreadful consequences? Evidently He who said: "This is My body; this is My blood." Christ Himself, therefore, the Founder of the Church, would be the responsible author of this universal error and all its revolting effects. In that case Christ could make no reproach to His Church; but the Church could justly reproach Christ. She could say to Him: By Thy omniscience, O Lord, Thou hast foreseen that Thy words would mislead millions of men to idolatry. Why, then, hast Thou uttered these words? Why hast Thou not, at least, explained them? Why hast Thou not corrected their evident misunderstanding? Didst Thou not see how they had been misconceived by the Jews, and by Thy own disciples? Why didst Thou not correct the error at least at the Last Supper? And why didst Thou reveal this mystery in the same words to the Apostle St. Paul? And if such a reproach of having invincibly led millions of men into idolatry should fall upon Christ Our Lord, what would be the logical consequence? It would necessarily follow that Christ was not God; for God could not lead men into idolatry. It would follow that Christ was an impostor, that our religion was not divine, that Christianity was a fraud. Deny this one truth, and you undermine the very foundation of Christianity. If we profess to be Christians, then we must believe, and firmly believe, that Jesus Christ is really and truly present in the Most Holy Sacrament of the Altar.

As Holy Scripture and Tradition are explicit in their teaching concerning the Real Presence, so as to leave no room to doubt of its truth, the difficulties which are brought forward by unbelievers can only be apparent, not real. Let us examine a few of them.

III. FUTILITY OF THE OBJECTIONS.

The doctrine of the real presence of Jesus Christ in the Most Holy Sacrament is above, but not contrary to, our natural reason. It contains mysteries and miracles, which we are unable fully to conceive; but no contradictions. And this is quite in keeping with the object which God had in instituting this Holy Sacrament. For, according to the words of the Psalmist, which I have taken for my text, in this Sacrament the all-merciful and all-gracious Lord has given a memorial of His wonderful works. Therefore it is intended by Almighty God to be a continual remembrance of His miracles—in the first instance, of His miracles in the order of grace; but, at the same time, of those in the order of nature. But in order to be the most perfect remembrance of God's wonderful works, it was befitting that this mystery should comprise in itself a series of striking miracles. And this is actually the case; for it contains a number of the most stupendous miracles. I shall call your attention only to three of these miracles.

1. The first great miracle we meet in this mystery is *the change of the substance* of bread and wine into the body and blood of Jesus Christ; not into His dead

body and blood—for Christ being once risen from the dead, as the Apostle assures us, dieth now no more— but into His living flesh and blood. And since the body and blood of Christ in the Holy Eucharist are His living body and blood, His soul is also present; and where His soul and body are, there, in virtue of the hypostatic union, is likewise His Divinity. Hence the Church teaches that Jesus Christ is wholly and entirely present—with body and soul, Godhead and Manhood—under each species: under the species of bread as well as under that of wine; in the sacred host as well as in the consecrated contents of the chalice. Whence you may see, by the way, why the faithful, who communicate under the species of bread alone, receive the same Jesus Christ wholly and entirely as does the priest at the altar, who communicates under both species.

Now, this miracle is not seldom a *stumbling-block* for those who are weak in faith; *but unjustly*. For, as I have said, this doctrine is not against reason, but only beyond the comprehension of the human mind. It implies no contradiction, but is only an incomprehensible miracle, a remembrance of the wonderful works of God. Christ is God, the *Creator* of the universe, at whose bidding in the beginning all things came forth from their nothingness into existence. But, if by His creative power He has been able to call forth the things that were not from their non-existence, why should we deny Him the lesser power of changing one thing into another—the power of replacing the substances of bread and wine by His own flesh and blood?

As God Christ is also *the author of the laws of nature*. It was He who devised the laws according to which substances are daily changed in the universe. It was He who framed the law by which living beings, men, beasts, and plants, continually transform into their own substance those objects which serve for their nourishment. Christ Himself, who deigned to become like to us in all things, sin alone excepted, changed, in virtue of this law, other substances into His sacred flesh and blood. Now, since this marvellous law of substantial changes still exists, and continually operates in nature, who, then, can reasonably take offence at the miraculous change of bread and wine into the body and blood of Christ? Here we have only a memorial of the wonders of the universe. The merciful and gracious Lord "hath made a remembrance of His wonderful works; He hath given food to them that fear Him."

2. The second great miracle in this mystery is the *simultaneous presence* of Jesus Christ in various places. This, again, involves no contradiction; it is a great and inexplicable miracle, a remembrance of the wonderful works of nature. My dear friend, can you explain the marvellous velocity of light or of electricity? Can you explain how the sound of the bell, or of the human voice, rings at the same time in the ears of thousands who are within its sphere, nay, how it is wholly, with all its peculiarities, present in the millions of assignable points of a large space? Are these marvels of nature not inexplicable and incomprehensible? True, the simultaneous presence of Jesus Christ is a much greater miracle; yet it is also true that it is only a memorial of the wonderful works of His creation. "He hath made a remembrance of His wonderful works, being a gracious and merciful Lord; He hath given food to them that fear Him."

3. The third miracle which strikes us in this inscrutable mystery is the presence of Christ in the *narrow space* of a tiny host. But this miracle is likewise a remembrance of similar marvels in nature, which, of course, are much less wonderful than that displayed in

the Real Presence. Is not the entire plant contained in a marvellous manner in a small germ? Does not the All-powerful enclose the mighty oak in a little acorn? And look at the growth of a plant. Is it not an incomprehensible mystery? Consider the wonders of the human eye. You survey from an eminence a large tract of country, covered with the most varied scenes. There lie before you mountains and valleys, rivers and lakes, fields and forests, towns and villages. And all those various objects are most distinctly delineated on the tiny retina of your eye. Not a single object is wanting; the entire scene is depicted in your eye with the greatest accuracy and minuteness. Is that not a most wonderful process? Who, then, shall marvel that He who devised the laws by which this wonder of nature is worked can condense His own body in such narrow space? It is only a memorial of His wonderful works. "He hath made a remembrance of His wonderful works, being a gracious and merciful Lord; He hath given food to them that fear Him."

Our faith in the real presence of Jesus Christ in the Most Holy Sacrament, therefore, rests on the clearest evidence of Scripture and Tradition, and all the objections which unbelief can muster against it are vain and ineffectual. Therefore we believe it, and to-day we profess our faith in it openly before the world. With what joy and devotion, then, should we take part in this holy celebration, in which we give public expression to our faith, our love, and our gratitude to Jesus Christ for the infinite love and condescension which He has shown us in this wonderful mystery! Therefore, beloved brethren, during this solemn procession in which Jesus Christ goes forth in triumph to scatter His blessings amongst you, throw off all human respect, and without reserve give expression to the faith, and love, and gratitude of your hearts, and give joy to that Sacred Heart which throbs for you under this lowly species. He who is not unmindful of the least service done to Him will reward you a thousandfold. If you confess Him openly and without fear before men in this world, He, who is true to His promises, will acknowledge you before His heavenly Father, in the presence of the whole court of heaven, before the eyes of all His angels and saints, and will lead you in triumph into His heavenly kingdom, and crown you with the crown of everlasting glory. Amen.

Feast of the Sacred Heart of Jesus.

DEVOTION TO THE SACRED HEART.

"You shall draw waters with joy out of the Saviour's fountains."—Is. xii. 3.

THE feast we celebrate to-day, beloved brethren, naturally suggests the subject of my discourse—*the devotion to the most Sacred Heart of Jesus.* It is our duty on each recurring feast of the Sacred Heart to renew ourselves in this devotion. For this end I shall endeavor to put before you the excellence of this devotion. The excellence of the devotion to the Sacred Heart will appear—

1. *From the authority on which it rests;*
2. *From its sublime nature;*
3. *From its salutary effects.*

I. AUTHORITY.

The authority on which this devotion rests is such that we may thence justly infer its superior excellence. For the devotion to the Sacred Heart is not only holy in its origin, but it is also sanctioned by the example and testimony of the greatest saints, and by the authority of the Church, the representative of Christ on earth.

1. It is holy in its *origin.* It would be a mistake to consider this an altogether new devotion, that has originated in latter times. The manner in which it is at present practised in the whole Church is indeed new; but in its substance the devotion itself is as old as Christianity itself. When Christ says: Learn of Me, because I am meek, and humble of heart" (Matt. xi. 29), does He

not invite us to conform our hearts to his own Sacred Heart? Does that not suppose that we, on our part, should make the Divine Heart the subject of our study and meditation? And is this not a principal feature in the devotion to the Sacred Heart? And when St. John at the last supper reclined on the Heart of his Divine Master, was he not drawn by his love and devotion to the Sacred Heart? Again, what was the intention of our Divine Saviour in allowing His Heart to be opened with a lance on the cross? Was it not to reveal to us the infinite love of His Sacred Heart, to invite us to the contemplation of its infinite treasures, and to prepare for us an abode in which we might take refuge in all our afflictions and temptations? So among other Fathers and Doctors of the Church St. Augustine and St. Thomas teach us. "The soldier," says St. Augustine, "has opened for me the side of my Lord. I have entered, and dwell therein with security." St. Thomas invites us to look through this gaping wound into the bleeding Heart of our Redeemer, and then he exclaims in the most tender expressions: "O Heart, that hast shed Thy blood to enliven and inflame us, quicken and inflame my heart with this life and love!" It is evident, therefore, from the practice and teaching of the saints, that the devotion to the Sacred Heart in its substance is as old as Christianity itself, and, consequently, that it is venerable and holy in its origin.

2. But it is, at the same time, sanctioned by the example and *testimony of the greatest saints.* Besides the authority of St. Augustine and St. Thomas already quoted, I could cite passages from many other saints in recommendation of the devotion to the Sacred Heart. St. Bernard, for instance, says: "Since we have come to the amiable Heart of Jesus, and since it is so sweet to dwell there, let us not suffer ourselves to be sepa-

rated from it.... O how good, how sweet it is to dwell in this Heart!" "O sacred wounds," says St. Bonaventure, "through you I have entered into the inmost sanctuary of the love of Jesus Christ!" The venerable Lansberg, surnamed the Just, writes: "Always endeavor to incite yourselves to the devotion to the most Sacred Heart of Jesus, a plenteous fountain of love and mercy; practise this devotion assiduously." Finally, St. Francis of Sales, who copied from the Sacred Heart that meek, and active, and self-sacrificing love which characterized his conduct and all his doings, exclaims: "How good is the Lord, and how amiable is His Heart! Let us always dwell in this holy abode! Oh, may this Sacred Heart always live in our hearts!"

3. But the highest sanction has been given to this devotion by the *Church* itself. After the devotion to the Sacred Heart had been thus practised for centuries by individuals, and began to spread in the Church, opposition was raised against it especially by the heretical sect known by the name of Jansenists, or followers of Jansenius. The propagation of the devotion was brought about in the following way. Towards the decline of the seventeenth century our blessed Lord repeatedly appeared to a holy religious of the Order of the Visitation by the name of Margaret Mary Alacoque. The best guarantee for the sanctity of this spouse of Christ is that in 1864 she was beatified by the Church. To her our blessed Lord revealed His Sacred Heart, from which issued flames of fire as from a burning censer. He charged her to propagate the devotion to His Heart, promising at the same time the fulness of His graces to all those who would dedicate themselves to His Sacred Heart. "Announce," He said, "and have it made known to the whole world, that I will set no limit and no measure to My spiritual blessings in

favor of those who seek graces in My Sacred Heart." It was these apparitions and revelations which gave an impulse to the propagation and to the general practice of the devotion to the Sacred Heart, but in consequence of its spread a violent storm of opposition was raised against it. This opposition caused the Church to interfere in behalf of the devotion. Pius VI. solemnly condemned the offensive propositions established against it by the Jansenists in their synod held in Pistoia. Several subsequent popes declared the devotion lawful and commendable. Clement XIII. granted permission to various churches to celebrate the feast of the Sacred Heart. And, finally, Pius IX., of glorious memory, ordered the feast to be annually celebrated in the whole Church, thus making the devotion to the Sacred Heart a universal devotion of the Church.

But what ultimately secured for this devotion the sanction of holy men and the approbation of the Church was the true worth inherent in its nature. Let us, therefore, in the second place, briefly consider the devotion to the Sacred Heart in its—

II. NATURE.

The nature of any devotion may be determined from its object and its end or purpose.

1. What is the *object* of the devotion to the Sacred Heart, or, in other words, what is it that we honor in this devotion? It is, as the name itself implies, the Heart of Jesus Christ, Our Saviour; that heart of flesh and blood, which upon the cross was pierced with a lance for us; the real and true Heart of the God-man, not a mere figure or symbol of it; the living Heart of Jesus, which throbbed and still throbs for us in the bosom of the Son of God; the Heart of Jesus Christ

arisen, and glorified, and seated at the right hand of God His Father.

But since, not only the heart, but every portion of the sacred Humanity of Christ is substantially and inseparably united with His Godhead, and therefore deserves divine honor, or supreme adoration, the question arises: *why* do we choose precisely His Sacred Heart as the special object of our devotion? The reason is plain. It is because our Divine Lord wished to give us in this devotion a living and permanent symbol or remembrance of His incomprehensible love. And there is nothing which so forcibly reminds us of the infinite love of our dear Saviour as does His Sacred Heart; for the heart, as you know, is the seat and the natural symbol of love; and, consequently, the Sacred Heart of Jesus is a living memorial of His inexhaustible love. While, therefore, the physical, human Heart of Jesus is the visible object and symbol of this devotion, its soul and substance, its invisible and chief object, is the infinite love of Jesus Christ, which is symbolized in His human Heart.

To put it in as few words as possible, the object of the devotion to the Sacred Heart is *the infinite love of Jesus Christ for us, symbolized by His human Heart*, or, in other words, *the heart of our Redeemer glowing with love for us.* Can there be a grander, a holier, a more excellent object of our devotion than the adorable Heart and the infinite love of Jesus Christ? Is there any devotion, then, which can compare in the sublimity and holiness of its object with the devotion to the most Sacred Heart?

2. No less sublime and holy is the *purpose* of this devotion. What is the end or purpose of the devotion to the Sacred Heart? It is to make some return for the infinite love of **Jesus** Christ towards us; it is to

make reparation to Jesus Christ for the indifference, the hatred, the outrages of so many souls; it is to inflame our own hearts and those of others more and more with love and devotion to the sacred Person of Jesus Christ. The end of this devotion, then, as you may perceive, is higher, more universal, and more perfect than that of any of the other special devotions to our Divine Saviour. Nay, it comprises in itself the special purposes of all the other devotions to Our Lord —of the devotion to the Infant Jesus, to the Passion of Our Lord, to the Five Wounds, to the Holy Cross, and even to the Most Holy Sacrament of the Altar. For, while these several devotions have the special aim of honoring our blessed Lord in some particular manifestation of His love for us—say, in His childhood, or His passion—the devotion to His Sacred Heart has the more universal purpose of honoring Him in the very source and motive of all the manifestations of His love, that is, in the infinite love of His Sacred Heart itself. Since, therefore, the devotion to the Sacred Heart comprises in its universal aim the special purposes of the several devotions to our Divine Lord, we must conclude that in its purpose, and consequently in its nature, it far surpasses all other devotions; that it is the chief of all devotions—the devotion, by way of excellence, of all Christendom. This conclusion is justified, in the third place, by its most salutary—

III. EFFECTS.

That the devotion to the most Sacred Heart of Jesus is productive of numerous and great spiritual blessings we have the strongest assurance, both in the nature of the devotion itself and the express promises made by Jesus Christ to His servant, Blessed Margaret Mary.

1. *Effects naturally following from the devotion itself.*

While the grand and holy object and purpose of this devotion entitle us to hope for the most copious fruits, its practice is the most efficacious means of realizing our most sanguine hopes.

a. What is the *strongest motive of hope* which we can have in this life? Is it not the infinite love of Jesus Christ? And is this not precisely the object that is held out to us in this devotion—the loving Heart of Jesus, the infinite love itself of Jesus Christ, Our Saviour? And what love is revealed to us in the Sacred Heart! Is it not the Heart from which flowed our Redemption? Is it not a Heart that has always been most faithfully attached to its friends? Is it not a Heart full of tenderness? Is it not that Heart from which have issued all the graces and blessings that our Redeemer has purchased for us by His life, passion, and death? Is it not that Heart which still pleads for us in its glory before the throne of the Most High, and sacrifices and annihilates itself for us in the Most Holy Sacrament of the Altar? Should this loving Heart, thus revealed to us in this devotion as an ocean of love and bounty, not inspire us with the most confident hope?

b. But, as the nature of the devotion to the Sacred Heart inspires us with the greatest confidence, its practice offers us the best *means of realizing the hopes* which it inspires.

To the practice of this devotion belongs, first of all, that we *honor*, adore, and praise the Sacred Heart of Our Lord. And what can be more efficacious to convert the heart of the sinner to penance, or to move the loving Heart of Jesus to mercy, than this honor, adoration, and praise? The honor paid to the Sacred Heart is in such glaring contradiction with the life of the sinner, is such a continual and bitter reproach to him, that it cannot but bring him to better sentiments, change his heart, and make him susceptible to the influence of grace. And what can be better calculated to call down upon the sinner the divine mercy than those sublimest acts of religion?

To the practice of this devotion belongs, in the second place, that we *make amends* to the Sacred Heart for the many outrages which have been and still are inflicted upon it, particularly in the Most Holy Sacrament of the Altar. But is this act of reparation not an eloquent and touching lesson to ourselves? Can we make satisfaction for the sins of others without being reminded of our own sins, without being moved to shame and sorrow for them, without conceiving an ardent desire and firm purpose of amendment?

Finally, this devotion consists in the *familiar intercourse* and intimate union with the Sacred Heart; in recurring to it with confidence in all our temptations, troubles, and dangers; in meditating upon its virtues, in endeavoring to conform our hearts to the Heart of the God-man, Jesus Christ. What stronger incentive to a pure and holy life can there be than this continued converse with the Sacred Heart? If one single conversation with Jesus Christ sufficed to convert the sinful Samaritan woman, and to make her the herald of His goodness and mercy, what must be the efficacy of frequent and familiar intercourse with the Sacred Heart of Jesus! Must not such celestial conversation gradually conform our hearts to the Heart of our Divine Master, and make us true and perfect Christians, fill our hearts with the spirit of Jesus Christ?

The devotion to the Sacred Heart is, therefore, in itself a most powerful aid towards appropriating to ourselves those spiritual fruits which it so copiously extends to us. Must we not thence conclude that this devotion is, of itself and independently of the special promises of Our Lord, most fruitful for our salvation? And this conclusion, which follows from the very nature of the devotion, is more than confirmed by—

2. *The special promises given by our blessed Lord.* These assuring promises of Jesus Christ to those who honor His Sacred Heart refer partly to this life, partly to the hour of death, and partly to the future life.

a. With regard to this *present life*. Our Saviour promises to all *sinners* who have recourse to His Sacred Heart the grace of conversion and perseverance in His friendship. Blessed Margaret Mary—who in this matter deserves our full credence, since the Church itself has set the seal of its approval upon the revelations which Our Lord vouchsafed to her—tells us expressly that Jesus Christ has revealed this devotion " to destroy the realm of Satan; to restore life to many; to open to men the treasures of grace, of sanctification and salvation, deposited in His Sacred Heart; to extend His mercy to numberless poor, ungrateful, and unfaithful souls, that are on the way to eternal ruin." What surer pledge of the grace of conversion could be given to the sinner? The promise of the grace of perseverance is no less explicit. "I cannot believe," says the blessed servant of God, "that those who have dedicated themselves to the most Sacred Heart of Jesus will by grievous sin come under the dominion of Satan."

But the promises of Our Lord are not confined to sinners; they extend also to God-fearing and *pious Christians*. The devotion to the Sacred Heart, Blessed Margaret Mary assures us on the testimony of Jesus Christ, her Spouse, is an inexhaustible fountain of salvation, contains an infinite treasure of love and of grace for the accomplishment of the work of our salvation. By this devotion, she says, it is the intention of Jesus Christ to procure for Himself a large following of faithful servants, true friends, and grateful children.

Besides those spiritual treasures, Our Lord promises also *temporal blessings* to those who honor His Sacred Heart. "Those living in the world," says the servant of God, "will in this beautiful devotion find all aid necessary for their state in life: light and encouragement in their labors and toils, success in all their undertakings, and comfort in all their adversities." Beloved brethren, are these not grand and consoling promises? Do they not fully bear out the boldest and most sanguine hopes which we can conceive in this life? What greater earnest of happiness, then, can we possess in this life than a tender devotion to the Sacred Heart of Jesus?

b. Still more consoling are the promises given by Our Lord to the devoted of His Sacred Heart for the *hour of death.* "The souls dedicated to the Sacred Heart," says Blessed Margaret Mary, "shall not be lost; . . . if they only surrender themselves wholly to the Sacred Heart; if they only endeavor, to the best of their power, to honor, love and glorify it, and to conform themselves to its maxims. . . . This Sacred Heart is a stronghold and safe refuge for all sinners, whither they may safely flee to escape the wrath of divine justice. . . . Oh, how sweet it is to die after a long and continued practice of the devotion to the Heart of Him who is to judge us!" In one of His apparitions to the servant of God, as she herself relates, Our Lord, moreover, promises the grace of true penance and conversion at their death to all those who on the first Friday of nine successive months devoutly receive holy Communion in honor of His Sacred

Heart. And He promises, likewise, that those who have devoutly made those nine Communions will not die in the state of sin, nor without the sacraments; that His Sacred Heart will be their protection in their last struggle.

c. If the fruits of the devotion to the Sacred Heart in this life and in the awful moment of death are so abundant and precious, those which it produces for the *life to come* must be of corresponding value. And in reference to these fruits of eternal glory the promises of our blessed Lord are no less explicit. Here I must confine myself to a single passage from the writings of Blessed Margaret Mary. To a fervent promoter of the devotion to the Sacred Heart she writes: " You may depend upon it that all you have done for the honor of the Sacred Heart will be for all eternity remembered with benevolence by Our Lord. . . . You shall be abundantly rewarded for it in the next life. Nay, you have done nothing in your life that will be so amply repaid. The resolve to devote yourself entirely to the honor and glory of the Sacred Heart will have greater merit for you than all else besides. . . . Your name shall be engraven in indelible characters upon the Sacred Heart of Jesus."

Let us, then, beloved brethren, thank our blessed Lord for having in this our day revealed to us a devotion so pleasing to Him and so salutary for us. And what will be the most acceptable tribute of thanks to Him for this inestimable favor? That we dedicate ourselves wholly and entirely to His Sacred Heart; that we honor His Sacred Heart ourselves, and do all we can to promote this devotion in our families, among our friends, and among all those over whom we possess any influence. Thus we shall show our blessed Lord, in very deed, how highly we appreciate this priceless benefit, and render Him due thanks for this singular favor. O sweetest Jesus, Our Saviour, we beseech Thee by Thy Sacred Heart, grant us the grace thus to show our gratitude to Thee, that, having devoted ourselves to the honor and glory of Thy Sacred Heart here on earth, we may eternally love and praise that inexhaustible source of love and grace and glory in heaven. Amen.

Feast of St. Peter and St. Paul.

ST. PETER THE VISIBLE HEAD OF THE CHURCH.

"Thou art Peter, and upon this rock I will build My Church."—Matt. xvi. 18.

TO-DAY, beloved brethren, as you are aware, we celebrate the feast of the Princes of the Apostles, Saints Peter and Paul. The reason why the memory of both these saints is kept on the same day lies in the fact that, according to a well-founded tradition, both suffered and gained the palm of martyrdom on the same day and at the same hour. Following, however, the example of the Church, who on this day gives her attention almost exclusively to St. Peter, while she defers the commemoration of St. Paul to the following day, I shall speak only of the former. Now, what makes St. Peter in a special manner worthy of our interest and deserving of our honor, it seems to me, is comprised in the one fact of his being chosen by Christ, in preference to all the other apostles, as the *supreme head of the Church*. This elevation of St. Peter, I maintain, was—

1. *A well merited distinction;*
2. *A most happy choice.*

I. A WELL MERITED DISTINCTION.

The elevation of St. Peter to the primacy of Christ's Church was a well deserved honor, because St. Peter distinguished himself among the apostles by two great virtues, which were particularly necessary for the head of the Church, and, at the same time, eminently qualified him for this exalted position—I mean a lively faith, and an ardent love for the sacred Person of Jesus Christ. That these two virtues precisely were particularly necessary for the head of the Church may be easily understood. For the Church, as you know, is a society, the union of all the faithful in one body, under one common head. Hence her members must be united, both among themselves and with the head. Now, what is the tie that binds the members of the Church together? It is faith; whence they are called the faithful. And what is it that unites them with their head? It is, above all, the bond of charity. Therefore it follows that the supreme head of the Church must be pre-eminent in these two virtues, on which chiefly depend the stability and well-being of the Church. Or should not he whose first duty it is to confirm his brethren signalize himself in faith and charity? And, in fact, we find that St. Peter distinguished himself above all the other apostles by his lively faith and by his ardent love and devotion to his Divine Master.

1. *St. Peter's faith.* It is not my intention, beloved brethren, here to dwell upon those features of St. Peter's faith which were common to all the apostles, but only on those that were peculiar to him alone. I shall, therefore, say nothing of the ardent desire which he manifested of becoming acquainted with Jesus Christ, as soon as he had learned from Andrew, his brother, that He was the Messias that was to come. I shall say nothing of the promptness with which he abandoned his nets and followed Jesus Christ; nothing of the readiness with which he left all that was nearest and dearest to him for Christ's sake. For, although these are grand manifestations of faith, yet they were not peculiar to St. Peter alone, since the other apostles, too, gave proof of similar faith. But what is peculiar

to St. Peter, and suffices to convince us that he surpassed all the other apostles in faith, is the *solemn profession* of faith which he, first and alone of all the apostles, made in the Godhead of Jesus Christ.

Having arrived in the region of Cæsarea Philippi, the Gospel tells us (Matt. xvi.), Jesus asked His disciples: " Whom do men say that the Son of Man is?" Having received various answers, He further asked: " Whom do you say that I am?" Thus He wished to give them an opportunity of professing their faith in Him. But Peter alone answered, and spoke the memorable words: " *Thou art Christ, the Son of the living God.*" Here St. Peter alone openly professes his belief in the Godhead of Jesus Christ; not a mere human faith, but a heavenly, a divine faith—a faith that was divine in its object, for it was the Divinity of Jesus Christ that he confessed; a faith that was divine in its motive, for it rested on divine authority. Hence the words which Christ immediately added: " Blessed art thou, Simon Bar-Jona; because flesh and blood hath not revealed it to thee, but My Father who is in heaven." And upon this public profession of his faith in the Godhead of his Master, Christ conferred upon him the highest office in His Church, the highest dignity upon earth. " I say to thee: that thou art Peter, and upon this rock I will build My Church; and the gates of hell shall not prevail against it. And I will give to thee the keys of the kingdom of heaven; and whatsoever thou shalt bind upon earth, it shall be bound also in heaven; and whatsoever thou shalt loose on earth, it shall be loosed also in heaven." This prerogative of supremacy over the entire Church which Christ conferred upon St. Peter was, therefore, well deserved on his part. It was a meet reward of that lively faith by which he distinguished himself among the apostles.

But did not Peter subsequently *deny* his Lord and Master? And did he not thereby lose all his former merits, and by the grave scandal which he gave make himself utterly unworthy of this great prerogative? True, Peter denied his Lord, and thus lost all his previous merits; but not irrevocably. For, according to the teaching of the holy Fathers of the Church, all the merits which the sinner loses through his sins are again restored on his conversion. Accordingly, St. Peter on his repentance regained all his lost merits. And as to the grave scandal which he gave by the denial of his Master, it was more than repaired by the illustrious example of penance which he gave by his conversion, and the public profession of his attachment to his Divine Master. This is the verdict of Jesus Christ Himself, the Son of God, who is certainly the most competent judge in this matter. For, despite the fall of St. Peter, Christ did not hesitate to confer upon him the promised dignity. After His resurrection, in the presence of the other apostles, having exacted from St. Peter a threefold profession of his love, to repair the scandal given by his threefold denial, Jesus Christ said to him: " Feed My lambs, feed My sheep" (John xxi. 15-17), thus making him supreme pastor of His entire flock, of the sheep as well as of the lambs. And what is this flock of Jesus Christ? It is His Church, comprising the bishops, who are the successors of the apostles; the priests, who are their assistants in the ministry; and the whole body of the faithful. With these words, therefore, " feed My lambs, feed My sheep," St. Peter was constituted the supreme head of the whole Church, of the apostles as well as of the faithful; as his successor, the Roman Pontiff is the supreme head of the bishops, the successors of the apostles, as well as of the priesthood and the laity of the Church.

2. *St. Peter's charity.* St. Peter, however, was no less conspicuous for his ardent love towards his Divine Master than for his lively faith in His Divinity. No other of the apostles gave so many proofs of special love and attachment to Jesus Christ as did St. Peter. Hence he always loved to be in the blissful presence of our blessed Lord. From the moment he first resolved to follow Jesus Christ we find him almost continually near His sacred person. This singular attachment of St. Peter to the person of Our Lord was shown on the occasion on which Christ revealed to the Jews that He would institute the Sacrament of His body and blood. Many of His disciples on this occasion, alarmed at the apparent incredibleness of this doctrine, left Our Lord, and conversed with Him no more. Whereupon Jesus addressed Himself to His apostles and said: "Will you also go away?" But Simon Peter immediately answered: "Lord, to whom shall we go? Thou hast the words of eternal life" (John vi. 67-69). To similar sentiments of love and attachment he gave expression on occasion of the Transfiguration of Our Lord on Mount Tabor. For, was it not chiefly his great attachment for his Divine Master that made him unwilling to quit that place of blissful memory, and caused him to exclaim: "Lord, it is good for us to be here; if Thou wilt, let us make here three tabernacles"? (Matt. xvii. 4.) For this same reason, we find him disconcerted as often as our blessed Lord speaks of His impending sufferings. And, again, when on several occasions, even at the risk of his life, he plunges into the water to go to meet his Lord, while the other apostles either await His arrival or row to meet Him, was he not, in like manner, prompted by his ardent and impetuous affection towards his Divine Master?

These and many similar manifestations of his love

justify us in asserting that St. Peter surpassed all the other apostles and disciples of Our Lord in his ardent affection towards his Master. And we make this assertion with less hesitation, because the *holy Fathers* of the Church do not hesitate to make the same statement. Thus St. Chrysostom says: "No one loved Christ as ardently as did St. Peter." And St. Augustine says: "The Lord was well aware that Peter loved Him more than His other disciples did."

But what need have we of the testimony of the holy Fathers, where we possess the clearest evidence of *Holy Writ?* Have we not the evident testimony of the Holy Ghost Himself that St. Peter was first in affection and devotion to his Master as he was the foremost in rank and power? One day, after His resurrection, St. John tells us (John xxi.), Christ appeared to His disciples; and after having taken a repast with them He addressed Himself to Simon Peter personally and said to him thrice: "Simon, son of John, lovest thou Me more than these?" And Peter thrice answered: "Yea, Lord, Thou knowest that I love Thee." And Jesus Christ, the searcher of hearts, accepted his answer as true and sincere; and, to confirm the truth of the fact, and to reward the excess of Peter's love, He publicly and solemnly conferred upon him that power and dignity which He had already promised him: "Feed My lambs; feed My sheep."

Thus the ardent love and attachment to his Divine Master, in which St. Peter excelled all the other apostles and disciples of Our Lord, as well as his lively faith, rendered him worthy of the highest place in the Church of Christ, and secured for him the highest power and dignity upon earth—that of supreme head of God's Church, and vice-gerent of Jesus Christ on earth. Is it not true, then, that his elevation to this exalted office was a well merited distinction?

II. A MOST HAPPY CHOICE.

The choice of St. Peter as supreme head of the Church of Christ was a happy one for this reason, because he made a fruitful use of the power that was vested in him for the advancement of Christ's kingdom on earth. Let us, then, as far as time and the scanty records of his deeds permit, review the *apostolic works* of the Prince of the Apostles.

1. *In Jerusalem.* According to the design of God, the Church of Christ was to take the place of the Jewish Synagogue, or Church of the Old Law. Hence we find that it was the first object of the apostles, and of St. Peter in particular, to preach Christ crucified in the City of Jerusalem, the centre of Judaism, and to convert the ungrateful city to the religion of Jesus Christ. It was therefore in Jerusalem that he began his apostolic career. And this he did with a courage and success truly marvellous. He who but a short time before trembled at the voice of a maid-servant, and denied his Lord from human respect, on the memorable day of Pentecost goes forth and fearlessly preaches Christ crucified before that same people who had crucified Him, and whose hands were still stained with His blood. And with what success? Such was the power of his word that on that very day thousands believed, were baptized, and received into the Church of Christ; and, as the Acts of the Apostles record, "the Lord increased daily together such as should be saved" (Acts ii. 47). And how great was the zeal and piety of those neophytes may be learned from the same record. "They were persevering in the doctrine of the apostles, and in the communication of the

breaking of bread, and in prayers. And they that believed were together and had all things in common They sold their possessions and goods, and divided them to all, according as every one had need" (Acts ii. 42-45).

And what frankness and intrepidity did Peter show before the *Chief Council* of the Jews! Having cured in the name of Jesus a cripple, who lay helpless at the temple-gate, and having made use of the occasion to exhort the people to penance and faith in Jesus Christ, he was seized and cast into prison. On the following day he was brought before the council and asked: "By what power, or by what name, have you done this?" And Peter, filled with the Holy Ghost, fearlessly answered: "Be it known to you all, and to all the people of Israel, that by the Name of Our Lord Jesus Christ of Nazareth, whom you crucified, whom God hath raised from the dead, even by Him this man standeth here before you whole" (Ibid. iv.). And he goes on to show them that in the name of Jesus alone is salvation, and that there is no other name under heaven given to men whereby they must be saved; so that they were all filled with amazement at his constancy and at the miracle he had wrought, and knew not what to answer. Thus, not daring to lay hands upon him, they dismissed him and St. John, his companion, charging them "not to speak at all, nor teach in the name of Jesus." But they fearlessly answered: "We cannot but speak the things which we have seen and heard." Need we, then, wonder at the marvellous fruit of St. Peter's work? Need we wonder that he rose from day to day in the esteem and veneration of the people? Need we wonder to see them bring their sick from a distance and lay them along the streets, that when St. Peter passed by his shadow might fall upon them, and cure them?

2. *Outside of Jerusalem.* St. Peter's activity, however, was not confined to Jerusalem and its inhabitants. Like St. Paul he, too, was a debtor to all men. Therefore, when after the martyrdom of St. Stephen the storm of persecution burst upon the flock of Christ in Jerusalem, and the Christians were dispersed, we find St. Peter in Samaria, a region which he declares ripe for the Gospel. Peace being restored, we meet him again in the neighborhood of Jerusalem, visiting and confirming the newly formed Christian communities. Later on he betakes himself to Antioch, where for some years he fixes his seat, and from whence he governs the Church. Here his followers were so distinguished by the spirit of Christ that they were the first to be called Christians. His work at Antioch, however, did not prevent him from visiting other places, whither the spirit of God had called him. Thus he visited Jerusalem, where in council with the other apostles he frames the first laws for the universal Church. There it was that, when his death had been resolved upon by the Jews, God at the prayers of the faithful miraculously delivered him from prison. Finally, after traversing the vast tracts of Pontus, Galatia, Cappadocia, Asia, and Bithynia, he directed his journey to Rome, the capital of the world, in order that from that great centre the light of the Gospel might the more effectually be diffused over all the nations.

This being *the most glorious enterprise* of St. Peter, let us briefly consider the difficulties which it involved. What was the object of Peter's journey to Rome? It was nothing less than the conversion of the whole Roman Empire to Christianity. For this end he had to bring the Romans to believe in the Divinity of Jesus Christ, and not only to believe, but also to embrace His doctrine with willing hearts. What a bold enterprise!

To bring the proud Roman people to believe in the doctrine of a foreigner of despised nationality, who had been condemned and put to death as an impostor and blasphemer by His own countrymen—to bring the proud Roman people to embrace a doctrine and to shape their lives according to a new religion which was diametrically opposed to all their views, customs, and inclinations; a religion which despises riches, honors, and pleasures, and commends poverty, humiliation and self-denial—does this not seem, naturally speaking, a visionary project? And who were those to whom he was to preach this doctrine? A nation that never bowed to a foreign foe; a nation that suspected and despised everything foreign; a nation that was steeped in the grossest and most unnatural vices. On whose authority are they to accept this religion? On the authority of a poor, despised, illiterate fisherman, who had never frequented the schools of philosophers or rhetoricians. Thus all circumstances are against him; not a single one, naturally speaking, inspires the least hope of success.

Yet St. Peter does not shrink from the difficulty. Like a solid rock amid the dashing waves he stands unshaken in his purpose. And what was the *success* of his undertaking? Almighty God prospered his work. He had the consolation of seeing at Rome a numerous and fervent Christian community spring up, which served as a model for the whole Christian world. And, what most of all he coveted, here it was his lot to follow his Master to the death of the cross; for it was at Rome that St. Peter laid down his life in evidence of the faith he preached. And by what manner of death? By a death that was worthy of the Prince of the Apostles, and of the most devoted follower of his Master. Like Him he was crucified, but his reverence and humility asked and obtained one favor, to be crucified head downwards.

True, St. Peter did not live to see the full fruits of his apostolic labors in Rome. But we, beloved brethren, see them in all their fulness. We have only to turn our eyes to the *Eternal City*. There, upon the summit of the Capitol, where once waved triumphantly the Roman Eagle, the radiant Cross of Jesus Christ sheds its benign light on the City of the Popes. Rome. the centre of the pagan world, has become the centre of Christendom. In Rome the Church of Christ was built on Peter, the rock, and cemented with the blood of more than twelve millions of martyrs. From Rome it was extended to the utmost ends of the earth. St. Peter triumphed over the Roman Empire; Christ triumphed over the Roman gods. Such was the success of the apostolic work of St. Peter.

Is it not true, then, beloved brethren, that the choice of St. Peter, and his elevation to the highest place in God's Church, was as happy as it was well merited? Has he not proved this by his indefatigable apostolic labors, by his glorious death on the cross, and by the wonderful fruits of his work? Is St. Peter, then, not worthy of our highest admiration and honor? Does he not inspire us with the greatest confidence in his power and intercession? But, my dear friends, while we invoke St. Peter, the supreme head of the Church of Christ, let us not forget his glorious companion and co-worker, St. Paul, who labored and died with him in the same cause. Let us look up with admiration and reverence, and invoke with confidence this glorious double-star on the bright firmament of heaven; but, above all, let us live according to the spirit and teaching of the Princes of the Apostles, that we may in this life be true children of that holy mother for whom they lived, labored, and died, and that we may in the life to come share their glory in heaven. Amen.

Feast of the Assumption.

MUTUAL RECEPTION OF MOTHER AND SON.

"And a certain woman named Martha received Him into her house: and she had a sister called Mary."—Luke x. 38, 39.

AMONG the feasts of the Mother of God there is none that is more suited to inspire us with a true longing for heavenly goods than that of the Assumption, which we celebrate to-day; for it clearly shows us the possibility of attaining to them, and traces out before us the way we have to pursue. It reveals, as it were, to our wondering gaze how the Blessed Virgin, who is neither God nor angel, but a human being like ourselves, is taken up into heaven, and raised to a throne at the right hand of her divine Son, above all the angels and saints of God. A similar though less glorious mansion is prepared for every one of us. But how are we to gain it? We must pursue the same course which our glorious Mother adopted. She received our blessed Lord in a befitting manner in this life; and, therefore, her divine Son received her into glory at her death. This, it seems to me, is the reason why the Church has chosen for this feast the Gospel which describes the reception given to our blessed Lord by Martha and her sister Mary in the hamlet of Bethania. For these two sisters, of whom the one waits on Our Lord with active service, while the other sits at His feet in holy contemplation and listens to His words, are a fit representation of the Blessed Virgin, who in her reception of her divine Son unites active service with heavenly contemplation. The Church would therefore direct our attention to this reception which the Mother of God gave to her divine Son in this life. Now, why does the Church do so precisely on this day? Evidently to insinuate that the reception which the Blessed Virgin gave to her Son in this world was the cause of the glorious reception which He gave her in heaven. Let us, then, following this hint of the Church, consider—

1. *How the Blessed Virgin received her Son on earth;*
2. *How Jesus Christ received His Mother in heaven.*

I. HOW MARY RECEIVED HER SON.

How, then, beloved brethren, was the Son of God received on earth by His most holy Mother? While He came into His own, and His own received Him not, His loving Mother prepared for Him a *suitable dwelling-place*, in which He loved to abide.

1. *What are the qualities* of an appropriate dwelling-place of the Most High? According to St. Augustine, a habitation befitting the abiding presence of God must have its foundation in faith, must be built up in hope, and must be completed in charity. The same thought we find expressed in one of the prayers of the Church. "Almighty and eternal God," thus the Church prays, "increase in us faith, hope, and charity, and that we may merit to obtain what Thou promisest, make us love what Thou commandest." Now, what is it that God promises us? A glorious mansion in heaven, provided only we prepare Him a suitable dwelling-place on earth. When, therefore, the Church prays for the increase of faith, hope, and charity within our hearts, she does so with the intent that we may thus prepare a suitable mansion for God in our hearts, a temple worthy of the Most High. The meaning of the Church's prayer, accordingly, is this: Grant, O Lord,

that we may prepare for Thee a befitting mansion in our hearts, that we may merit to be received by Thee into the eternal mansions of heaven. Blessed are those who prepare in their souls such a temple for the Most High! Such a soul is the seat of the Eternal Wisdom and the dwelling-place of the Almighty. All the efforts and all the ministries of the Church are directed towards the erection and completion of this spiritual edifice in our souls. This is the object of the Church's preaching, of her prayers, her divine worship, her sacraments. This is the object of the Church herself, of the whole scheme of Redemption, of all God's dealings with man.

If we would, then, prepare in our hearts a dwelling-place for the Most High, we must begin with the deep, and broad, and solid *foundation of faith*. For faith is the foundation and the beginning of salvation; and "without faith," as the Apostle assures us, "it is impossible to please God" (Heb. xi. 6). But our faith must rest, not on the drifting sands of the opinions of men, but on the unshaken rock, which is Christ Jesus Our Lord, who speaks to us by the mouth of His Church.

On this solid foundation of faith we must *build in hope*. As the edifice rests on its foundation, so hope is based upon faith. For as soon as we believe that God exists; that He is our Redeemer; that He promises eternal happiness to those that love and serve Him—we have the strongest motives to hope in His goodness and mercy, that we shall once by our co-operation with His assistance obtain the rewards which He has promised us. It is hope that gives us strength and courage to undergo all toils and hardships in the work of our salvation, according to the words of the Prophet, "They that hope in the Lord shall renew their strength; they shall take wings as eagles; they shall run and not be weary; they shall walk and not faint" (Is. xl. 31).

But the spiritual edifice which is a meet dwelling-place of the Most High must be *finished in love.* For, as an unfinished building is liable to decay and to totter, so this supernatural structure, though based on faith and reared up in hope, must still be consummated in charity, if it should be a durable and permanent mansion of Him who deigns to take up His abode with us. Such must be the quality of the spiritual temple which God chooses for His dwelling-place.

2. Such, in fact, was the dwelling-place which the Blessed Virgin prepared for her divine Son. It was based on the solid foundation of *faith.* So great was the faith of the Mother of God, that St. Elizabeth, the mother of St. John the Baptist, filled with the Holy Ghost, on meeting her, exclaimed in wonderment: "Blessed art thou that hast believed; because those things shall be accomplished that were spoken to thee by the Lord" (Luke i. 45). How deeply must she have laid the foundation of faith! In her humility she was thoroughly convinced that she was a poor, lowly handmaid of the Lord, unworthy of any distinction; and yet she believed that she was chosen by God as the instrument of the most inscrutable mystery; that she was to be raised to the most intimate communion with God; that she was to be the subject of the most unheard-of miracle of God's infinite power, that of motherhood and perpetual virginity in the same person; that she was really and truly to become the Mother of her Creator. If the faith of Abraham was so eloquently commended in Holy Scripture, if the Apostle, filled with admiration at the patriarch's faith, exclaims: "By faith Abraham offered Isaac, accounting that God is able to raise up even from the

dead; whereupon also He received him for a parable [that is, as a type of Jesus Christ]" (Heb. xi. 17-19), what words can suffice to extol the faith of the Mother of God! Did she not offer a greater sacrifice than Abraham? Did she not offer in faith her only-begotten Son—not a type of Christ, but the true Christ Himself—at the foot of the cross on Golgotha? Solid, therefore, was the foundation of faith upon which rested that grand supernatural structure which the Mother of God prepared as a dwelling-place for her divine Son.

No less conspicuous was her *hope*. To her may be justly applied the words of the Psalmist, "Thou, O Lord, singularly hast settled me in hope" (Ps. iv. 10). And, in fact, how could it be otherwise? How could she who was so favored of God, who had received so many marks of His predilection, be otherwise than thoroughly confirmed in hope? If we, who are only poor servants of God, have every reason confidently to hope in the goodness and mercy of God, how much stronger grounds had she, the Mother of the Eternal Word, to hope all things from her divine Son! And if she so despised all earthly things that she surrendered all for God's sake, and generously sacrificed even her beloved Son to His heavenly Father, how confident must have been her hope of once possessing the heavenly joys and being inseparably re-united with her divine Son! Mary, the Mother of God, was therefore singularly settled in hope; and in this hope she prepared a suitable mansion for the Son of God.

And what shall we say of the *love* of our blessed Lady? If love is the queen of all virtues, must it not have glowed pre-eminently in the heart of her who is the Queen of heaven and earth, of angels and of men? And if it consists, not in mere sentiment and words, but in action, in the endurance of labors and sufferings for the beloved, what must have been the love of the Mother of God, who took an active part in all the hardships and sufferings of her divine Son! If that love is most perfect which knows no fear, how perfect must have been the love of her who forced her way through the infuriate mob to the foot of the cross, there persevered for three long hours with her son, amid the bitterest and grossest reproaches, when almost all His friends had fled for fear! If, according to the words of Our Saviour, true love consists in the observance of the Commandments, what shall we say of the love of the Mother of God, who not only observed the law of God, but with the greatest eagerness and promptness fulfilled His every wish and obeyed all His inspirations! And if, again, there can be no greater show of love than to give one's life for one's friends, where shall we find words to characterize the charity of that Mother who gave her Son, much dearer to her than her own life, not only for His friends, but even for His enemies! With this unspeakable love, which the tongue of angels could not describe, the holy Mother of God completed and adorned the dwelling-place of the Most High in her immaculate heart.

Such was the mansion which the Son of God found prepared for Him in her heart—a dwelling-place that was firmly based on the unshaken foundation of faith, strongly cemented with unwavering hope, and finished and fitted out with the most perfect charity. No wonder, then, that the Eternal Word, enamored of this holy habitation, descended from the bosom of His Father, was made flesh, and took up His abode in this sacred dwelling-place. And because she prepared such a habitation for Him, He now receives her into the mansion of glory.

II. HOW JESUS RECEIVED HIS MOTHER.

1. After the Ascension of Our Lord, His blessed Mother, who loved Him so ardently and tenderly, had but one longing, to be dissolved and to be with her divine Son. Her only comfort was to visit, either actually or in spirit, those places that had been hallowed by the footsteps of her Son, to converse with Him in spirit, to recall the sacred memories which clustered around the holy places. When the hour of her dissolution had come, and she heard the consoling words of the Spouse in the Canticle: "Arise, make haste, my love, and come; for winter is now past, the rain is over and gone; the flowers have appeared in our land; arise and come!" (Cant. ii. 10-12), she is not startled, as when first she was greeted by the angel; but she placidly and joyfully *yields up her spirit;* not in pain or agony, but in holiest ecstasy of love. Oh, who can describe or even conceive the delight of this holy Mother in that happy moment when she breathed forth her loving soul into the hands of Divine Love, before the hosts of jubilant angels, who had come to escort her to the mansions of glory! Who can depict her triumphant entrance into the heavenly court, as she ascends like a luminous cloud from the desert of this earth toward the glorious firmament, flowing with delights, leaning upon her Beloved (Cant. viii. 5)!

2. But not only her soul, but also her body was taken up into heaven. It was not meet that that immaculate body, which was the true ark of the covenant, the habitation of the Eternal Word, the temple of the Holy Ghost, should see corruption, should be resolved into dust. And do you think, beloved brethren, that if the spotless body of the blessed Mother of God had been left on this earth, it would for so many centuries have remained unknown and unhonored, that it would lie

concealed in some obscure corner of the Holy Land? If God does not permit that the bodies of His martyrs and confessors should be deprived of due honor, if He has so often, in the course of centuries, discovered the remains of His servants by miracles, could He permit the stainless body of His own beloved Mother for so long a time to remain in obscurity, and to be bereft of all honor? No, beloved brethren; such a thing is incredible. But it is highly credible, nay, certain beyond the shadow of a doubt, that Jesus Christ, the Son of God, in fulfilment of the words of His heavenly Father, spoken by the Psalmist: "Arise, O Lord, into Thy resting place, Thou and the ark, which Thou hast sanctified," took up into heaven that spotless body which He had sanctified as His tabernacle here on earth. Such is the teaching of the holy Fathers of the Church; such is the constant tradition; such is the belief of the Church; and although the Church has not yet defined this truth as an article of faith, yet it is so certain that nothing stands in the way of its definition whenever occasion may demand it.

3. And what transports of joy and exultation filled the court of heaven, when Mary, the Mother of God, entered into the glory of her Lord, her God, and Son! What joy and delight filled the immaculate heart of that heavenly Mother, when she entered into that New Jerusalem, the splendor and glory of which no eye hath seen, nor ear heard, nor heart of man conceived! Whithersoever she turns her eyes, she perceives joy and delight without measure, power and splendor and glory without end. She beholds the paradise of pleasure, the glorious choirs of the angels, and the ranks of the saints. She beholds her Son sitting on His throne of glory and majesty at the right hand of His heavenly Father, crowned—not by the Jews with thorns—but

by His Eternal Father with power and majesty, His face radiant as the sun, and His glorious wounds beaming like so many precious stones. And if she reflects upon herself, she beholds herself raised to the dignity of Queen of heaven and earth, elevated over all the angels and saints of God, surrounded with unspeakable glory and majesty. "Go forth, ye daughters of Sion," says the Canticle, "and see king Solomon in the diadem wherewith his mother crowned him in the day of his espousals, and in the day of the joy of his heart" (Cant. iii. 11). But greater than Solomon is here—the Mother of God, crowned not by an earthly hand, not with an earthly crown, but by the hand of her divine Son, with an imperishable crown of unspeakable glory! What wonder, then, that the daughters of the New Sion, the blessed in heaven, enraptured at beholding her glory, burst into a new canticle of praise to the Almighty, who has conferred such glory on a human creature!

4. *This glory* it was that St. John saw in spirit when in his Revelations he penned the words: "And a great sign appeared in heaven; a woman, clothed with the sun, and the moon under her feet, and on her head a crown of twelve stars" (Apoc. xii. 1). This woman, beloved brethren, is the Mother of God arrayed in the radiance of the Sun of justice, that robe of glory with which her Son clothed her, who had once clothed Him with the lowly garb of our humanity. The crown of twelve stars is the lustre of her virtues. For she embodies in one all the virtues that distinguish the various ranks of the blessed. She combines the faith of the patriarchs, the hope of the prophets, the love of the apostles, the fortitude of the martyrs, and the purity of the virgins; and all those virtues and the numerous others expressed in the mystic "twelve" now shine

like so many stars in her crown of glory: "And on her head a crown of twelve stars." "And the moon under her feet." As the sun in which she is clothed symbolizes Jesus Christ, her Son, so the moon represents the Church of God, the hierarchy of the saints, over whom she is raised as the mediatrix between them and her divine Son. She is the Queen of the Church militant on earth, suffering in purgatory, and triumphant in heaven. Therefore she is represented with "the moon under her feet." But the moon symbolizes also the sinners, according to the words of the Scripture: "A fool [i. e., a sinner] is changed as the moon" (Ecclus. xxvii. 12). She is the refuge of sinners; the sinner finds safety if he casts himself at her feet in penance; therefore, also, she is represented with "the moon under her feet."

Such is the glorious reception which the Son of God gave to His holy Mother in return for the loving reception which she had prepared for Him on earth. If then, beloved brethren, we would behold the glory of our holy Mother Mary, and receive a similar welcome at the hands of Jesus Christ, let us prepare a similar habitation for Him in our hearts; a dwelling-place based on faith, built up in hope, and fitted out in charity. And let us pray to the divine Architect, without whom the builders labor in vain, and to His glorious Mother, to consummate this divine work in our souls, that we may be the living temples of God in this life and be crowned with the Mother of God after death. Amen.

Feast of the Nativity of the Blessed Virgin.

CONFIDENCE IN THE MOTHER OF GOD.

And Jacob begot Joseph, the husband of Mary, of whom was born Jesus, who is called Christ."—Matt. i. 16.

THE festival of to-day is the commemoration of that joyful day on which our blessed Lady first saw the light. Her birth brought joy to the whole world—to her holy parents, St. Joachim and St. Anne, whose old age was, as tradition tells us, miraculously gladdened by this beauteous babe; to the holy patriarchs, who had departed this life in the friendship of God, and to whom she was the herald of deliverance; to those who then lived upon earth, to whom she, as the morning-dawn, was the harbinger of the Sun of justice; nay, even to the angels of God, who greeted her as their new-born queen. Therefore the Church on this day sings: " Thy Nativity, O Virgin-Mother of God, has brought tidings of joy to the whole world; for from thee hath gone forth the Sun of justice, Christ the Lord; who loosing the curse hath given benediction; and vanquishing death hath bestowed life everlasting." Of the many causes of rejoicing which the memory of the birth of our blessed Lady suggests to us I shall for the present direct your attention to one only : viz., that in her is born to us a powerful patroness—a patroness who next to Christ, the supreme Mediator, is worthy of our *greatest confidence.* For Mary, the Mother of God, surpasses all the saints in power as well as in love for us, and is, therefore, more powerful and more disposed to aid us than are the rest of God's saints. It will,

therefore, be my endeavor to show you that the Blessed Virgin excels all the other saints—
1. *In power, because she is the Mother of God,*
2. *In love to us, because she is our Mother.*

I. MARY'S POWER.

I said that the Blessed Virgin surpassed all the other saints of God in power. For why are the saints so powerful with God? Why is their intercession so effectual? Is it not because they are holy, because they are saints? But the Blessed Virgin, being the Mother of God, is not only holy, not only a saint, but she is the holiest of God's saints, the queen of all the saints. Holiness, above all other things, is the work of grace or is identical with grace itself; and grace was much more abundantly conferred upon her by Almighty God than upon all the other saints. Why?

1. Because God is wont to confer His graces in *proportion to the dignity* to which He has called His servants. For, the greater the dignity conferred on any one the greater are also his duties and responsibilities; and as God never imposes a duty or responsibility without at the same time giving the graces necessary for its fulfilment, it is manifest that the dignity to which one is raised is a standard according to which God confers His graces upon him. But the Mother of God, as we all know, has been raised by God to the highest dignity of which a mere creature is capable; a dignity which exalts her above all the choirs of the angels and the ranks of the saints. For what angel or saint can say to the Most High: Thou art my son, to-day have I borne Thee? Therefore we must conclude that God has much more abundantly conferred His graces upon her than upon any of His angels or saints. And here, beloved brethren, I do not speak merely of

the grace of assistance necessary to enable her to fulfil the duties attaching to her exalted dignity, but also all those graces that go to constitute the most eminent personal sanctity. And it is by this personal or habitual sanctity, most of all, that the Mother of God surpasses all the other saints.

Unlike the other saints, who were all once children of wrath and slaves of Satan, Mary, the Mother of God, was from the very first moment of her existence *free from sin*, stainless, immaculate. The dignity of Mother of God is incompatible with sin. If she had ever been under the influence of sin, the Son of God would have to acknowledge that His Mother had been once a sinner, His enemy, the object of His hate, the slave of Satan. And who does not see at once that such a supposition is inconsistent with the sanctity of the Son as well as the dignity of the Mother?

But the Blessed Virgin was not only exempt from sin, but also, from the first moment of her conception, *adorned with all supernatural gifts and graces*. Does not human reason itself teach us that this must have been the case? My dear friend, if you had been free to grace your own mother with all imaginable gifts and virtues, would you have left her deprived of any given grace or excellence? If you had the power thus to fashion and fit out your mother, how fair, how perfect, how glorious would she not be! But Jesus Christ, being the Son of God, had the power to form His Mother according to His own heart, and to enrich her with all heavenly graces and favors. Can we, then, imagine that He withheld from her a single gift or virtue which would tend to make her the master-work of grace as well as of nature? Is it not unreasonable to think that the Divine Wisdom and Omnipotence and Sanctity would create and fit out for Himself a mother unworthy of His infinite majesty?

If we compare Mary, our Mother according to the spirit, with *Eve, the mother of all the living* according to the flesh, we arrive at the same conclusion, that the Mother of God far surpasses all the saints in grace and sanctity. Eve is the mother of all mankind; Mary is the Mother of God Himself. Now, I ask, beloved brethren, can God have withheld anything from His own Mother which He has liberally bestowed upon the common mother of mankind? Certainly not; all graces and gifts which Eve possessed before the fall must have been given to Mary, the second and greater Eve, in still greater measure. The first Eve, as we learn from Holy Scripture, went forth spotless and without blemish from the hands of the Creator. So Mary, the second Eve, proceeded without spot or stain from the hands of the Most High, and as she, unlike the first Eve, was never for a moment unfaithful to her sublime vocation, she never made herself guilty of the slightest sin or imperfection. Eve, as she came forth from the hands of her Creator, was adorned with all supernatural gifts and virtues. Mary must, therefore, in the first moment of her existence have possessed all supernatural graces in a much higher degree. Thus the Mother of God was, in consideration of her unspeakable dignity, from the very beginning enriched with a treasure of graces which elevated her far above all the angels and saints in heaven.

2. But God is, moreover, wont to confer His graces on His rational creatures *in proportion to their co-operation.* As long as we are in the state of sanctifying grace, and with the aid of the helping grace of God perform good works, we merit for ourselves not only an eternal re-

ward in heaven, but also an immediate increase of sanctifying grace or internal sanctity. If, then, the just man always, to the utmost of his power, co-operates with God's grace, sanctifying grace or internal sanctity will be continually augmented within his soul. Since, therefore, the Blessed Virgin was never guilty of the least imperfection and always most faithfully co-operated with God's grace, sanctifying grace was continually increased in her soul throughout the whole course of her mortal life. Now, if the first gift of grace conferred upon her in the moment of her conception, as we confidently believe, had raised her to a degree of sanctity which far transcends that of the holiest of God's angels and saints, what fulness of grace and sanctity must she not have possessed at the end of her earthly career! Justly, then, did the angel salute her with the glorious title "full of grace." She is, in truth, full of grace, an overflowing ocean of grace. As is the boundless and unfathomable sea compared with the fountains, rivers, and lakes, such is the sanctity of the Mother of God compared with that of the other saints.

If, then, the saints, owing to their sanctity, are so powerful with God, how powerful must be the Mother of God, who is the Queen of all the saints! Yes, beloved brethren, the Mother of God is, in a certain sense, almighty, that is, she can by her intercession obtain all things for us from Him who is almighty. Or do you think that her divine Son has lost any portion of His former child-like piety towards her? Do you think He has forgotten the many loving services which she rendered Him? Has He forgotten her grief at the foot of the cross? Oh, no, beloved brethren; the most loving and grateful of all sons bears in mind all this, and cannot refuse to hear His own beloved Mother, when she intercedes for her children. The Mother of God is, therefore, in a true sense almighty by her power of intercession. She *can*, therefore, aid us; nay, she can aid us more than all the angels and saints of God, because she is the Mother of God. But she is also, in the second place, *willing* to aid us; for, being likewise our Mother, her love for us is incomparably greater than that of all the other saints.

II. MARY'S LOVE FOR US.

1. Almighty God has given to His holy Mother such a position in our regard as to secure for us her most tender, affectionate, and active love. She is, by the very place she occupies in the plan of our salvation, *our Mother*, the mother of all Christians who have once been received into the household of God's Church. According to the original plan of God our supernatural as well as our natural life was to be transmitted to us through the instrumentality of our first mother Eve. Through her sanctifying grace, as well as life and existence, was to be communicated to mankind. By the sin which she committed and to which she seduced our first father Adam, she frustrated this design of the Most High, and forfeited the sublime vocation and dignity of spiritual motherhood. But God in His mercy raised up for us another spiritual Mother, a second Eve, more perfect than the first, to take the place of the first Eve in our regard. Through her instrumentality we were to receive that spiritual life which we had forefeited through the sin of our first mother. This second Eve, the spiritual Mother of all the living, is Mary, the Mother of God. This spiritual Motherhood of the Blessed Virgin is clearly implied in the words which God addressed to the serpent after the fall of our first parents: " I will put enmities between thee and the woman, and

thy seed and her seed; she shall crush thy head" (Gen iii. 15). Mary's vocation was, therefore, to vanquish the serpent that in our first mother had robbed us of our spiritual life, to undo the work of Satan, and, consequently, to restore to us in her divine Son the spiritual life which we had lost. Is it not evident, then, that, being the Mother of the Redeemer, who is the giver of eternal life, the true life itself, she is in the truest sense the spiritual Mother of all the living, as Eve is the mother of all according to the flesh? Hence our blessed Lord in His last will upon the cross, according to the well founded and pious belief of many eminent writers, commended her to all of us as our Mother in the person of His beloved disciple St. John, when He spoke the words: Behold thy mother" (John xix. 27).

2. This being the case, Mary being in the strictest sense our spiritual Mother, is it not manifest that *she loves us* with an incomparably more tender and affectionate love than all the other saints do, who are only our brothers and friends? And has she not given us manifest proofs of her most tender affection and active love? Has she not borne an active part in the work of our Redemption? Did she not freely and readily surrender her divine Son to the death of the cross for our salvation? Oh, who can measure the greatness of this sacrifice! Who can describe the sorrows which she endured during this ordeal, while standing at the foot of the cross! There she stood for three long hours, as in the agony of death, the sword of grief transfixing her soul.

"*There stood by the cross of Jesus His Mother*" (John xix. 25). Her Son, her dearly beloved, hangs upon the cross, upon the tree of shame, between two thieves; she sees it with her own eyes, and yet she stands at the foot of the cross! His most tender hands and feet are pierced with rough nails; she sees it, and yet she stands at the foot of the cross! On His head is pressed a crown of sharp thorns, and His blood trickles down to the ground on all sides; she sees it, and yet she continues to stand at the foot of the cross! His most sacred body is disfigured with livid and bleeding wounds, and racked so cruelly that all His bones may be numbered; His Mother sees it, and yet she stands at the foot of the cross! Her divine Son, the King of heaven and earth, is mocked and scoffed at by the populace; the Mother sees their fury, and hears their blasphemies, and yet she stands at the foot of the cross! Her Son, the joy and comfort of her life, bows His head and yields up His spirit in death; the Mother sees Him breathe His last, yet she stands at the foot of the cross! The sacred body of her Son, cold and lifeless, and disfigured with wounds, is taken down from the cross and laid on her lap. She looks into His face: His eyes are glazed in death, His lips are mute, His face is covered with blood; she can hardly recognize those divine features, so familiar and so dear to her! Oh, what grief! What a sea of sorrows!

And who is *the cause of this sorrow*, beloved brethren? Let us all strike our breasts in contrition, and acknowledge it: we are the cause! Our sins are the cause! It was our sins that caused the bitter passion and death of her Son. It was our sins that pierced the heart of the Mother. Was it not we who by our sins crucified her Son? Who else but ourselves, then, has thrust the sword of grief into the Mother's soul? Could, then, a Mother who has thus loved us, who has borne such a martyrdom of sorrows for our sake, who has sacrificed amid the most cruel tortures her own divine Son for us—could such a Mother, I ask, be unwilling to aid us? It were as impious to doubt her willingness to help us, as it would be to doubt her unfathomable love for us.

If, then, beloved brethren, Mary, the Mother of God, is of all God's elect the most powerful and at the same time the most ready to help us, is she not next to her divine Son the safest anchor of our hope? Have we not good reason, then, to rejoice in her nativity, to rejoice that in her such a powerful and loving Mother has been given us? But while we justly rejoice, let us not neglect to show our gratitude to God and to His blessed Mother by proving ourselves children worthy of so great and good a Mother. Amen.

Feast of St. Michael the Archangel.

DEVOTION TO ST. MICHAEL.

"And behold Michael, one of the chief princes, came to help me."—Dan. x. 13.

To-day, on the feast of St. Michael, the glorious chief of the heavenly hosts, I feel that it is my duty to contribute something towards the renewal of your devotion to him and of your confidence in his powerful intercession. For this end we shall in the present discourse put to ourselves two questions, the answers to which will supply us with ample motives of honoring and confidently invoking this great prince of God's angels, who is the patron of our Church and congregation. We shall, therefore, ask ourselves—

1. *Why should we pay special honor to St. Michael?*
2. *Why should we invoke him with special confidence?*

I. HONOR DUE TO ST. MICHAEL.

1. In the first place, it is meet that we should pay special honor to St. Michael on account of the *extraordinary merits* obtained by him in his victorious struggle in the cause of the Most High against the rebellious archfiend Lucifer.

This fallen chief, as is commonly believed, was the highest and mightiest of God's angels; the most excellent, most beautiful, and most highly endowed of all creatures that had proceeded from the hands of the Almighty. He was, according to the words of the prophet Ezechiel, of all creatures the most perfect likeness of God's greatness, wisdom, and beauty; richly endowed with all gifts and excellences: "Thus saith the Lord God: Thou wast the seal of resemblance, full of wisdom, and perfect in beauty; thou wast in the pleasures of the paradise of God; every precious stone was thy covering" (Ezech. xxviii. 12, 13). Great, then, were the natural and supernatural endowments which God had conferred on this rebel angel. But instead of acknowledging his endowments as gifts bestowed upon him by the munificence of God, instead of showing himself grateful to the bountiful giver of all good gifts, and loving Him as his supreme benefactor, he abused the gifts so liberally bestowed on him, gave to himself the honor due to God, and went so far in his vain self-glorification as to affect a throne equal in glory to that of God Himself. "Thou saidst in thy heart," says the prophet Isaias, "I will exalt my throne above the stars of God, I will sit in the mountain of the covenant, in the sides of the north. I will ascend above the height of the clouds, I will be like the Most High" (Isa. xiv. 13, 14). Yet he went still farther; he gave open expression to his rebellious sentiments, and endeavored to gain over to his designs and involve in his impious revolt all the choirs of angels. Such were the baneful effects produced by his bad example and seduction that, according to a well founded opinion, one third of the angels of God followed his standard and fell off from their allegiance to God.

But St. Michael, filled with zeal for the cause of the Almighty, *arose as the champion of God's glory*, strengthened in their allegiance those good angels that had not yet joined the standard of Lucifer, and, taking for his war-cry "Who is like God?" thrust the rebellious spirits together with their apostate leader from heaven's courts into the abyss of hell. By this grand victory St. Michael gained unspeakable merits in the cause of the Most High. If the merits of St. Paul or of St. Francis Xavier are so great, because by their apostolic labors they gained so many souls for heaven, how great must be the merits of St. Michael, who by his efforts preserved in their loyalty to God so many millions of glorious angels as would outweigh in worth and number many worlds of human beings? Therefore Almighty God, according to a very common opinion of divines, conferred on St. Michael all those gifts and prerogatives which Lucifer possessed before his fall; now, he possesses all that greatness and power and majesty with which Lucifer was then endowed. Hence the saints and doctors of the Church do not hesitate to assert that none of God's angels is greater or even equal in merit to St. Michael; that St. Michael may, therefore, be justly considered the prince of the heavenly hosts. And this opinion is confirmed by the Church herself, who gives him the title "Prince of Paradise," and adds that all the angels pay him the tribute of honor. A special honor is, therefore, due to St. Michael for his extraordinary merits in the cause of the Almighty, and on account of that high position to which he has consequently attained. But we shall the more readily pay him the due tribute of our honor when we further consider how God Himself has honored him, and how He wishes us to honor him.

2. In what honor St. Michael stands with Almighty God Himself and how *God has honored him above all His other angels*, we may conclude from the important missions and offices which He at various times entrusted to him. It was to him, as is commonly admitted, that God confided the guardianship of the Church of the *Old Law*, and the protection of His chosen

people. Therefore we may safely admit that, as often as God in the Old Dispensation sent an angel for the defence of His people, the angel chosen for such a mission was St. Michael (Origen, hom. 13 in lib. Num). It was St. Michael, then, that appeared to Josue before the taking of Jericho, and promised him aid from on high; it was he who aided the Israelites against the hosts of Syria and slew the mighty army of Sennacherib; it was he who withstood Satan, when, to seduce God's people to idolatry, the fiend endeavored to discover to them the grave of Moses; it was he who opposed Balaam and changed his curses into blessings, when this impious prophet went forth to curse the people of God; it was he who chastised Heliodorus for his intended profanation of the temple (Jos. v. 13; IV. Kings xix. 35; II. Mach. xv. 22; Jude ix.; Num. xxii. 31; II. Mach. iii. 25). In short, he was like a two-edged sword in the hand of God for the destruction of the enemies of His people.

But Almighty God entrusted to the patronage of St. Michael not only the Church of the Old Law and His chosen people, but also in the *New Law* the Church of Christ and the whole Christian flock—His dearest and most costly possession, which He purchased by the toils and labors, by the sufferings and death, by the ransom of the precious blood of His only-begotten Son. Does this fact not show to evidence that St. Michael stands higher in honor with God than all the other legions of His angels?

3. Since Almighty God Himself has thus honored St. Michael above all other angels and archangels on account of his extraordinary merits, gained in the vindication of the divine glory, it must be His earnest wish that *we, too, show him special honor.* Hence we see that He has glorified His faithful servant St.

Michael by divers apparitions and miracles of the most striking character, in order that our attention might in a special manner be directed to him, that we might conceive great admiration and reverence for him, and honor him above all the heavenly hosts. And, in fact, we find that in all ages of the Church extraordinary honor was paid to St. Michael by all nations and in all countries. An evidence of this special devotion to the prince of angels are the numberless churches and altars dedicated to him, the many confraternities and pious associations established under His patronage, the various devotions to him practised by the faithful, and the two great festivals yearly celebrated in his honor by the universal Church. Let us, then, beloved brethren, who owe an especial debt of devotion to St. Michael, as the patron of our church and congregation, following the example given us by the universal Church, and obeying the wishes of the Most High, pay special honor to the glorious chief of the heavenly hosts, in accordance with the high place which he occupies in the hierarchy of God's angels, and the great services which he has achieved, and still continues to achieve, in the cause of Almighty God. And let us have confident recourse to him in the struggle for our salvation; for, while special honor is due to him on our part, he deserves likewise our greatest confidence.

II. INVOCATION OF ST. MICHAEL.

The more willing and powerful a patron or advocate is to aid us, the greater must be our confidence in his assistance. But who in the court of heaven, if we abstract from the Mother of God and, perhaps, her holy spouse St. Joseph, is more willing and powerful to aid us than the great leader of God's heavenly forces?

1. His *willingness* to aid us is as great as is his interest in the affair of our salvation. But his interest for our salvation is most intense. Why?

a. On account of *his great love for us.* He loves us as the friends, the spiritual brethren of Jesus Christ; as the heirs of Christ's kingdom, of which he is the patron, the protector, the champion. He loves us, therefore, as he loves Jesus Christ Himself and the glory of His kingdom.

b. His interest in our salvation is, likewise, great on account of his intense *hatred against Lucifer*, the archenemy of God and man. In virtue of this implacable hatred of the enemy of mankind he has no interest more at heart than to thwart his malicious plans. And what are the designs of the evil one? As his attempts against the Most High Himself have proved ineffectual, all his plans are directed against us, all his intentions are now bent on our spiritual ruin; his only interest, therefore, is to make us miserable for time and eternity. Now, St. Michael has declared a never-ending warfare against Satan; his glorious task is to defeat his fiendish purpose, to rescue us from his snares, to aid us in the attainment of a complete victory over the devil, and to help us to secure the final safety of our souls.

c. Finally, his interest in the work of our salvation is great, because we have been placed by Almighty God *under his patronage* and protection. He is the patron of the universal Church, and as such he is the guardian and protector of every one of us in particular. Hence we may understand the forcible words which the Church, in the name of Jesus, addresses to him: " Michael, Archangel, (thus she exclaims) I have appointed thee leader of all those souls that are to be assumed," i. e., of all the souls that are to be adopted to grace and to glory. How great, then, must not be the desire of the mighty leader to bring all souls entrusted to his care to their glorious end, and lead them in triumph to the throne of God! And if such is his eagerness for the salvation of all, what must be his zeal for your salvation, my dear friends, who are in a still more special way placed under his protection?

2. If Almighty God has given St. Michael such a lively interest in our salvation, we may rest assured that He has given him *no less power* to aid us. There is no doubt, beloved brethren, but St. Michael is one of our most powerful intercessors before the throne of the Most High. And the reasons for this belief are manifest.

a. The first cause of St. Michael's power of intercession with God is his extraordinary *sanctity*. Why are the angels and saints so powerful with God? Whence comes the efficacy of their intercession? Evidently from their sanctity. For it is their sanctity which makes them the friends and favorites of God, and moves Him to make them partakers of all His attributes and perfections, and, consequently, also of His omnipotence. But St. Michael is not a saint merely, but is, as we have seen, most eminent in sanctity. Therefore he in an eminent degree partakes of the infinite power of God.

b. Another cause of his extraordinary power with God is the *high place* which he occupies. For, if God has entrusted a special office or dignity to any one, according to the teaching of St. Thomas, He gives him at the same time all the requirements necessary for its fulfilment. Now, the dignity which God conferred on St. Michael is that of patron of the universal Church. Under his protection are placed, not merely a single congregation or community, but the whole Catholic Church with its various dioceses and congregations. His office is to guard and protect all these against the fearful and the continual assaults of Satan and his forces. The safety, the well-being, and the increase of the entire Church are entrusted to his care. What a momentous charge is his! And what power is necessary to discharge such an important office! And this extensive, immeasurable power has actually been conferred upon him by Almighty God. If, therefore, St. Michael, on the one hand, has nothing more at heart than to extend his aid to us, and if, on the other hand, he possesses such unlimited power to do so, if he is able and willing to help us, should we not have an unshaken confidence in his intercession?

Having now considered the reasons why we should pay special honor to St. Michael, and invoke him with special confidence in all our spiritual wants, and having convinced ourselves that it is our duty as well as our advantage thus to honor and invoke him, it only remains for us to act according to the conviction which we have gained. Above all, then, let us endeavor to imitate the illustrious example which our great and glorious guardian spirit gives us—particularly imitate his intense hatred and abomination of all that is offensive to Almighty God, and his invincible courage in the struggle against the archenemy of God and man.

One thing more: forget not, beloved brethren, often to recommend to this prince of the heavenly hosts the sufferings and distress of the Church militant on earth. For St. Michael is, as you know, the invincible champion in the spiritual combat, the victorious leader of the forces of the Most High, commissioned by God to wield the sword of the spirit against the enemies of His Church. Pray to him that he may obtain strength for our Catholic brethren all over the world, not only to bear up with patience under affliction and persecution, but also, where the interest of the Church requires it, bravely to combat, in public and in private, in the cause of God and of His holy Church. Thus, under the leadership of the great Archangel St. Michael, we shall fight the good fight on earth, and when our course shall be finished, and the priest at our death-bed shall invoke to our aid the prince of the heavenly hosts, he shall come and lead us triumphantly into the glorious ranks of his followers in heaven. Amen.

Feast of the Holy Rosary.

EXCELLENCE OF THE DEVOTION OF THE ROSARY.

" Queen of the most holy Rosary, pray for us."

THE Church's object in the institution of the feast of to-day was to keep in our remembrance the numberless favors which have been and still are bestowed on Christendom at large through the instrumentality of *the devotion of the holy Rosary*. It is the wish of the Church to foster and promote this form of prayer among her children. We cannot, therefore, better respond to the wishes of Holy Church than by endeavoring on this occasion to increase our esteem for this beautiful devotion, and to renew ourselves in the fervent and fruitful practice of it. For this end there is no more efficacious means than the inward and firm conviction of the surpassing *excellence* of this devotion. Its excellence will appear if we consider (1) its *introduction* in the Church, (2) its *nature*, and (3) its salutary *effects*.

I. ITS INTRODUCTION.

When I speak of the introduction of the devotion of the holy Rosary I mean its propagation in the Church as well as its origin.

1. The *origin* of this form of prayer was as follows. In the beginning of the thirteenth century St. Dominic, at the request of Pope Innocent III., betook himself to the south of France to preach against the heretical sect known by the name of Albigenses. These ruthless heretics were perverting the teachings of the Gospel,

blaspheming the most sacred mysteries of the faith, profaning the sacraments, undermining the faith, and corrupting the morals of the faithful. After St. Dominic had long preached to no effect against the spreading contagion, the Blessed Virgin one day appeared to him in a vision, revealed to him the devotion of the holy Rosary, and charged him to preach it and introduce its practice everywhere among the heretics. "You know, my son," said our blessed Lady to St. Dominic, "what means Almighty God used to redeem mankind. The first step was the salutation which the archangel Gabriel brought to me; then followed the gracious birth and holy life of Jesus Christ; after that came His bitter passion and death, and finally His glorious resurrection and ascension into heaven. Thus the world was redeemed, and the gates of heaven were re-opened to mankind. These mysteries of the life, passion, and resurrection of Jesus Christ, interwoven with the angel's salutation and the Lord's Prayer, constitute my chaplet of roses. Preach this Rosary to the heretics. It will be the instrument of their conversion."

Consoled and strengthened by this assurance, St. Dominic arose, and having, according to the instruction of the Queen of heaven, arranged in order the chief mysteries of the life, passion, resurrection, and ascension of Our Lord, and the principal events of the life of our blessed Lady, went forth with renewed vigor on his mission. He *preached* the devotion of the holy Rosary with irresistible eloquence, and repeated again and again its prayers and mysteries with the people, until it became a familiar exercise to them. The fruits were marvellous. What neither fire, nor sword, nor human eloquence could effect was brought about by this tiny instrument, the holy Rosary. Such was the origin of the devotion of the holy Rosary—a marvellous and holy origin, which of itself warrants its excellence.

2. As was the origin, so also was the *propagation* of this devotion marvellous and holy. Scarcely had the saint begun to preach the new devotion, when the people in countless multitudes flocked to hear him and joined by thousands in the recital of the holy Rosary. No church was large enough to contain the masses that followed the saint, and the praises of the Mother of God and the prayers of her holy Rosary resounded under the broad canopy of heaven. During the life of St. Dominic the devotion was spread over the whole of France; it was soon carried beyond the French confines and became the common property of the whole Christian world. All Christians joined their voices in this universal prayer that ascended to God and His holy Mother. It became the practice not only of the common people, but also of the most illustrious personages—of popes and cardinals, bishops and priests, kings and princes, founders of religious orders, saints and apostolic men—all united their efforts to glorify the Mother of God in this devotion and to propagate it to the ends of the earth. Thus it soon became the favorite and universal prayer of Christendom. You see, then, beloved brethren, that the spread of this devotion is no less wonderful than its origin is marvellous and holy. The holy Rosary has, therefore, from its very origin proved itself a devotion of the highest excellence; but what constitutes its intrinsic excellence we shall see more clearly when we consider—

II. ITS NATURE.

The nature of this devotion, beloved brethren, may be determined from the prayers and mysteries of which it is composed, and the order in which they are arranged. Both of these, its contents as well as its arrangement, go to show its transcendent excellence.

1. The devotion of the holy Rosary *is composed* of prayers and meditations. The prayers used in this devotion are the most excellent we possess: the Apostles' Creed, which summarizes the principal truths of our faith; the Lord's Prayer, which Our Saviour Himself has taught us; the Angelical Salutation, which is made up of the words of the angel Gabriel, of St. Elizabeth, and of the Church, addressed to the Mother of God. Are these not the most excellent of all prayers? The meditations have as their subject matter, as we have seen, the chief mysteries of our faith, viz., the Incarnation of Our Lord, His birth, His sufferings, His death, His resurrection, His ascension, and His glorious life in heaven. And these mysteries, according to the unanimous consent of the saints and divines of the Church, afford the most suitable and most fruitful subjects of meditation. The contents of this holy devotion are therefore of surpassing excellence.

2. These eminently rich and holy contents are likewise *arranged* in the most excellent and suitable order. The arrangement is not only the best suited to foster recollection and devotion, but also such that the simplest and most illiterate of the faithful, even the little children, can easily understand them, and without effort impress them on their memory.

First comes the *introduction* to the devotion, which is well calculated to put us in the proper disposition to pray devoutly. It begins with the Sign of the Cross, the profession of our faith in the Triune God, the Father, the Son, and the Holy Ghost. Then follows the Apostles' Creed, briefly comprising the chief articles of the faith. Next comes the doxology, or "Glory be to the Father" etc., that grand anthem of praise to the

Holy Trinity with which the Church is wont to close her psalms and chants. The introduction closes with the recital of the Lord's Prayer and three "Hail Marys," to implore the fruits intended by the devotion—an increase of faith, hope, and charity.

After this introduction the *Rosary properly so called* begins. It consists in the meditation of fifteen mysteries of our Redemption—five joyful, five sorrowful, and five glorious mysteries. And, while the mind is engaged in the meditation of each of these mysteries successively, the devout worshipper recites one "Our Father" and ten "Hail Marys" and closes the decade with "Glory be to the Father." Is it not manifest, then, beloved brethren, that this devotion is most suitable, and at the same time eminently adapted to the capacity of all the faithful without exception?

The holy Rosary is, therefore, both according to its contents and its arrangement, a most excellent form of prayer. The richness of its contents and the simplicity of its arrangement render it the profoundest and at the same time the most popular book of meditation and prayer; whence it has been justly termed the *breviary of the laity.*

3. But like all good things the devotion of the holy Rosary has had, and still has, its *adversaries.* What they object to it is mainly this: It is rather simple, they think, for the more intellectual class of the faithful; and its frequent repetitions are tedious and tiresome: whence it commonly degenerates into a thoughtless and mechanical routine.

To this I answer that it is precisely in the *simplicity* of this form of prayer that its chief excellence consists —in this simplicity, which makes it alike suited to the learned and unlearned, to the child and the adult. It is this simplicity which makes it eminently suited for recitation in common, whether publicly in the Church or privately in the family circle; and we all know what importance our blessed Lord attaches to common prayer, in which several join in His name. If we except the Litanies sanctioned by the Church, we can hardly find any other form of prayer so well adapted to common devotion as the holy Rosary. And the reason of this is its simplicity.

And with regard to the *frequent repetitions*, it is very true; they would become tiresome and tedious, if the mind had not at the same time ample matter for consideration and reflection. But this is far from being the case; for the prayers of which the holy Rosary is composed contain inexhaustible matter for meditation; and, besides, they are accompanied by the sublimest mysteries of our religion, whose depth the most assiduous and protracted meditation cannot exhaust, from whose treasures the profoundest minds have drawn life-long spiritual nourishment. If, then, this devotion is a thoughtless and mechanical exercise for some, the fault lies not in the Rosary, but it lies in their own spiritual weakness, negligence, and lukewarmness. But what completely refutes all objections against this devotion, and shows its excellence in the brighest light, are—

III. ITS FRUITS.

These precious fruits refer partly to this life, and partly to the life to come.

1. In the *present life* the devout practice of this devotion is, above all, most productive of spiritual blessings.

a. First among these spiritual blessings is the *grace of conversion* for those who are in the state of sin. We have the most striking proof of this efficacy of the holy

Rosary in the case of the Albigenses, who had not only fallen off from the faith, but in their blind fury had taken up arms against the children of the Church, demolished churches and convents, and shed torrents of Christian blood. Such an infuriate sect was certainly little disposed to be converted to the true faith. Even the eloquent preaching of the apostolic St. Dominic was of little avail with them. But as soon as at the instigation of the Mother of God he began to preach the holy Rosary, behold, those obdurate sinners, who had thus far frustrated all his efforts, began to enter into themselves, to see their errors and crimes, and to return by thousands to the true faith and to a Christian life. "Not more quickly," says St. Alphonsus Liguori, "did the walls of Jericho fall at the sound of Josue's trumpets than error and heresy disappeared before the holy Rosary of the Blessed Virgin." And this Rosary is the same to-day as it was in the days of St. Dominic. Are we, then, not entitled to hope from it the same marvellous effects? However deeply, therefore, a man may have fallen into sin, he will most certainly obtain the grace of conversion if he only have confident recourse to the practice of the devotion of the holy Rosary.

b. Moreover, the prayer of the holy Rosary secures for us the grace to lead a truly *Christian life*. It amply supplies us with motives and means to lead a pious and holy life. It brings to our remembrance the chief mysteries of our faith—the Incarnation of the Eternal Word for our salvation, the just punishments due to sin, our deliverance from sin, and our justification through the passion, death, and resurrection of the Son of God. But the frequent remembrance of these holy mysteries is a most powerful incentive to love God, to hate sin, and to strive with all our energies after the eternal goods of heaven. Or can anything incite us more effectually to the love of God than the consideration of the infinite love which He has shown for us in the mystery of the Incarnation? Is there anything that can inspire us with greater hatred for sin than the contemplation of the God-man Jesus Christ suffering and dying for us on the cross? Can anything fill us with greater longing for the everlasting glory of heaven than the meditation of the glorious resurrection and triumphal ascension of Jesus Christ? And, while this devotion holds out to us the strongest motives to lead a pious and holy life, it also puts before us the grandest and most inspiring models, in the persons of Jesus Christ and His immaculate Mother. Finally, this devotion directs our attention to Jesus Christ, the true and inexhaustible fountain of divine grace, and to the powerful intercession of His holy Mother, who has never been invoked in vain; whence we are filled with courage and confidence, and strengthened for the practice of Christian virtue. The holy Rosary is, as it were, an open book, in which all may read the profoundest and most consoling truths, the most illustrious and encouraging examples of Christian virtue, and the most powerful exhortations to the practice of good works. Can there be a more efficacious means of guiding us on the path of Christian virtue?

c. Finally, the constant practice of the devotion of the holy Rosary secures for us the greatest of all graces—the grace of *final perseverance*, or of a happy death. This is a special grace, beloved brethren, which we cannot merit by any work of ours, but which is to be obtained by humble and persevering prayer. But thus we can infallibly obtain the grace of final perseverance. For Almighty God has set no limits to the efficacy of prayer, as far as our eternal salvation is concerned. But it is not sufficient to pray for this grace incidentally, or from time to time; we must pray for it without ceasing, according to the teaching of Our Lord, "that we ought always to pray and not to faint" (Luke xviii. 1). Now, it is certain that there is no more suitable way of practising this continual prayer than by frequently saying the Rosary.

As a proof of this assertion, instead of the many arguments I might advance, I shall adduce the following simple, but well authenticated *fact*. A celebrated preacher of the last century was one day summoned to the death-bed of a young nobleman, who was well known to be of dissolute habits. Not without much misgiving in his heart did he obey the summons. But how great was his surprise to find the dying man most contrite for his sins, and fully resigned joyfully to offer the sacrifice of his life as an atonement for his errors! He confessed his sins and received the last sacraments with the most ardent devotion. The confessor, unable to explain this miracle of grace, asked him the cause. The sick man, amid tears and sobs, answered: "Oh, my Father, this grace must be ascribed to the intercession of the Mother of God. When my mother lay on her death-bed, she called me to her bed-side and made me promise that I would daily say the Rosary. I have kept my promise, though for the last ten years I performed no other act of religion. The Mother of God has saved me." He soon breathed his last in the greatest peace of soul, and the priest took his departure, blessing the mercy of God and the power and efficacy of the holy Rosary.

That the holy Rosary is also a powerful means of obtaining *temporal blessings* we have the most striking evidence in the very existence of this feast. It was to commemorate two great temporal favors obtained

Excellence of the Devotion of the Rosary. 231

through its instrumentality that this feast was instituted. These memorable events are the two great victories over the Turks—one at Lepanto (1571), the other at Temesvar in Hungary (1716)—both miraculously obtained through the intervention of the Queen of the most holy Rosary.

2. But the fruits of the holy Rosary are not confined to this life; they extend also to the *life to come*. As a penitential work, and an exercise which enjoys the privilege of many indulgences, the Rosary is a most effectual means of cancelling the temporal punishment due to sin. Besides, it secures for ourselves and for the suffering souls in Purgatory the powerful intercession of the Mother of God, which appeases the divine wrath and moves Almighty God to shorten or alleviate the pains of the suffering souls. Such are, in brief, the fruits of the devotion of the holy Rosary.

It is a subject, beloved brethren, on which much more might be said. But is not the little I have said sufficient to convince you of the excellence of this devotion, to fill you with a high esteem for it, and inspire you with renewed confidence in its effects, and fervor in its practice? The least I can expect of you, then, and what your heavenly Mother expects of you, is that all of you—also the men—have your beads and use them; that those who are not yet enrolled in the confraternity of the holy Rosary become members. The duties it imposes are slight, while its advantages are great. Besides, I would earnestly entreat you, Christian parents, for the benefit of your own souls and those of your children, daily to assemble your children around you for the recitation of the Rosary in common. If you cannot recite all five decades, it will not be too much to ask you to recite one or two every day. Thus you and your household will be under the special protection of the Queen of heaven, the Queen of the most holy Rosary. She will bless you in this life, plead for you before the judgment-seat of God, and receive you into the mansion of everlasting bliss. Amen.

Feast of the Guardian Angels.

DEVOTION TO OUR GUARDIAN ANGELS.

"Behold, I will send My angel, who shall go before thee, and keep thee in thy journey, and bring thee into the place that I have prepared."—Exod. xxiii. 20.

THE intention of the Church, beloved brethren, in celebrating the feast of the guardian angels, is to keep the fact before our minds that we have been entrusted by God to their care, to keep in our remembrance what we owe to them, and to remind us of our duties towards them. I cannot, therefore, better comply with the wishes of Holy Church to-day than by endeavoring to impress these three truths upon you. I shall, therefore, briefly show you—

1. *That we have each his guardian angel;*
2. *Why we should honor our guardian angels;*
3. *How we should honor them.*

I. THE EXISTENCE OF GUARDIAN ANGELS.

1. Has each of us his guardian angel? In the first place, it is most certain that *the just*, that is, those who are in the state of sanctifying grace, have each his guardian angel. This we find clearly expressed in the words of St. Paul in his Epistle to the Hebrews: "Are they [the angels] not all ministering spirits, sent to minister to them who shall receive the inheritance of salvation?" (Heb. i. 14.) And when our blessed Lord says that the innocent child has his guardian angel, He certainly implies that adults, who in innocence are like to those little ones, have also theirs. This was also

the belief of the disciples of Our Lord, as we learn from the Acts of the Apostles. For, when the news was brought that St. Peter was miraculouly released from prison, the disciples, thinking his deliverance impossible, said it was not Peter who was asking for admittance, but his angel (Acts xii. 15). It is, therefore, a truth evidently contained in Holy Scripture that the just have each his guardian angel.

2. Nor is there any reason to doubt, in the second place, that every *individual*, whether in the state of grace or in the state of sin, has his guardian angel. This is absolutely certain, at least as far as the faithful are concerned; but we have not the same evidence in regard to pagans and infidels. It has been the constant belief in the Old as well as in the New Testament. In the Old Law we find that pious and holy men and women speak of the protection of the angels as one of the common and ordinary favors of God to all without distinction. Thus Judith says: "As the same Lord liveth, His angel hath been my keeper, both going hence, and abiding there, and returing from thence hither" (Judith xiii. 20). The saints and doctors of the New Law are still more explicit on this point. St. Jerome, commenting on the words of Our Saviour (Matt. xviii. 10) concerning the angels of the little ones, says: "Such is the dignity of our souls that each has an angel appointed for its protection." The teaching of the Fathers and ecclesiastical writers on this point is so universal and so positive that it must be considered as the common belief of the Church that each individual, at least of the faithful, is entrusted to the keeping of a guardian angel. Therefore the Roman Catechism, which enjoys the highest authority as an exponent of Catholic belief, says that God has given to " *all* men, . . . to *each* one of us " a guardian angel.

3. This fact, beloved brethren, shows in a most striking manner the loving providence of God towards us, and wonderfully contributes to the *glory of God*. It displays in the clearest light the power and wisdom of God in the government of the universe. To illustrate this truth, imagine two different clock-works; the one is so perfect in its design and construction that, being once set in motion, it moves indefinitely, without the interference of the artist, while the other requires the artist's constant and direct attention. Now, I ask, beloved brethren, which of the two mechanisms is more deserving of your admiration, and reflects most credit on the artist? Is it not the one that moves without his direct interference? Is it not evident, then, that the power and wisdom of the Creator are more strikingly manifested by the fact that in this great universe, which is a most wonderfully complicated mechanism, one creature is moved and guided by the influence of another? Does this not show the greatness of God in a clearer light than if He dispensed with the mutual influence of creature upon creature, and directed every individual being of the universe by Himself alone? By this loving provision of Almighty God, by which He has given us in charge to His holy angels, His power and wisdom are, therefore, manifested in the most striking manner, and, consequently, His glory is promoted in a wonderful degree with His rational creatures. But this provision not only promotes the glory of the Creator, but also our welfare, as we shall see from the fruitful services of the guardian angels in our behalf.

II. MOTIVES OF HONORING OUR GUARDIAN ANGELS.

Why should we honor our guardian angels? Though they deserve our honor and esteem on account of their own intrinsic perfection, and on account of the high position they occupy in God's creation and in the order of grace and glory, yet the motives which appeal most forcibly to us are the *services* which they render us. In what do those services consist?

1. According to the design of Almighty God our guardian angels are to *aid us in the attainment of our last end*. This may be inferred from the words of the Apostle already cited: "Are they not all ministering spirits, sent to minister to them who shall receive the inheritance of salvation?" (Heb. i. 14.) By these words it is plainly signified that God has appointed His angels for the service of man, to aid him in the attainment of his eternal salvation. But if this is true of the angels in general, it is most especially true of our guardian angels, who have received a special charge from Almighty God in our regard.

2. Our guardian angels, *in particular*, render us the following services—

a. They *pray* for us. "When thou didst pray with tears and didst bury the dead," said the angel to Tobias the elder, "I offered thy prayer to the Lord" (Tob. xii. 12). And St. John assures us in his Revelations (Apoc. v. 8) that our prayers are presented to God by the hands of the angels, not, of course, because our prayers without the ministry of the angels would be unknown to God, but in order that, being united with the prayers of the angels, they may be a more pleasing offering to the Divine Majesty. Therefore it is that the priest in the divine sacrifice prays as follows: "We humbly beseech Thee, Almighty God, bid this offering be carried by the hands of Thy holy angel to Thy high altar, in the sight of Thy divine majesty." The first function of the holy angels in our behalf is, therefore, to unite their prayers with ours and to present them before the throne of the Most High.

b. They *exhort* us to do good. Was it not an angel that admonished Cornelius, the centurion, to send for the apostle St. Peter to instruct him in the truths of faith, and direct him on the way of salvation? (Acts x. 3, sqq.) Was it not an angel that, after miraculously delivering the apostles from prison, exhorted them fearlessly to continue their apostolic labors? " An angel of the Lord, by night opening the doors of the prison, and leading them out, said: Go, and standing speak in the temple to the people all the words of this life" (Acts v. 19, 20). But it is only in exceptional cases that the angels appear in visible form and speak with audible voice, as they did to the apostles and to Cornelius, the centurion; their ordinary way of admonishing us is by holy inspirations, whereby they enlighten our understanding and move our will, to think and to do what is good.

c. They *protect* us in body and soul. That they guard us against the dangers of the *body* is certain from the testimony of the Psalmist, who, full of joy and confidence, exclaims: " There shall no evil come to thee; nor shall the scourge come near thy dwelling. For He hath given His angels charge over thee, to keep thee in all thy ways. In their hands they shall bear thee up, lest thou dash thy foot against a stone" (Ps. xc. 10–12). Whether we wake or sleep, and wherever we are, the protecting angel of God is always by our side. Do we not find this truth confirmed by many facts in Scripture? You all remember how an angel rescued Lot and his family from the destruction of Sodom; and how the archangel Raphael accompanied the younger Tobias on his journey, protected him against all dangers, and brought him back in safety to his aged parents.

If the holy angels are so much concerned for the

safety and welfare of the body, how much greater must be their care for our immortal *souls!* One of their chief duties is to protect us from the assaults of the evil spirits, who, as St. Augustine teaches, are subjected to their power. And if they do not effectually frustrate all the malicious efforts of the evil one, it is because in this they follow the instructions of the Almighty, who for wise reasons makes the victory, as a rule, depend upon our co-operation. Hence you see, beloved brethren, that the ministry of the guardian angels in our behalf not only promotes the glory of God, but is, at the same time, most advantageous for our bodily and spiritual well-being, and a most effectual aid towards the attainment of our eternal salvation. Such being the case, we owe them a special tribute of honor. What, then, are—

III. OUR DUTIES TOWARDS OUR GUARDIAN ANGELS?

1. The first duty we owe to our guardian angels is that of *reverence* for their sacred presence. For they are princes of the heavenly court, familiar friends of God, before whose awful throne they stand, and whom they contemplate face to face. If, according to the words of Our Saviour, reverence is due to a child because of the angel who stands by his side, how much more should we revere the holy angels themselves, who, though invisible, always accompany us! This awe and reverence for our guardian angels we can show best by carefully avoiding everything that could grieve or offend them—every wilful offence against God, and particularly every sin against the angelic virtue of purity. For, if the sight of sins of the flesh produces a loathing even in sinful man, what a horror and abomination must they not awaken in God's holy angels! "Dare not," says St. Bernard, "to do in the

presence of your guardian angel what you would be ashamed to do before men." But, alas! how often are deeds done before the eyes of the guardian angels of which the most shameless would blush even before the eyes of the most wicked men! Oh, remember, my dear friend, that, while you gratify your passions even in the most secret place, where the eye of man cannot reach you, your guardian angel is near, and is witness of your unhallowed deed! Let us, then, beloved brethren, often call to mind the presence of our guardian angel, and we cannot but be filled with awe and reverence towards him, and be restrained from grieving him by deliberate sins.

2. The second duty we owe to our guardian angels is that of *gratitude* for their loving services. Our sentiments towards them should be such as were those of Tobias. "Father," said the holy youth, "what wages shall we give him [the angel who had been his guide]? Or what can be worthy of his benefits? He conducted me and brought me safe again; ... he delivered me from being devoured by the fish; thee also he hath made to see the light of heaven; and we are filled with all good things through him. What can we give him sufficient for these things?" (Tob. xii. 2-3.) Similar should be our gratitude towards our guardian angels. For, how numerous and how great benefits have they not bestowed upon us! Since the moment you first saw the light your guardian angel has stood by your side, protecting, admonishing, exhorting you. He has borne your prayers to heaven, supported them with his own intercession before the throne of God, and joyfully returned laden with heavenly blessings for you. Great was the friendship which Jonathan cherished for David; yet our guardian angel is a better friend of ours. For, while Jonathan, notwithstanding

his great love for David, was unable to ward off all dangers from his friend, our guardian angel can, if we ourselves only wish, frustrate all attacks and snares of our enemies. Beloved brethren, must we not acknowledge that we have been thus far very remiss in the discharge of this duty of gratitude to our good guardian angel? Have not days and even weeks passed without our thinking of this great love of our holy angel, much less thanking him for his kind services? Should we not be ashamed of our ingratitude? Let us, then, now at least ask pardon of our holy angel, and make the resolve in future not to let a day pass without thanking him for his benefits.

3. We should, moreover, *invoke* the aid of our guardian angels. Though our guardian angels have been sent by God for our service, though they joyfully undertake and discharge their duty, and are always willing and eager to assist us, yet they wish to be invoked by us. In this they imitate the example of God Himself. For, although God desires nothing more eagerly than to dispense His graces and favors to us, still He wishes, as a rule, that we should ask for them ourselves. Do not neglect, then, beloved brethren, frequently and confidently to invoke your guardian angels in your spiritual wants, especially in dangers and temptation.

4. Lastly, we owe our guardian angels the duty of *obedience*. It is the will of God that we follow their inspirations. The Lord once spoke to the Israelites in the desert: "Behold I will send My angel, who shall go before thee, and keep thee in thy journey, and bring thee into the place that I have prepared. Take notice of him, and hear his voice, and do not think him one to be contemned" (Exod. xxiii. 20, 21). These words apply also to us, beloved brethren. Are we not

in a similar condition? Are we not also wandering in the desert of this world, in search of the land that God has prepared for us? And is our guardian angel not charged by God to conduct us to that promised land? Is it not the will of God, then, that we take notice of him, and hear his voice? God wishes, therefore, that we listen to and obey the inspirations of our guardian angel. But, in order to notice him, and to hear his voice, we must cultivate an inward life of recollection. For thus only can we hear the whisperings of our good angel in our hearts, and give ear to his admonitions.

Such are the duties we owe to our guardian angels: a holy awe and reverence for their invisible presence; an inward and an active gratitude for their loving services; a strong confidence in their protection; a willing obedience to their inspirations. Now, allow me to make one more remark, before I close. It is a sad fact, beloved brethren, that there are many apparently good Christians who, wholly or in great part, neglect all these duties to their guardian angels. Whence comes this? There are, doubtless, many reasons; but the chief one, it seems to me, is the *neglect of parents*. If the parents seldom, or never, direct the attention of their children to their guardian angel; if they neglect to speak to their children, while they are still small, about their guardian angel, and to admonish them daily to honor him, and to pray to him, the devotion to the guardian angel will not take root in their young hearts; and, when they have grown up amid the tumult of the world, they will hardly ever think of honoring him; nay, they will hardly ever think that they have an angel by their side. Therefore, my dear Christian parents, beware of neglecting a duty of such importance to your children, a duty the neglect of which would deprive your children of so many blessings. Neglect not from this day forward, night and morning, to invoke the guardian angel with your children. The holy angels will amply reward you; they will be your and your children's faithful companions through life, and at the end of your pilgrimage they will lead you into the promised land of everlasting joy. Amen.

Feast of All Saints.

THE REWARD OF SANCTITY.

"Be glad and rejoice, because your reward is very great in heaven."—Matt. v. 12.

THE chief object of the Church in celebrating this festival in honor of all the saints is to direct our attention to the reward which God has promised to, and actually bestows upon His faithful servants; and thus to incite us to follow in their footsteps, that we may gain the same exceeding great reward. For the same reward is held out to all of us, if we only imitate the example of the saints. In accordance with the intention of the Church, I shall endeavor to show you the greatness and excellence of the *reward of sanctity*, while I contrast it with the reward which the world gives to its followers. While the recompense of the world is uncertain, the reward of sanctity is absolutely certain; while the recompense of the world is insignificant and unsatisfactory, the reward of sanctity is great and all-sufficient; while the recompense of the world is fleeting and perishable, the reward of sanctity is permanent and everlasting. The reward of the saints has, therefore, three great advantages over the petty remunerations of this world: (1) absolute *certainty*, (2) surpassing *greatness*, and (3) *duration* without end.

I. CERTAINTY.

The first quality of the reward of the saints, that is, of the true followers of Christ, is its infallible certainty. This attribute, beloved brethren, is one of surpassing excellence. For there is nothing that so sustains and consoles one in toils and hardships as the prospect of certain remuneration, as there is nothing, on the other hand, that is more likely to discourage one than the probability of the fruitlessness of one's labors, the uncertainty of remuneration. When I speak of reward, I mean a recompense which is strictly merited, and to which the claimer has a strict right. Now, the servant of the world, as well as the faithful follower of Christ, has a right to his due recompense. But, while the reward which Christ holds out to His followers is infallibly certain, that which the world promises is most doubtful. It is an acknowledged fact that many services rendered in the cause of the world remain unrequited; but no merits obtained in the cause of Christ go without their due reward. There are chiefly three classes of merits which remain unrewarded by the world.

1. In the first place, there are numberless services rendered in the cause of the world which *are never acknowledged*. Are not many services, rendered to the world, utterly overlooked? How many are there the remembrance of which is effaced by time? How many glide into everlasting forgetfulness? How many are misrepresented by hatred and envy? But the case is different with those merits which are obtained in the cause of Christ. None remains unknown; all are recorded in the all-comprehending mind of God. He is omniscient; nothing can escape His notice. He knows each and every one, even of our least and most hidden merits—those merits which the world ignores and despises; those merits which, perhaps, we ourselves have never noticed, or have long since forgotten. He looks into the heart, and acknowledges and rewards not only our good deeds, but also our good will and our desire to please Him, according to the words of

the Psalmist: "The Lord hath heard the desire of the poor; Thy ear hath heard the preparation of their heart" (Ps. Heb. ix. 17). He acknowledges and rewards the least actions done in His service; not even a cup of water given in His name (Matt. x. 42), not even the widow's mite (Mark xii. 43), goes unrewarded. And, since God is not only all-knowing but also all-just, His rewards are strictly proportioned to our merits, while the rewards given by men are often in no proportion to the services rendered. Moreover, while men are often forgetful of past services, the memory of Almighty God is infallible, so that even our most insignificant meritorious actions are always before Him, as He assures us in the words of the Psalmist: "I will not reprove thee, for thy sacrifices; and thy burnt-offerings are always in My sight" (Ps. xlix. 8).

2. A second class of merits which are not rewarded by the world are those that are, indeed, known and acknowledged, but *unfavorably received*. And to this class, as experience shows, belong many of the services rendered in the cause of this world. How could it be otherwise, since among the followers of the world there are so many proud, selfish, and envious men, who look with jealousy on the merits of others? But with God the case is different. There is no merit which is displeasing to Him. For, as God of necessity hates evil, so of necessity He loves what is good. Among the numberless merits of the saints there is none but is pleasing to God; because merit itself is a gift of God, who gives us both to will and to perform what is good.

3. A third class of merits which go unrewarded are those which, although acknowledged and appreciated, *cannot be sufficiently rewarded*. Such merits are of no rare occurrence in the service of the world—merits

which, on account of their greatness or their character, exceed all remuneration that man can bestow in this world. Can any earthly reward sufficiently compensate the man who for the benefit of his fellow-men sacrifices his health or even his life? And yet how often does it not happen that health and life are sacrificed in the cause of the world? What earthly treasure can repair such a loss? How, then, can the world reward such services? But God, whose power and liberality are infinite, can reward all merits obtained in His service, however numerous and great they may be; He can reward them not only adequately, but also superabundantly.

While, therefore, the rewards of the world are uncertain, the reward of God is infallibly certain. How great, then, is the folly of those who are so engrossed in the service of this world—in the pursuit of riches, honors, and pleasures—that they neglect the service of God, and seek the uncertain recompense that the world gives, instead of the certain reward which God holds out to His servants! But what makes their folly still greater is the fact that, while the recompense which the world promises is paltry and insufficient, the reward which God gives is exceeding great.

II. GREATNESS.

A reward is justly called great, says St. Jerome, when it exceeds, or at least equals, the merits for which it has been obtained, and St. Augustine calls that reward great which makes the receiver perfectly happy. A reward that is truly great must, therefore, possess these two qualities. But the reward which God gives to His saints possesses these two attributes in the highest degree, while the reward promised by the world is neither equal to the merit for which it is offered, nor capable of rendering its recipient truly happy.

1. The reward of the saints *exceeds their merits*, while that of the servants of the world is inferior to their merits. To the recompense of the followers of this world may be applied the words of the Prophet: "You have sowed much and brought in little, you have drunk, but have not been filled with drink; you have clothed yourselves, but have not been warmed, and he that hath earned wages put them into a bag with holes" (Agg. i. 6). You have sown much: Oh, what have you not done in the service of the world to obtain temporal happiness or success! What sacrifices have you not made—sacrifices of your rest and comfort, sacrifices of your freedom and independence, sacrifices of your peace and domestic happiness! What toils and hardships have you not undergone! To what trials and dangers have you not exposed yourselves! What patience and endurance have you not practised! You have sown much. But what have you reaped? Where is your reward? All you can show is disappointment and discontent. Or, let us suppose you have gained your object—that you have attained to wealth, honor, and worldly enjoyments—did you then feel that you were fully compensated? Or must you not, on the contrary, confess that "you have brought in little"? With wealth you reaped only greater cares and anxieties; with worldly honors only greater responsibilities, and perhaps criticism, envy, hatred, and ridicule; with sensual enjoyments only loathing, weariness, and remorse. The result was disappointment and dissatisfaction. You have sown much and reaped little; you put your wages in a bag with holes.

How different is *the case of the followers of Christ!* They too have sown much. They have labored and suffered much in the cause of Christ. Their lives were austere. They crucified their flesh, mortified their bodies, denied themselves. But they consoled and strengthened themselves with the prospect of the reward that awaited them, and said to themselves, with the Apostle: "I reckon that the sufferings of this time are not worthy to be compared with the glory to come, that shall be revealed in us" (Rom. viii. 18). Oh, how great is that reward compared with the little they have done and suffered in this life! Hear the assuring words of our blessed Lord Himself: "Well done, good and faithful servant; because thou hast been faithful over a few things, I will place thee over many things; enter thou into the joy of thy Lord" (Matt. xxv. 21). Little it is, therefore, that they have done and suffered compared with the greatness of the reward which is in store for them. Their reward is, consequently, incomparably greater than their merits. As, therefore, the rewards offered by the world are inferior to the merits of its followers, so the reward of the servants of Christ is infinitely superior to their merits.

2. But, however great the rewards of the world may be, they cannot make their recipients *completely happy*—a condition which, I said, was essential to a truly great reward. That this necessary attribute is lacking in the reward which the world bestows is evident from the fact that we find not a single one among the followers of the world who can say that he is perfectly happy. Or have you ever met a votary of the world who was truly happy? True, we sometimes meet such as enjoy the fulness of riches, honors, and enjoyments, who lack nothing that this world can supply. But is there one amongst them who is perfectly happy; who has no afflictions, no cares, no

longings—in short, who has everything his heart desires? No; not even one. And the reason is, as St. Chrysostom tells us, that it is an unchangeable and eternal truth that all the treasures of this life, even taken together, are not able to satisfy the longings of the human heart.

The *reward of the saints*, on the other hand, has this property of conferring on the possessor the fulness of happiness, and is, therefore, a truly great reward. For it is the teaching of faith that it satisfies every longing of the human heart, and produces perfect happiness. "I shall be satisfied when Thy glory shall appear," says the Psalmist (Ps. xvi. 15); viz., till then, whatever the world may afford me, I shall be hungry and thirsty; my yearning shall not be appeased; but as soon as I shall become partaker of Thy glory, all my longings shall be satisfied, and my soul shall find rest. Thy glory shall at once deliver me from all evil, and put me in the full possession of all good. Thus thought King David, the man according to the heart of God. And how could it be otherwise, since the reward of the elect, this glory of which the Psalmist speaks, is the full and undivided possession of God, according to the words of the Lord Himself: "I am thy reward exceeding great" (Gen. xv. 1). And does not the Psalmist, in another place, say: "They shall be inebriated with the plenty of Thy house; and Thou shalt make them drink of the torrent of Thy pleasure"? (Ps. xxxv. 9.)

Judge, then, beloved brethren, whether the reward which God gives to His servants is not exceeding great, compared with the wages which this world offers to its followers, and whether it is not the greatest imaginable folly to prefer the service of this world to the service of God. But this folly must appear utter madness if we, furthermore, consider that the recompense of the world is of short duration, while the reward of God is eternal.

III. DURATION.

1. *The rewards which the world offers* us are fleeting and perishable, because they either sooner or later escape our grasp, or we, at least, are some time or other called upon to abandon them for good. There is nothing easier than to lose those worldly goods of which we have with great efforts possessed ourselves. How often does this not actually happen? Or is it a thing of so rare occurrence that a man all at once loses all he possessed? How often do we meet such as once lived in affluence again struggling to earn their bread in the sweat of their brow even at the most humble occupation! Or is it a thing unheard of that men who had been raised to high positions, and were once renowned, have fallen into oblivion, or even into contempt? The reward of the world, therefore, however secure it may seem, may easily escape our grasp. But though we should manage to keep our hold of it during the short span of this life, yet implacable death will one day wrest it from our hands. When death once knocks at our door, we must obey his summons; we must go, leaving all behind. The world claims again as its own whatever it has given us. So shortlived, so fleeting, is the world's reward!

2. *The reward of the saints* is, on the other hand, an imperishable, eternal one. It will never be taken from them, nor will they be called upon to relinquish it. It will not be taken from them, because it consists in the possession of God, which can be lost only by sin; and the saints, when once admitted into glory, can sin no more. They will not be called upon to relinquish their reward;

for "death shall be no more; nor mourning, nor crying, nor sorrow shall be any more; for the former things are passed away" (Apoc. xxi. 4); and "the just shall live for evermore" (Wis. v. 16), says the Holy Ghost. Nothing can, therefore, separate them from their exceeding great reward, from the inexhaustible source of never-ending joy.

The reward of the saints is, therefore, absolutely certain and exceeding great; it is imperishable; it cannot be lost or wrested from them; it will last forever. As long as God is God, those who have served Him faithfully to the end will be surrounded by a sea of unspeakable bliss and delight. It was this prospect of the eternal reward that, next to their pure love of God, stimulated the saints to give themselves up wholly to God's service; that sustained them in all their toils and sufferings and struggles; that filled their hearts to overflowing with the sweetest consolations in the midst of their afflictions. Beloved brethren, the same reward is in store for each one of us. Should the prospect of this reward not have the same effects upon us? Were the saints not men and women like ourselves? Had they not the same human nature, with all its evil inclinations, the same difficulties to overcome, the same obstacles to surmount? Let us, then, to-day, in view of this infinitely great and eternal reward, make the firm resolution henceforth, according to the example of the saints, to devote ourselves wholly to the service of God, carefully to avoid sin, and faithfully to fulfil our Christian duties. And this generous purpose, aided by the grace of God, will secure for us the final victory over all the enemies of our salvation, will lead us to the never-ending bliss, which is the infallible, unfathomable, and eternal reward of God's saints. Amen.

All Souls' Day.

DEVOTION TO THE SUFFERING SOULS.

"It is therefore a holy and wholesome thought to pray for the dead, that they may be loosed from sins."—II. Mach. xii. 46.

THE commemoration of all the departed, which we celebrate to-day, has been ordained by the Church to foster in our hearts a devotion to the holy souls. All the ceremonies of the day are directed to this end. The decoration of the altars, the sacerdotal vestments, are suggestive of mourning, and invite us to compassion for the suffering souls. The Church's hymns and chants remind us of the just judgment in which we all have to give a strict account of our actions, while the catafalque represents to us the graves of the dead. The lights which burn around the tomb symbolize the faith of the departed, and the hope with which the prayers of the living ascend to the throne of God in their behalf; and the holy water and incense are expressive of the ardent desire of the faithful that their prayers and offerings for the dead may be acceptable to the Divine Majesty. I can, therefore, do nothing more in keeping with the spirit and the wishes of Holy Church to-day than endeavor to strengthen you in your devotion to the suffering souls in purgatory. This devotion, however, does not consist merely in remembering the dead, and, perhaps, shedding a few fruitless tears over their graves; it consists chiefly in the endeavor to assist them and relieve their suffering by our prayers and other good works. "It is a holy and wholesome thought to pray for the dead." Now, what are the

chief motives that should urge us to come to the aid of the suffering souls?
1. *The love we owe to them;*
2. *Our own interest.*

I. THE LOVE WE OWE TO THE SUFFERING SOULS.

The first motive which should stimulate us to come to the aid of the holy souls in purgatory is the love we owe them. The duty of charity does not, it is true, under all circumstances oblige us to relieve the sufferings of our neighbor. If, for instance, his suffering is uncertain or insignificant, or if it is of such a kind that it still leaves him the possibility of helping himself, in that case charity does not oblige us to go to any considerable inconvenience to tender him our assistance. But if, on the other hand, his sufferings are certain; if they are great; if they are of such a character that he cannot help himself, while we can easily render him effectual assistance; and if he, moreover, stands in the closest relation to us, we are certainly bound in charity to tender him our active assistance. In such a case it is uncharitable and inhuman to withhold our aid from him. In the case of the suffering souls we find all these circumstances combined.

1. Their sufferings are *certain*. For, that there is a purgatory, or place of atonement and purgation, in which the departed souls undergo the temporal punishment still due to their sins, is an article of faith not only defined by the Church, but also clearly contained in the sources of Revelation.

a. In Holy Scripture. In the Old Testament this truth is clearly set forth in the words of My text, "It is a holy and wholesome thought to pray for the dead;" this is the teaching of the Holy Ghost Himself. But, if there were no purgatory, no possibility of making satisfaction for the punishment due to sin in the next life, how, then, could it be a holy and wholesome thought to pray for the dead? Would it not rather be a useless and superfluous work? But this same doctrine is likewise contained in the New Testament. Christ Our Lord clearly supposes this truth, when He says (Matt. xii. 32.) that there are certain sins so grievous that they shall not be forgiven either in this world or in the world to come. Whence it manifestly follows that there are certain light sins that can be remitted in the next life as well as in this; else the words of Our Saviour would be without sense, or misleading. There is, therefore, actually a remission of sins, and, therefore, an atonement for the punishment due to them in the next world as well as in the present life. The place, or condition, in which this atonement is made, is called purgatory.

b. The teaching of the Church, and our faith in the existence of purgatory, rests, moreover, on the clear evidence of *Tradition.* It were an easy matter to cite the testimonies of the Fathers and ecclesiastical writers of all ages to prove the constant and unanimous tradition on this point. But, for the sake of brevity, I shall only refer to St. Cyprian and Tertullian, who in the first ages of the Church earnestly exhort the faithful to pray for the dead. Tertullian, moreover, bears testimony that the pious custom of praying for the dead dates back to the time of the apostles.

c. This consoling article of our faith is also the teaching of *reason.* For, since it is, on the one hand, most certain that nothing unclean can enter the kingdom of heaven; and, on the other hand, very few even of the holiest Christians die altogether free from venial sins, it would follow that, if there were no future atonement, all men, with very few exceptions, would be forever excluded from heaven. For without satisfaction God, who is infinitely just as well as merciful, will not remit the temporal punishment. After death God deals with His creatures according to the rigor of His justice, and gives to each according to his works (Matt. xvi. 27). To deny the existence of purgatory, therefore, would be to exclude from eternal salvation almost the whole human race, which is contrary to reason as well as faith. Hence the sufferings of the departed souls are an indisputable, an absolutely certain fact.

2. But their sufferings are, furthermore, *great* beyond measure. For what is purgatory?

a. Purgatory is a place where no longer mercy, but only stern *justice* reigns. The sufferings of the souls in purgatory must, therefore, be such as completely to satisfy the infinite justice of God. Hence they must be strictly proportioned to the offences committed against God. But who can measure the greatness of even the smallest offence of a miserable creature, such as man is, against the infinite holiness and awful majesty of God? Does not the malice of even the slightest sin surpass our understanding? Must not, therefore, the punishment due to the slightest venial sin go beyond our comprehension? Oh, how true, then, are the words of the Apostle, " It is a dreadful thing to fall into the hands of the living God!" (Heb. x. 31.)

b. Purgatory is a place of *penance.* And of what manner of penance? A penance with which no earthly penance, no rigor or austerity practised by the saints, can be compared. The reason is evident; for every penance practised in this life, however severe it may be, is undergone to escape the dreadful punishments of purgatory. Whence we must conclude that the sufferings of purgatory are much greater than any voluntary or divinely-sent punishments to be met with in this life. If, then, the saints exercised such austerities; if penitent Christians in by-gone ages submitted to long and severe ecclesiastical penances; if the faithful servants of God have borne without a murmur the heaviest crosses sent them by God Himself; they did so in order to avoid the severer penance of the life to come. How dreadful, therefore, must be the sufferings of purgatory, which in their severity so far exceed all the penances, austerities, and chastisements of this life! How dreadful it is to fall into the hands of the living God!

c. Purgatory is a place of *atonement*—of atonement from which the most fervent penitents and greatest lovers of the cross would shrink with terror. And why is this process of purgation so terrible? It is because the satisfaction rendered in purgatory is quite different from the atonement made in this life. The atonement made in this life consists of penitential works which are eminently meritorious and satisfactory through the merits and satisfactions of Jesus Christ, and at the same time most consoling in view of the sufferings of our crucified Lord and Saviour. But the atonement in purgatory is without merit and without consolation—a just and condign punishment which man has merited by his sins, his lukewarmness and negligence in the service of God; a debt which must be paid to the last farthing. Hence the royal prophet David prayed: "O Lord, rebuke me not in Thy indignation, nor chastise me in Thy wrath " (Ps. vi. 2.), that is, according to the interpretation of St. Augustine, grant me the grace not to merit Thy wrath in purgatory, where sins must be atoned for according to the rigor of Thy justice. The sufferings of the holy souls in purgatory are, therefore, not only certain, but also great beyond measure and beyond conception.

3. And *who* are those holy souls who thus suffer such dreadful torments? True, most of them are unknown to us; but still they all stand in the closest relation to us. For they are all without exception closely united with us by the bond of sanctifying grace, and are, consequently, *our brothers and sisters in Christ*. As we would gladly succor our own brother or sister in distress, though we had never seen their faces, so we should be always ready and willing to aid those poor souls in their sufferings, particularly since they are unable to help themselves, and we have ample means at our disposal to succor them.

Are there not among those suffering souls many who are *closely related to us?* Are there not amongst them, perhaps, your parents, who have been once so dear to you; brothers and sisters; near relatives; friends and benefactors? Does not the love you owe them imperatively demand of you to come to their assistance? Does not the close relation in which they stand to you give them a special right to your aid? And is this duty not all the stricter on your part, since it may easily happen that you yourselves have been, to a great extent, accessory to the sins for which they have now to atone—by provoking them to anger, impatience, or other faults? Do you, then, not hear their voice crying to you from the depth of their sufferings, in the words of the afflicted Job: " Have pity on me, have pity on me, at least you, my friends : because the hand of the Lord hath touched me "? (Job xix. 21.) Have you, then, really these sentiments of compassion for your departed friends? Is it their distress and misery that make you grieve for them? Or is it your own interest —the loss of their society, their support, the services they rendered you?

You weep at the remembrance of your departed

friends and relatives, and justly so; but, my dear friends, your tears are of little avail to them if you do no more. Our sympathy for the suffering souls must be an *active sympathy*. Our tears must be accompanied with the sacrifice of our prayers and good works for their relief. Thus Jesus wept for Lazarus; but His tears were followed by good works. For, as St. Jerome says, grieved as He was, He immediately inquired for him whom He loved. "Where have you laid him?" (John xi. 34) asked our blessed Lord. He causes the barriers to be removed that stand in the way of His friend's welfare. "Take away the stone," He says. He commands the by-standers to remove the winding-sheets that bound him: "Loose him and let him go." And He cried out with a loud voice: "Lazarus, come forth." In other words, Jesus wept not useless, but effectual tears. For in the midst of His tears and His grief He forgot not what was necessary to raise Lazarus to life, and restore him to his friends. Such, beloved brethren, must be your tears for the dead; such your mourning; they must be fruitful tears and mourning. It is not enough to weep bitter tears for your deceased friends, to provide for them a gorgeous funeral, to erect a splendid monument to their memory. All the solemnity of your mourning, and the grandeur of your funeral display, and the costliness of your monuments will neither preserve their bodies from decay nor relieve their souls from the pains of purgatory.

If, then, beloved brethren, you would escape the just reproach of harshness and injustice towards your deceased friends, *employ those means which the Church offers you* for the relief of their souls: pray incessantly for the repose of their souls, approach the holy sacraments worthily, and offer the holy Communion for them; have Masses offered for them according to your means—

in the holy sacrifice of the Mass Jesus Christ Himself is offered as a sacrifice of atonement for the dead as well as for the living—endeavor to gain for them the indulgences which the Church so liberally bestows in their behalf; and offer up as many good works as you can for their repose, for all our good works can be of advantage to them. If we thus fulfil our duty towards the faithful departed, we will not only relieve them from their sufferings, but at the same time most effectually promote—

II. OUR OWN SPIRITUAL INTEREST.

What we do for the suffering souls in purgatory, beloved brethren, will all turn to our own spiritual advantage. It will be more than amply repaid. Those holy souls, as you know, are the friends of God, the elect of God, whose eternal crowns are secured, and who shall be admitted into the glory of the heavenly court. As soon as they are delivered from their sufferings they will reign with power and authority in the kingdom of God. But even now in their sufferings they already reign in the affection of God on account of their merits and their love. Therefore we have every reason to hope that the services rendered to them will be generously requited both by their gratitude and by the bounty of God, which will not be surpassed by our liberality.

1. The poor suffering souls will once *reign in heaven*. If we now by our prayers and good works hasten their deliverance and entrance into glory, shall we not thereby make to ourselves powerful friends and intercessors, both for this life and the life to come? For it is evident that they will have the power to help us from the very fact of their being saints of God and members of His glorious household; and it is no less certain that

they will be willing to help us, since the gratitude of the saints is as certain as their holiness. It is, therefore, most certain that the sacrifices which we make for the suffering souls will secure for us prompt and powerful advocates with God. Is this not consoling as well as advantageous for us?

2. The holy souls in purgatory already *reign in the affection of God*, who loves them with the most tender love. It is, therefore, the ardent desire of God that we appease His justice by our prayers and good works, and thus shorten the sufferings of those souls that are so dear to Him. They are His children, and He is their most loving Father. If a cup of water given in the name of Our Lord shall not be left unrewarded, how amply will Almighty God reward those who by their prayers and satisfactions relieve those suffering souls He loves so tenderly, and bring them to His loving embrace!

Let us, then, beloved brethren, have pity on the poor suffering souls. The love we owe them and our highest interest demand it. Oh, if we could only behold them to-day, in the midst of their torments, suppliantly stretching forth their hands to us, and invoking our aid! O children, behold your father, whose too great anxiety for your welfare has, perhaps, brought him to an untimely grave; behold your mother, who loved you so tenderly and watched over you with such care, whose death you mourned with so many tears! They now invoke your aid. Or is it a brother or a sister who was so kind to you, and whose death you so keenly felt? Or is it your departed wife, who was the comfort and happiness of your life; or a loving husband, who was your support and the stay of your dear little ones? Or is it your friends, relatives, benefactors, from whom you experienced so much kindness in life?

Behold them in their dreadful sufferings, unable to help themselves, and crying for your assistance! Turn not a deaf ear to them while they cry with plaintive voice: " Have pity on me, have pity on me, at least you, my friends!" Amen.

Feast of the Dedication of a Church.

A DAY OF JOY AND GRATITUDE.

"This day is salvation come to this house."—Luke xix. 9.

IF at any time, surely to-day, beloved brethren, we have reason to rejoice and give thanks to Almighty God from our hearts. Yes, joy and gratitude should be the distinguishing features of this festival. For to-day we commemorate an event which has rendered our church particularly dear to us; which has made it an object of our veneration and a source of unspeakable blessings to us. We commemorate the dedication (consecration) of our church, a sacred ceremony which bestowed on it an inestimable value, that converted it into our most precious treasure on earth. Therefore we may in truth apply the words of Our Saviour to our church: "This day is salvation come to this house." Let us, then, in order to arouse in our hearts this joy and gratitude, consider what a great treasure we possess in our church; or, in other words, with what character it was invested by its dedication to divine service. The effects of its dedication on this material structure may be summed up in the two following sentences. By this sacred ceremony it became—

1. *The house of God;*
2. *Our own house.*

I. THE HOUSE OF GOD.

1. Our church, beloved brethren, has by its dedication become, in a true sense, the house of God. For

from that moment it has been exclusively *set apart for divine worship*, so that it may not be used for any other purpose. This is manifest from the ceremonies employed in the consecration of a church. The various prayers, the exorcisms, the sprinkling and washing with holy water, the numerous applications of the holy cross, the incensing and other ceremonies—all point to the withdrawal of the sacred edifice from profane purposes, and its appropriation to sacred uses, to the removal of the influence of the evil spirits—in short, to the sanctification of the house of God. The church which has once been dedicated to divine worship is, consequently, in the truest sense, the house of God.

2. But it is, furthermore, the house of God, because on its dedication Almighty God chose it in a special manner as *His dwelling-place*. At that moment it became the abode of the Most High, even though for some reason the Most Holy Sacrament may not have been preserved in it. God, it is true, is everywhere present, according to the words of Wisdom, " The Spirit of the Lord hath filled the whole world " (Wis. i. 7); but places exclusively consecrated to His service are sanctified in a special manner by His awful presence. This truth is confirmed by the belief of all ages and of all nations. Hence it is that, even in the remotest times, sacrifices were offered to God in places especially set apart for this purpose. Thus Abel, Abraham, and Noe sacrificed on altars erected for this end. For the same purpose Moses constructed the holy tabernacle, according to the design that God had shown him on Mount Sinai (Exod. xxv. 40).

For this end Solomon built that magnificent *temple* which was the pride and glory of God's people, and dedicated it to the Most High with pomp and splendor never before witnessed. The celebration, which lasted for a whole week, was well suited to convince the people of the presence of the Almighty. The thousands of victims offered, the clouds of incense that ascended to heaven, the multitudes prostrate in adoration before the Most High, the miraculous fire that descended from heaven and consumed the offerings, the glory and majesty of God enshrouded in the cloud which surrounded the Holy of Holies—all this combined to impress upon the people the fact that the Lord had chosen this place for His abode; that there His name should be sanctified; that from thence He would pour forth His blessings upon all those who worshipped Him in that holy place. And, in fact, the Lord appeared to Solomon, and said to him: "I have heard thy prayer, and I have chosen this place to Myself for a house of sacrifice. I have chosen and have sanctified this place, that My name may be there forever, and My eyes and My heart may remain there perpetually" (II. Paral. vii. 12, 16).

If the presence of God was so conspicuous in the temple of Solomon, which was only the figure of the temples of the New Law, what shall we say of His presence in *our churches*, which are not only consecrated to the service of God, but in which the Incarnate Son of God, the Second Person of the Most Holy Trinity, is really, truly, and substantially present under the appearance of bread? May we not, then, point to our altars and say in all truth: "Behold the tabernacle of God with men, and He will dwell with them"? (Apoc. xxi. 3.)

3. This being the case, what should be *our behavior* in the house of God? Should it not be in keeping with our belief, and with the sanctity of the place? Should we not behave with the greatest respect in the divine presence, express our inward reverence towards the

Divine Majesty in our outward deportment? But where is our reverence for the Divine Majesty, if we utterly forget that we are in the awful presence of God, if our minds and hearts are taken up with worldly, or even sinful, thoughts and desires? Where is our reverence for the divine presence, if in His house we take a posture which we would be ashamed of in the society of respectable men? Where is our inward and outward reverence for the divine presence, if we allow our eyes freely to gaze at every distracting object within our view? Where is the reverence due to the house of God, if there we so far forget ourselves as to laugh and talk, to the great disturbance of our neighbors? Where, finally, is our reverence for the awful presence of God, and the sanctity of His dwelling-place, if, to the great scandal of the whole congregation, we habitually come late for the services, or leave the church before divine service is ended? Let us to-day, beloved brethren, examine ourselves on these points; and, if we find that we have been guilty of any of these faults, let us resolve to avoid them for the future, to behave as is becoming the sacredness of the house of God and the awful presence of the Divine Majesty, and thus to repair the scandal we have given in the past, and to appease the wrath of God, which we have deserved by our sins. But I said, moreover, that the church once dedicated to divine service is in a special manner—

II. OUR OWN HOUSE.

Our church is our true home, the place where we should love to dwell. It is a place connected with numberless sweet and consoling memories, a place where we assemble around our common Father to receive His blessings and His graces. Our church should, therefore, be particularly dear to us; it should be the common centre of attraction for us, especially for two reasons: because it is to us the house of prayer, and because it is the store-house of God's graces.

1. *The house of prayer.* When I say that the church is the house of prayer I do not wish to be so understood as if I meant to imply that it is the only place where we should pray. For God is everywhere present, and can hear our prayers in any place whatsoever; and Christ, moreover, exhorts us always to pray, and, accordingly, to pray wherever we are. The church, however, is by way of excellence the house of prayer. Why?

a. According to the promises of God, there is no other place where we may so confidently *hope that our prayers will be heard*. "My eyes shall be open," says the Lord, "and My ears attentive to the prayer of him that shall pray in this place" (II. Paral. vii. 15). This promise, of course, refers in the first instance to the temple of Solomon, but it applies still more fully to our churches, since the temple was but the type or shadow of which our churches are the reality. Hence the eye and the ear of the Most High are still more intently bent towards the prayers which are offered Him in the temples of the New Law.

Besides, in the church everything tends to *awaken our devotion*, so that there we are more than anywhere else apt to pray with fruit. The altar, upon which day after day the Son of God descends and offers Himself as a living holocaust for us; the baptismal font, at which we have been freed from the slavery of Satan, made children of God and heirs of His heavenly kingdom; the Communion table, at which we all unite in brotherly love to partake of the same divine banquet; the confessional, that tribunal of penance, in which we so often sought and found the peace of our souls; the pulpit, the chair of truth, from which the teachings of our holy religion are announced to us, our Christian duties impressed upon us, and their faithful fulfilment urged upon us; the pictures and images of the saints, which continually remind us of their heroic virtues and unfading glory, and exhort us to imitate their example; finally, the impressive ceremonies of the Church, and the mutual edification of the faithful—do not all these circumstances combine to arouse our devotion, to dispose us to pray with fruit, and thus to gain for us the benevolence of God and secure us the graces we implore?

Add to this the special efficacy of *common prayer*, to which Our Lord Himself attributes such extraordinary power. "Where there are two or three gathered together in My name," He says, "there am I in the midst of them" (Matt. xviii. 20). Now, this efficacy is peculiar to the prayer that is offered in the church. Here it is not our own individual selves that pray, but the whole congregation gathered in the name of Jesus Christ; and Christ Himself, who is really present in the tabernacle, or sacrifices Himself upon the altar, prays with us. The prayer offered in the church, especially during divine service, is pre-eminently a common, a public prayer, offered not only in the name of the whole community, but in the name of the whole Catholic Church, and has, consequently, the greatest efficacy. The church is, therefore, pre-eminently our house of prayer.

b. What a *happiness* for us, beloved brethren, to possess such a sanctuary, such a home of sanctity, where we can with confidence gather around our loving Father and hopefully present all our petitions to Him! How easy is our access to the throne of mercy! How easy is it for us to visit our church, and there, where God's eye and ear and heart are inclined to hear our prayers, to find aid, and consolation, and strength in all our necessities, trials, and afflictions! But should we not be ever grateful to Almighty God for this blessing, of which so many are deprived? And is it not meet that we show our gratitude to God by deriving the greatest possible advantage from this signal favor? Would we not make ourselves guilty of the greatest ingratitude, if we neglected to do so? What, then, must we think of those who even on Sundays and festivals of obligation, I will not say neglect to hear Mass, but regularly absent themselves from the other services of the church? They are, to say the very least, ungrateful, ignoble, lukewarm, followers of Christ, unworthy to bear the name of Christians.

2. *The store-house of God's grace.* What unspeakable treasures are deposited in this holy place! What treasures can equal them in magnitude and worth! No prince, no king, no realm, no empire can boast of such a treasury as we possess within these sacred walls.

a. Earthly treasures, be they ever so great, are soon exhausted; but our treasury is *inexhaustible.* However largely, however frequently you may draw from it, it remains full as before; the store is not diminished. For it is the treasury of the infinite merits and satisfactions of Jesus Christ.

b. The several treasures of this store-house of grace are of *infinite value.* Every single one of them has been purchased at the infinite cost of the precious blood of Jesus Christ. The grace of Baptism, which of children of Satan makes us children of God, and brothers and joint-heirs of Jesus Christ; the grace of Confirmation, whereby the fulness of the Holy Ghost is imparted to us; the grace of the sacrament of penance, which reconciles the sinner with God, restores sanctifying grace to the soul, or augments it, if it still exists; the grace communicated by the worthy reception of the body and blood of Jesus Christ; the graces which Almighty God showers down upon those who devoutly assist at the holy sacrifice of the Mass, and the other services of the Church—every single one of them is purchased at the infinite price of the entire blood of Jesus Christ.

c. And this infinite treasure, beloved brethren, is *all our own*. It is ever open to us; we may appropriate to ourselves as much as we please. The supreme treasurer Jesus Christ invites us to come, and to draw largely. The more of these heavenly treasures we appropriate to ourselves, the better He is pleased with us.

d. And does He impose hard conditions upon us? No; *the conditions are easy* to be fulfilled. He only requires of us to frequent the church and pray devoutly; regularly to attend the devotions and services of the church, especially the holy sacrifice of the Mass; worthily and frequently to approach the holy sacraments of penance and the Eucharist.

Now, I ask you, beloved brethren, is there a treasury on earth to be compared to that which we possess in our church? And this infinite, inexhaustible treasury is all our own, ever open to us. Were it not the greatest folly on our part, then, if we failed to enrich ourselves with its heavenly treasures?

Let us rejoice and give thanks, therefore, beloved brethren, that God has thus deigned to set up His tabernacle, to erect His throne of mercy in our midst, where we can confidently approach Him, and enrich our souls with His heavenly treasures. But let us also show our gratitude practically by our fervor in frequenting the church and our reverential behavior in the house of God. Let us draw largely from this store-house of divine grace; and we shall experience the fact that on the day this church was dedicated salvation came to our house. Amen.

LENTEN SERMONS.

First Course.

On Prayer.

First Sermon.

NECESSITY OF PRAYER.

"Watch ye, and pray, that ye enter not into temptation."—Matt. xxvi. 41.

THE holy season of Lent, upon which we have just entered, is, according to the intention of the Church, not only a time of fasting, but also pre-eminently a time of prayer. Wishing, therefore, to comply with the intention of the Church, I have chosen *prayer* as the subject of these weekly Lenten sermons. And in order to give the subject as full a treatment as the time will permit, I shall explain to you in succession the *motives* which should urge us to pray, and the manner in which we should pray, or the *practice* of prayer. The first motive which suggests itself is the absolute *necessity* of prayer, which will be the subject of the present discourse.

Prayer, particularly prayer of petition, is necessary in two different respects: as (1) the fulfilment of an *indispensable duty*, and (2) as a *necessary means of salvation*.

I. AN INDISPENSABLE DUTY.

1. It is a duty imposed by the *natural law*, which God has written in the hearts of all men.

a. This duty is as evident as it is evident that man is bound by the law of nature to *worship* God, that is, by certain acts of his understanding and will to acknowledge God's supreme dominion over him, and his own total dependence on God. Who does not see that this tribute of the understanding and will is due to God, the Creator, from His creature? Is it not manifest that we owe to Him as our supreme Lord, as our sovereign benefactor, as the chief good, the tribute of reverence, gratitude, hope, and love? Does the creature owe less to the Creator than the child owes to his father? And who will dispense the child from the obligation of revering, thanking, loving, and confiding in his father? And what are such acts, if directed to God, else than prayer in its more general acceptation, that is, a pious elevation of the soul to God?

b. Again, how could man efficaciously *pursue his last end,* how could he resist sin and its allurements, without nourishing his intellect with religious truths, and his heart with religious sentiments? Would he not soon become the slave of his sensual passions if he neglected to cherish nobler sentiments and to check his sensual inclinations? Reason alone cannot control the rebellious passions. For, how easily is the understanding obscured by the depraved lusts of the heart! To obtain this victory over our passions both heart and mind must from time to time be raised to God, who alone can control our thoughts and affections; in other words, man, in order to gain his last end, must pray to God, his Creator and supreme Lord and Ruler.

c. That *prayer of petition,* in particular, is a strict duty is most evident. Or can we consider the power and goodness of God, on the one hand, and our own weakness and misery, on the other, without perceiving the necessity and obligation of invoking the assistance of God? Will a man whose life is in danger, or who is laboring under some great distress, not cry out for aid to his fellow-man who is able and willing to relieve him? The same natural law of self-preservation impels us almost unwittingly to have recourse to God in danger and distress; whence the very common saying: necessity teaches us to pray. It is, therefore, a duty imposed upon us by the law of nature that we should not only elevate our souls to God in prayer, but also have recourse to Him for aid and protection.

d. Hence, it has been the *custom of all peoples*, even of those who knew nothing of divine Revelation, to make prayer a part of their divine worship—a fact which shows to evidence that they considered prayer an indispensable duty, which they owed to the Supreme Being, or to those whom they considered their gods. This universal persuasion of all mankind can have no other cause than the general law which God has written in the hearts of all, and which we call the natural law. Prayer is, therefore, a strict obligation imposed upon us by the natural law, independently of any positive commandment of God.

2. But prayer is not only a prescription of the natural law; it is also a *positive command* of God, expressly and repeatedly enforced and inculcated in divine Revelation. In the Old Testament we find no duty more frequently and forcibly urged than that of prayer. And how often does Christ Himself exhort us to pray! "Ask and it shall be given you," He says; "seek and you shall find; knock and it shall be opened to you" (Luke xi. 9). And again, " He spoke also a parable to them, that we ought always to pray, and not to faint" (Ibid. xviii. 1). And in another place: "Pray, lest ye enter into temptation" (Ibid. xxii. 40, 46). That these and similar words of Our Saviour imply, not a mere counsel, but a precept, that is, a strict command, is both manifest in itself, and also the universal teaching of the divines of the Church. And what divine wisdom is

manifested in this command! How wonderfully does it promote our welfare and the glory of God!

a. It promotes *our welfare.* It fosters *humility* in us. For by prayer we acknowledge our total dependence on God. This commandment, which is always binding, forces us, as it were, frequently to make this humble acknowledgment and to present ourselves as poor, destitute, and helpless creatures before the throne of the Most High.

And while this commandment preserves us in humility, it shows at the same time the exalted *dignity of man*, who is not only permitted, but even morally constrained to approach the throne of the Almighty. If a poor subject had not only access to his sovereign at any moment, but was also urged under pain of his sovereign's displeasure to wait upon him, would he not justly consider himself greatly honored? What an honor and privilege it is, then, to be admitted at any moment we desire into the presence of God, to converse with Him, to beg His graces and receive His favors!

Besides, this divine commandment is well calculated to awaken our *gratitude* towards God, and to teach us to esteem His graces and carefully to preserve them; whereas, if we received His graces without asking, we would be apt to attach little value to them. Whence comes it that gamblers, for instance, place so little value on their winnings? It is because they have obtained them without trouble. So, it is to be feared, we would squander the graces of God, if we received them without earnest and incessant prayer. It is, therefore, most beneficial for our salvation that God has made prayer a strict obligation for us.

b. But while this commandment is most advantageous for our own spiritual welfare, it is likewise most effectual for the advancement of *God's glory*. It reveals God to us in all His greatness and majesty, as He really is, as the Sovereign Lord, and the Supreme Good, who is worthy of our supreme adoration, of our unbounded hope, and of all our love. The duty of prayer imposed upon us by the divine law, consequently, redounds to the glory of God as well as to our own spiritual advantage. Should not this fact be for us a powerful motive of faithfully discharging this obligation? Should it not inspire us with great love and esteem for prayer? Should it not make the exercise of prayer sweet and easy for us? Should it not make prayer a matter of the highest importance and interest to us?

II. A NECESSARY MEANS OF SALVATION.

While prayer is an indispensable duty, imposed upon us by the natural law as well as the positive law of God, it is also an absolutely necessary means of salvation, so that without prayer those who have come to the full use of reason cannot be saved.

1. Prayer is necessary to *obtain divine grace*, without which we cannot be saved. Without grace we cannot attain to our last end. So our blessed Lord Himself teaches us in the clearest terms. "Without Me you can do nothing," He says (John xv. 5); that is, without My supernatural aid, without My grace, you can do nothing that is productive of eternal life, nothing that will effectually lead you on the way to heaven. Grace is, therefore, absolutely necessary for salvation. But how is the grace of God to be obtained? According to the disposition of Divine Providence, divine grace can be secured by those who have attained to the use of reason only by prayer and the sacraments—the two great means of salvation according to the dis-

pensation of Almighty God. Both these means are necessary to secure the grace of God, and, consequently, to obtain eternal salvation. Without the sacraments prayer is not sufficient, and without prayer we cannot worthily and fruitfully receive the sacraments. Therefore prayer, as well as the sacraments, is a necessary means of grace.

This is *the way to grace* which our blessed Lord shows us, when He says: "Ask and it shall be given you; seek and you shall find; knock and it shall be opened to you. For every one that asketh receiveth; and he that seeketh findeth; and to him that knocketh it shall be opened" (Matt. vii. 7-8). By these words is clearly implied that he that asks not shall not receive, that he that seeks not shall not find, and that to him that knocks not it shall not be opened. For, although a man may obtain a thing without asking, yet he will not find without seeking, nor will a man be admitted into a house without seeking admission. Hence the choice of these words by our Divine Saviour. St. James, who best understood the meaning of Our Lord's words, teaches us that the reason why we do not receive is that we do not ask. "You have not," he says, "because you ask not" (James iv. 2). Hence you see that prayer is a necessary means of grace, and consequently, of salvation. It is, therefore, a universally admitted principle that, as without grace there is no salvation, so without prayer we cannot obtain sufficient grace to work out our salvation.

2. But does not God give us graces for which we have not prayed? True, we receive some graces from God independently of our prayers; but, as St. Augustine teaches us, these graces consist in the inspiration to pray; or they are the graces pertaining to faith, which must precede all salutary prayer. Man cannot

pray aright without a divine impulse and supernatural aid. This impulse is an antecedent grace, given without the intervention of prayer. But all succeeding graces, as a rule, are given in view of our prayers. Therefore the same St. Augustine says that God gives us some graces, particularly the beginning of faith, without our asking, but that ordinarily He reserves His other graces for those who pray for them. Finally, the graces which God gives independently of our prayers are commonly of an ordinary character. Great and extraordinary graces are promised only to those who earnestly and perseveringly pray for them. Whence we must conclude that those graces by which we are saved, according to the dispensation of Almighty God, practically depend upon our prayers as *a necessary condition.*

3. From what I have said it follows that prayer is necessary for all without exception, in order to attain to their last end. This will become still more evident if we consider the *different classes* of men in particular.

a. Prayer is necessary for *the sinner*. For, unless he is converted to God, he cannot be saved. But without prayer he cannot be converted. Without the aid of grace we can do nothing in the work of our salvation. And the ordinary way to the attainment of grace, especially the grace of conversion, is prayer. Among the many conversions recorded in Holy Scripture there is hardly one that has been effected without prayer. The publican in the Gospel was converted; but he first invoked the divine mercy, and prayed: "O God, be merciful to me, a sinner" (Luke xviii. 13). The Samaritan woman was converted; but she first asked our blessed Lord for the living water, "springing up into everlasting life," that water which washes away the sins of the world (John iv. 15). The penitent thief was converted on the cross; but it was not until he had invoked the grace of God, and prayed: "Lord, remember me when Thou shalt come into Thy kingdom". (Luke xxiii. 42). What, then, will be the fate of those sinners who neglect prayer altogether, who allow weeks to pass without invoking the mercy of God; who on Sundays and festivals either neglect to hear Mass, or, if they are present, allow their thoughts to dwell on all manner of worldly objects; who, instead of reflecting on the miserable state of their souls, spend all their spare time in drinking, gambling, godless conversation, and dissipation of every description? Beloved brethren, if they do not change their ways, if they do not enter into themselves seriously, and begin to pray, it is more than likely, unless at the pious prayers of their friends God gives them a special grace, that they will die in their sins, and be eternally lost.

b. But prayer is necessary, likewise, for *the just*, who have already entered on the way of salvation. For without prayer they can neither remain on the path of justice, nor make any progress upon it.

It is necessary for the just, in the first place, in order *to remain on the path of salvation.* It is an article of our faith, that no one, not even the just, who are in the state of sanctifying grace, can without the aid of a special grace overcome grievous temptations. And how many such temptations do we not encounter? There is hardly a day on which some one of our unruly passions, whether it be avarice, or pride, or lust, does not assail us, and threaten to drag us into the abyss of sin. Therefore our blessed Lord warns us to watch and pray, lest we enter into temptation (Matt. xxvi. 41). As soon, then, as we begin to relax our vigilance, to become remiss in prayer, we are sure to fall into sin and to swerve from the path of salvation. I am not astonished, says St. Augustine, that Peter, in the danger into which he thrust himself, fell into sin. For although Our Lord repeatedly admonished him to pray, yet he neglected to do so. The consequence was that he yielded to the temptation, and fell. And the cause of his fall was no other than that he neglected the grace of prayer that was offered him. If he had availed himself of this grace, if he had prayed, he would not have fallen. O beloved brethren, have you not made the same experience yourselves? Have your relapses into sin not always been preceded by neglect of prayer?

Prayer is necessary for the just, in the second place, in order *to advance* on the way of salvation, to make progress in Christian virtue. Sanctifying grace, which the just already possess, is not sufficient for this effect. According to the unanimous teaching of divines, actual graces are also necessary. But these graces are given, even to the just, only in answer to their prayers. If, therefore, you find that you have made little or no progress in virtue, that after many years you are as impatient and sensitive, as vain and sensual, as ever, you may ascribe this to your neglect of prayer, or to the carelessness with which you have practised it. If you had prayed as you ought, you would have long since overcome all these defects, and be now quite a different person. Now, at least, begin fervently to practise prayer, and you will soon prove its salutary effects.

c. Finally, prayer is necessary for all, whether they are in the state of grace or in the state of sin, to obtain that greatest of all graces—the grace of *final perseverance*, or the grace to die well. According to the teaching of the Church this is quite a special grace, that cannot be merited, in the strict sense of the word, even by the just. The most austere or the most innocent life cannot give us a strict right to this decisive grace. It is altogether a free gift of God's mercy. For God can, without the least injustice, permit one who has led a holy life to fall by his own fault into grievous sin, and to die in that state. This truth is well fitted to preserve us in humility, and to make us work out our salvation with fear and trembling.

But is there no effectual means to secure this grace, upon which all depends? Yes, beloved brethren (and that is the source of our consolation), there is an *infallible means;* and this means is prayer, and prayer only. For to prayer, and to it alone, has been promised the infallible efficacy of obtaining all things appertaining to our eternal salvation, and, consequently, also the grace of final perseverance. Jesus Christ, the Eternal Truth, expressly says: " Whatsoever you shall ask the Father in My name, that will I do " (John xiv. 13). Our final perseverance, therefore, depends upon our prayers; and the grace of salutary and effectual prayer is never wanting to us. Therefore St. Alphonsus Liguori says that our salvation depends almost entirely on our prayers; not as if prayer alone were sufficient, but because we shall always obtain the grace to fulfil our other duties and keep all God's commandments, provided we only pray well.

You see, then, beloved brethren, that prayer is absolutely necessary for our salvation; necessary as the fulfilment of God's law, necessary as a means of salvation; necessary for the sinner, necessary for the just; necessary for the beginner, necessary for the veteran in the service of Christ. Is this not a sufficient motive for us in future faithfully to discharge this duty towards God? O my dear friends, if we now neglect the duty of prayer, it is greatly to be feared that on our death-bed, when the decisive struggle, upon which depends our eternity, shall set in, we shall fail to wield this powerful weapon, and surrender ourselves into the hands of our enemy. Let us, then, resolve to-day henceforth regularly and devoutly to say our prayers night and morning, always, when possible, to attend the services of the Church, and often during the day to raise our hearts to God in prayer, especially in the moment of temptation. If we do so, we shall fulfil the command of Christ, always to pray; and this fervent and incessant prayer, together with the sacraments of the Church, will be for us an effectual means of salvation, and will lead us to that everlasting happiness which is the object and fruit of all our prayers. Amen.

Second Sermon.

EFFICACY OF PRAYER.

"Amen, amen I say to you: if you ask the Father anything in My name, He will give it you."—John xvi. 23.

PRAYER is a necessary duty imposed upon us by God, and a necessary means of salvation. It is indispensable for the just man as well as for the sinner, so that, in the present order of Divine Providence, practically no man who has come to the use of reason can be saved without prayer. This was the substance of the preceding discourse. And it certainly proved a powerful motive to urge us to the faithful fulfilment of this so necessary obligation of a Christian. But prayer is not only necessary; it is also a most *efficacious means* of saving our souls. It has the infallible virtue of obtaining for us all graces necessary for the accomplishment of the work of our salvation. This consideration should inspire us with a high esteem for prayer and an unbounded confidence in its efficacy.

The infallible efficacy of prayer for the attainment of all graces necessary for our salvation rests on three attributes of God—(1) His *faithfulness*, (2) His *justice*, and (3) His *mercy*—which will form the subject and division of the present discourse.

I. GOD'S FAITHFULNESS.

The foundation on which the infallible virtue of prayer rests is, first of all, God's fidelity in the fulfilment of His promises. God has promised to hear our prayers; God is faithful to His promises; therefore He will infallibly hear our prayers. This is the argument upon which the infallible efficacy of prayer and our unbounded confidence are based.

1. God *has promised* to hear our prayers. Our blessed Lord distinctly says: "Ask and it shall be given you; seek and you shall find; knock and it shall be opened to you" (Matt. vii. 7). This promise is universal; it refers to all the graces necessary for our salvation, as Our Lord expressly teaches in the words recorded by St. John: "Whatsoever you shall ask the Father in My name, that will I do" (John xiv. 13). It refers to all men without exception. Christ excludes no one, He makes no restriction. He does not say: the Father will hear you, if you do His will, keep His commandments, and lead a virtuous life. No; His words are directed to all, even to the greatest sinners. And having repeated the promise several times, He confirms it with the words: "Amen, amen I say to you"—words which, according to the teaching of St. Thomas, have the weight of a sworn statement; Jesus Christ has, therefore, given us the most solemn promise that He would hear our prayers.

2. But God *is faithful* in the fulfilment of His promises: He is both able and willing to fulfil what He promised. That He is able to keep His promises is evident from the fact that He is all-powerful. Nor is His good will less evident than His omnipotence. For what could induce Almighty God to swerve from His purpose? Will His bounty make Him poorer? God, the supreme and infinite Good, can by His munificence lose nothing of His boundless riches. Or is it any trouble to God to grant our petitions? It only costs an act of His almighty will; there is no labor, no effort in the actions of God. Or is it perhaps our sinfulness that would prevent Him from hearing our prayers? No; not even this; for our sinfulness only awakens His

compassion, and is one of the chief reasons why He has given us this assurance. What, then, could induce the almighty and all-bountiful God to withhold from us what He has promised?

Here, beloved brethren, *the honor and glory of God*, for which He created heaven and earth and all things, are at stake. If He failed to fulfil His promises He would forfeit His divine honor. Even a man who fails to keep his word is without honor in our eyes. If, then, man is in honor bound to keep his promises, what shall we say of God, who is the source of all honor and justice? How could He pronounce judgment on the world unless He were faithful to His promises? If the Judge of the living and the dead were unfaithful to His promises, would not many of those condemned in that case have just cause of complaint? Could they not say: we have prayed and yet we have not been heard, though Thou hast repeatedly promised to hear our prayers; we have asked and have not received; we have sought and have not found; we have knocked and it has not been opened to us. You see, then, beloved brethren, that it would be not only absurd but blasphemous in the highest degree for a moment to think that God, the almighty and all-bountiful, could be unfaithful to His promises.

The efficacy of prayer is, therefore, infallible, because Almighty God is able and willing, and His supreme divine honor is pledged, to hear our prayers. If a rich man, a powerful king or prince, made such a promise, and was thus disposed to fulfil it, what a rush there would be from all quarters to partake of his munificence! How many thousands of petitions he would receive daily! Should we, then, not be ashamed of our remissness? A man, whose riches, however extensive they may be, are yet limited, who offers nothing but fleeting and perishable goods, the continuance of whose good will cannot be relied upon—such a man is besieged by petitioners; and to Him who possesses inexhaustible and imperishable treasures, who has solemnly promised to hear all our petitions and grant our requests, to the almighty and all-merciful God, we pay no attention, or only with reluctance have recourse to Him! Let us now at least repent of our past neglect, and at last begin the fervent practice of prayer, and draw from the inexhaustible treasures of God's grace. I said that the infallible efficacy of prayer rested, secondly, on—

II. GOD'S JUSTICE.

Almighty God is not only pledged in virtue of His fidelity to His promises to hear our prayers, but also bound in virtue of His justice.

1. Christ Our Lord by His bitter passion and death has in the strict sense of the word satisfied the divine Justice for our sins. He has also *merited* for us in the strictest sense all the graces necessary for our salvation. If, therefore, a man is in grievous temptation, and needs the grace of God, even extraordinary grace, to overcome it, Christ has merited this grace. Again, if a man under the weight of suffering needs strength to suffer with patience and without murmuring, Christ has merited also this grace. In short, Christ has merited for us all the graces needful for the attainment of our last end.

God, therefore, in justice to His divine Son and to us for whom He suffered and died, must afford us the *means of appropriating* to ourselves those graces which are necessary for the work of our salvation. For what would those graces avail us unless we could obtain possession of them? What will it avail you, if a friend of yours deposits a sum of money in the bank for you, if you cannot draw it, if you have not the check in your possession? The sum of money is yours, but it remains useless as long as you cannot appropriate it. In like manner the merits of Jesus Christ would be of no avail for us; His sufferings and death would be ineffectual, unless God had given us a means of appropriating them. But if God has once given us a means, and we employ it according to His will, it is certainly a matter of justice on the part of God to grant us the necessary graces, just as it is an obligation of justice on the part of a banker to disburse a sum of money for which I present him a payable check.

Now, God has actually afforded us such a means. And this means of appropriating to ourselves the grace of God, this ever payable check on the treasury of God's grace, is prayer, according to the words of our Divine Saviour: "Whatsoever you shall ask the Father in My name, that will I do." If, therefore, we use this means, if we present this check to the heavenly Father in the name of Jesus, if we ask those graces that appertain to our salvation, the Father is in virtue of His divine justice bound to give them to us. This obligation He has in His love and mercy freely imposed on Himself; but this free disposition once supposed, it is, in a certain true sense, a duty on the part of God. To doubt the infallible efficacy of prayer, therefore, would be to call in question not only His unswerving faithfulness, but also His infinite justice, both of which would be equally an outrage against Almighty God.

2. From what I have said you will easily perceive that this obligation of justice on the part of Almighty God to hear our prayers rests exclusively on the *merits of Jesus Christ*, not on our merits or on our worthiness. And this fact removes a misgiving which is wont to

weaken our confidence in the efficacy of our prayers, viz., that we are conscious of no merits, but rather of great demerits with God, and, consequently, that we have no right to hope that our prayers will be heard. Is it our merits that move Almighty God to hear our prayers? Is it not, on the contrary, the infinite merits of Jesus Christ, the Son of God, which He has ceded in our favor? We must, therefore, take into consideration, not our own spiritual poverty and unworthiness, but the infinite riches and merits of the Son of God. Nor must we overlook the fact that Jesus Christ is still with us; that He always prays with us, and offers up His infinite merits and satisfaction to God in our behalf.

How firm, then, how unshaken, is the foundation upon which rests the efficacy of prayer! It is as unshaken and unchangeable as are the unvarying faithfulness and infinite justice of God Himself. But no less firm is the third foundation upon which our confidence is based—

III. GOD'S MERCY.

Abstracting from the promises of the Almighty and from His infinite justice; supposing for argument's sake that God had given us no promise to hear our prayers, or that He could be unfaithful to His promises; supposing He were not bound in His infinite justice to hear us, still His mercy would be a sufficient warrant for our unbounded confidence.

1. What is mercy? Mercy is the readiness to relieve the misery of others. Such is the power of the natural impulse of mercy that some trace of it is to be found even in the most depraved hearts. *How great*, then, must not be the mercy of God, or His readiness to relieve our misery! Have we not the most striking in-

stances of God's infinite mercy? We were all plunged in utter misery and ruin. What has the all-merciful God not done to rescue us from our doleful condition? He sent His only-begotten Son into the world, to become man for us, to labor and to suffer for us, to die amid the most cruel torments for our Redemption. "God so loved the world," says our blessed Lord, "as to give His only-begotten Son: that whosoever believeth in Him may not perish, but may have life everlasting" (John iii. 16). Could God have shown greater mercy to us, greater inclination to succor our misery? Is there anything He could have done for us that He has not done? How great, then, is the mercy of God!

It is His infinite mercy which *urges God to hear our prayers.* At the sight of our misery and helplessness His tender mercy moves the heart of God to such compassion for us that He cannot refuse to hear any petition of ours that regards our spiritual welfare. If parents are so compassionate towards their children that they can with difficulty refuse them any request, how could God, our tender Father, refuse to hear our prayers—the prayers of His children, whom He loves so dearly, and whose misery so strongly affects His Divine Heart with compassion! All the love of friends, all the tenderness of parents, is but, as it were, a tiny drop compared with that ocean of love and tenderness that swells in the bosom of the all-merciful and all-bountiful God. As soon as Almighty God perceives our misery, and our prayers reach His ear, He is seized with compassion for us, hastens to console us, to dry our tears, and to grant our petitions. Therefore the Psalmist exclaims: "Thou, O Lord, art sweet and mild, and plenteous in mercy to all that call upon thee. And Thou, O Lord, art a God of compassion, and merciful, and patient, and of much mercy, and true" (Ps. lxxxv. 5, 15).

But God shows the greatest mercy to *the sinner*, whose condition is the most lamentable, whose misery is the most pitiable. Also to the sinner Jesus Christ addresses His loving words: "Come to Me, all you that labor and are burdened, and I will refresh you" (Matt. xi. 28). If you are laden with sin and pressed by your enemy, despond not, but come to Me in confident prayer, and you will be relieved of the burden of your sins, and you will receive strength to vanquish your enemies. "If your sins be as scarlet, they shall be made as white as snow; and if they be red as crimson, they shall be white as wool" (Is. i. 18).

Confide, therefore, O sinner, in the mercy of God. Though you were the greatest sinner on earth, the all-merciful God will infallibly hear your prayers. How great were not the errors of the *prodigal son?* Having demanded and obtained his share of the inheritance, to which he had no right during the life of his father, he abandoned his home and carried his fortune into a strange land, where he spent it in riot and dissipation. He continued this life until he squandered his inheritance, and was reduced to beggary and to the deepest moral degradation. He began to be in want, so that he would fain appease his hunger with the husks that were thrown to the swine. Now he entered into himself; he remembered the love and gentleness of his father, and constrained by want he set out again for his father's house. And what is the request he makes of his father? Only to be received as one of his hired servants. And how is his petition received? His father, regardless of his son's errors and ingratitude, mindful only of his own paternal love and mercy, receives him again as his son. He thinks not of the disobedience of his son, not of his sinful life; he only reflects upon his misery, and scarcely allows him to present his petition before granting his request. But he not only grants his request, he gives him much more than he asked. He re-instates him in all his former rights as a son. And the father's joy is so great that he desires all his friends to share it. "Let us eat and make merry," he says, "because this my son was dead and is come to life again; was lost, and is found" (Luke xv. 24). Such, as our blessed Lord assures us, is the merciful disposition of Almighty God towards all, even the most degraded of His children.

Let us, then, beloved brethren, henceforth in all our necessities with unbounded confidence have recourse to God in prayer. And God the all-merciful, all-just, and all-faithful will hear our prayers and lead us to the final victory and to the crown of everlasting glory. Amen.

Third Sermon.

REQUISITES OF FRUITFUL PRAYER.

"This is the confidence which we have towards Him, that whatsoever we shall ask, according to His will, He heareth us."—I. John v. 14.

PRAYER, as we saw in our last discourse, has an infallible efficacy. This truth follows evidently from the infinite faithfulness, justice, and mercy of God. However, you will quite naturally ask: If the efficacy of prayer is infallible, whence comes it that our prayers are so often not heard? That you may be able to solve this question for yourselves, I shall put before you the requisites which our prayers must possess, in order that their efficacy may be infallible. The promises which God has given us in regard to the hearing of our prayers, though universal, are not absolute, or without conditions. These conditions, though not always expressed, are always supposed, and sometimes expressly added in Holy Scripture, when there is question of the efficacy of prayer. Thus, in the text which I have quoted, the efficacy of our prayers is made to depend upon the condition that we "ask according to His [God's] will." Now, when do we ask according to the will of God? We ask according to the will of God, when both the object for which we ask and the manner in which we ask are in accordance with the divine will. Whence the following two questions arise, which will give the subject and division of the present discourse: viz., in order that our prayers may have the infallible effect which God has promised them—

1. *What must be the object of our prayers, or for what must we pray?*
2. *What must be the qualities of our prayers, or how must we pray?*

I. THE OBJECT OF OUR PRAYERS.

For what must we pray, in order that our prayers may be infallibly heard?

1. First, we must pray for something which relates to our own salvation; in other words, *we must pray for ourselves.* This is the teaching of St. Thomas; for the promises made by God invariably refer to the person who prays, and therefore suppose that we pray for ourselves, that is, for something that refers to our own spiritual well-being. If we pray, for instance, for the conversion of a friend, it may easily happen, and often does happen, that he places such an obstacle in the way of his conversion that God cannot possibly hear our prayers in his behalf. Yet it were very wrong if, for that reason, we neglected to pray for others; for, although our prayers for others are not infallibly heard, yet they are often heard, and will, in every case, be pleasing to God and certainly bear their spiritual fruits in some way. Neither are our prayers for the dead always infallibly efficacious for those for whom they are offered; but let us not, on that account, fail to pray for them; for, though in certain cases they may not profit those for whom they have been especially offered, they will certainly be accepted by God for some other souls, who are no less in need of them. Besides, we must not forget that praying for others, whether for the living or for the dead, is one of the greatest acts of charity, and consequently a work of great merit for ourselves. Our blessed Lord Himself complained to St. Mary Magdalene de Pazzi of the remissness of His servants who neg-

lect to pray for poor sinners who are walking on the way to destruction. "You see, My child," He says, "how many Christians are under the power of Satan; if My elect fail to deliver them by their prayers, these miserable sinners will finally become a prey to the enemy." Do not neglect, therefore, fervently and perseveringly to pray for others, especially for your benefactors and for those who are placed under your care, though you cannot claim an infallible efficacy for your prayers in their behalf.

2. Besides, if our prayers should have the infallible efficacy promised by God, we must pray for something *that has reference to our eternal salvation.* For absolute efficacy is promised to our prayers only when we pray in the name of Jesus. "Whatsoever you shall ask the Father in My name, that will I do" (John xiv. 13). But in the name of Jesus we can ask only for those things which Jesus Christ, Our Saviour, has merited for us, and all that He has merited for us appertains to our eternal salvation. If, therefore, you ask for temporal blessings, the efficacy of your prayers is not certain; because it is doubtful whether the temporal blessings you ask for are conducive to your salvation, or not.

However, I would not have you understand that it is wrong or useless to pray for *temporal blessings*, for instance, to implore God to grant us a long life, good health, the necessaries and comforts of life; for this we are taught to do in the Lord's Prayer, which contains a petition for our material daily bread. Nay, it is not only lawful, but even a duty, to have a moderate care for our temporal concerns. But such care must not be excessive, must not be our chief object in life, and must not so engross our attention as if temporal prosperity were our chief good in this world. Therefore we must always pray for temporal blessings, not absolutely, but under the condition that such are conducive to our eternal salvation.

We must make the same restriction when we pray to God to deliver us from certain irksome *temptations.* God sometimes, despite our prayers, permits temptations to continue to molest us. And why? Because it is not the temptation, however grievous, disagreeable, and humiliating it may be, that renders us displeasing to God, but the consent of the will, in which alone is sin. Temptation, on the contrary, if we pray and resist it as we ought to do, is a powerful means of practising the opposite virtue, and an effectual warning for us to put our whole trust in God, and cling to Him for support. In our temptations, therefore, we must pray with perfect resignation to the will of God, and say: O God, if it is for my salvation, take away this temptation from me; if not, at least give me the grace efficaciously to resist it. If we thus pray with resignation to the will of God, who in His infinite wisdom knows what is for our salvation, we will soon experience the truth of the words of St. Bernard: "As often as we ask God for any grace, we either receive that grace, or something which is still more expedient for us."

If, therefore, our prayers should be infallibly efficacious, we must pray for ourselves, without, however, neglecting to pray for others; we must pray for those things which appertain to our eternal salvation. But this is not sufficient; we must, furthermore, pray in a manner that is pleasing to Almighty God.

II. THE QUALITIES OF OUR PRAYERS.

It is self-evident that, in order to have that infallible efficacy promised by God, our prayers must possess those qualities that render them pleasing to God.

Now, which are those qualities? They are, according to the teaching of St. Thomas, chiefly three: reverence, confidence, and perseverance.

1. We must, then, if we would claim infallible efficacy for our prayers, pray with *reverence*. An irreverent prayer is an insult to Almighty God. It resembles the behavior of certain beggars known by the name of tramps—a behavior which is not at all calculated to awaken sympathy or benevolence in their favor. How can we expect God to hear a prayer which is wanting in reverence?

a. In order that our prayers may have this attribute of reverence, we must, in the first place, when praying, assume a reverent *exterior posture;* whether we kneel at our prayers, which is the most becoming attitude, or stand, or sit, or even walk, as circumstances may demand, our outward deportment should always give expression to our inward reverence towards the Divine Majesty. This outward as well as inward reverence we owe to the Sovereign Lord and Master, to whom we address ourselves.

b. We must pray with *attention* and devotion. To pray without attention is to honor God with the lips only, while our hearts are far from Him—a species of honor for which God Himself expresses His abomination, and which cannot possibly be pleasing to God, or claim to be heard by Him.

Very true, some one will say; in order that our prayers may be pleasing to Almighty God, we must pray with attention; but for me it is a thing impossible to pray *without distractions.* My dear friend, the question is not whether you have distractions in prayer, or not; the question is, whether your distractions are wilful, or not. Unwilful distractions, though they mar our attention, do not render our prayers fruitless;

only wilful distractions render our prayers ineffectual; and against such we have especially to guard. And how are we to guard against them? First, we must remove the distracting thoughts, as soon as we become aware of them. Thus they become a source of merit to us; and the more we have to struggle against them, the greater is our merit. Secondly, we must endeavor to remove the causes of distraction, both during prayer and before it; else we are responsible for the effects. If, for instance, during prayer we allow our eyes full freedom to gaze at all objects within our view, we are evidently ourselves the cause of the distractions which naturally and necessarily arise. The same may be said of him who wilfully fosters an immoderate attachment in his heart, which engrosses his attention during prayer. What we have to do, then, in order to avoid wilful distractions is to cleanse our hearts, as far as possible, from immoderate desires, to keep guard over our senses during prayer, and to endeavor to remove the distracting thoughts that present themselves during our prayers; and, particularly, always to recollect ourselves before beginning to pray.

c. Finally, in order to pray with reverence, we must pray with *humility*, that is, with a lively sense of our own spiritual poverty and unworthiness. There is nothing more unbecoming and more hateful in a beggar than pride. Who will give an alms to an arrogant beggar? Now, we are all poor, helpless beggars in regard to Almighty God. It behooves us, then, to present ourselves before Him in all humility. How God regards the prayers of the proud has been illustrated by our blessed Lord in the parable of the Pharisee and the Publican. The humble publican returned to his house justified, while the proud pharisee found no favor with God. If, then, my dear friend, you behave in the house of God as did the pharisee in the temple; if you look down with scorn upon your neighbor; if you conduct yourself as if you were rendering a great service to Almighty God by your condescension in coming to church at all; if you come to church to be admired; if, like the pharisee, you make a display of your piety to seem better than your neighbors; is it to be wondered that you return to your home with empty hands? But if, on the other hand, you present yourself before Almighty God with the humility of the publican, you may hope to return enriched with the grace of God. External and internal reverence, therefore, and, accordingly, inward recollection and profound humility, are inseparable attributes of fruitful prayer.

2. The second attribute of fruitful prayer is *confidence*. If our prayers should be efficacious, we must pray with confidence. A prayer without confidence cannot but be offensive to Almighty God. For he who prays without confidence practically denies or doubts, either that God has promised to hear our prayers or that He is faithful to His promises, both of which are equally offensive to Almighty God. A confident prayer, on the other hand, is most pleasing to God, because it is a tribute of honor paid to His infinite faithfulness and goodness. Such a prayer is certain to be heard. "Therefore I say unto you," says our blessed Lord, "all things whatsoever you ask when ye pray, believe that you shall receive, and they shall come unto you" (Mark xi. 24). "What!" says St. Augustine; "could God deceive us? could He promise to assist us in all our necessities, if we confided in Him, and then abandon us, when we invoke Him?" A confident prayer constrains, as it were, the mercy of God to hear it. Therefore our blessed Lord

once revealed to St. Gertrude that he who prays with confidence does such violence to Him that He is necessitated to hear all his prayers. Blessed, therefore, is he who confides in God; for he can obtain all graces necessary for his salvation, and cannot suffer the loss of his soul.

But, you may say, it is written in Holy Scripture "that God doth not hear *sinners*" (John ix. 31); and you are a poor sinner, who can put no claim to the divine mercy. To this I answer with St. Thomas: these words are true only of him who prays precisely as a sinner, that is, who is not disposed to be converted to God; who, therefore, does not pray for his conversion, nor for graces that might lead to his conversion; but who prays for those things that tend to confirm him in his sinful state; for instance, revenge of his enemies, gratification of his passions, or salvation from God without employing the necessary means. Such prayers cannot be heard, because they are sinful and presumptuous. But the words of the Gospel have no reference to him who is eager to rid himself of his sins. If, then, the sinner who sincerely wishes to be converted confidently prays to God to loosen the bonds that fetter his soul in the captivity of Satan, and prays with perseverance, his prayer will infallibly be heard; for Our Lord says: Whoever—be he a just man or a sinner—asks, he shall receive. Be, then, of good heart, beloved brethren, and let not your sins prevent you from having confident recourse to God in prayer. Oh, wonderful power of prayer! Two sinners hang on either side of Jesus on the cross; the one prays, and obtains salvation; the other neglects to pray, and is lost!

3. The third quality of an efficacious prayer is *perseverance*. This attribute is indispensably necessary;

for, although our blessed Lord has pledged His word to hear our prayers, yet He did not determine the time He would grant our petitions. Sometimes He grants them without delay; but sometimes He delays for a longer or shorter time, according as He sees in His divine wisdom that it is for our advantage. The prayer of the centurion was heard at once by our Divine Lord. How differently did He deal with the Cannanæan woman! At first He gave no answer at all. When she repeated her petition, He answered apparently with a refusal: " I was not sent but to the sheep that are lost of the house of Israel" (Matt. xv. 24). Not discouraged at this answer, however, she threw herself at His feet and prayed: " Lord help me!" Hereupon Jesus spoke to her the seemingly harsh words: " It is not good to take the bread of the children, and to cast it to the dogs" (Ibid. 26). But she answered with admirable simplicity and humility: " Yea, Lord; for the whelps also eat the crumbs that fall from the table of their masters" (Ibid. 27). After having thus tried her perseverance and humility, Jesus granted her prayer, and exclaimed : " O woman, great is thy faith ; be it done to thee as thou wilt" (Ibid. 28). If God thus sometimes delays to hear our prayers, He does so, not through want of compassion, but to give us an opportunity to prove our faith and confidence. He wishes us to become inwardly sensible of our own misery and helplessness. He desires thus to make us esteem His graces the more ; for the more we have prayed for them, the higher we esteem them, and the more carefully we endeavor to preserve them.

Perseverance is necessary, above all, to obtain the grace of a *happy death*. For this signal grace, as St. Alphonsus Liguori teaches, is not a single grace, but a whole series of graces, which, combined, constitute the grace of final perseverance. And corresponding to this series of graces there must be a series of prayers. We cannot, it is true, in the strict sense of the word, merit the grace of final perseverance, but, as St. Augustine teaches us, we can, in a looser sense, merit it by prayer, that is, obtain it by constant supplication. The learned and pious divine Suarez adds, that he who prays will infallibly obtain this grace. But St. Thomas reminds us that our prayers to this effect must be persevering. Therefore our blessed Lord teaches that we ought always to pray and never to faint. It is, therefore, not enough to pray for the grace of final perseverance once, or at certain times in our lives; to secure this grace, we must pray constantly, our whole lives long. Let us not fail to pray, then, beloved brethren; let us constrain Our Lord, as it were, to hear our prayers. This importunity is pleasing to Him. St. Jerome assures us that prayer is the more efficacious with God, the more persevering and the more importunate it is.

In conclusion, if you wish your prayers to have an infallible efficacy with God, pray for those things that appertain to your salvation; pray in a manner that is pleasing to God—with reverence, confidence, and perseverance. This is the only way, but at the same time an absolutely sure way, to obtain all graces from Almighty God, and particularly the grace of graces—the grace of a happy death, crowned by everlasting bliss. Amen.

Fourth Sermon.

TIME AND PLACE OF PRAYER.

" We ought always to pray, and not to faint."—Luke xviii. 1.

THE subject which thus far occupied our attention were the motives which should induce us to pray. The first motive we considered was the necessity of prayer. We have seen that prayer is a necessary duty, imposed upon us by the natural law, which is inscribed on the hearts of all men, as well as by the positive law of God ; that it is, moreover, an indispensable means of salvation, because without prayer we can, in the ordinary providence of God, neither obtain nor preserve God's grace, much less secure the greatest of all graces, final perseverance. The second motive is the infallible efficacy of prayer, which rests on the firm foundation of God's infinite faithfulness, justice, and mercy. But as our prayers often, despite the infallible efficacy promised to them by God, are actually not heard, it was necessary to set forth the requisites of an infallibly fruitful prayer: whence we have learned that, if our prayers are not heard, the fault lies not with God, but with ourselves, namely, in the defective quality of our prayers. For our prayers, in order to claim an infallible response on the part of God, must have for their object something appertaining to our eternal salvation, and must be offered in a manner pleasing to God, i. e., with reverence, confidence, and perseverance.

It remains for us still to consider the *practice* of prayer. As the practice of any art or occupation is determined by the various circumstances of time, place, persons, etc., we shall consider in succession the principal circumstances of prayer. In the present discourse the circumstances of time and place will claim our attention, while we answer the two following questions—

1. *When ought we to pray?*
2. *Where ought we to pray?*

I. WHEN WE SHOULD PRAY.

1. To this question I must answer, first of all, according to the teaching of our blessed Lord, that we must pray *without ceasing.* "We ought always to pray, and not to faint." Thus also the Apostle St. Paul teaches expressly in the words: "Pray without ceasing" (I. Thess. v. 17). This doctrine contains, according to the teaching of divines, not a mere counsel, but a real command. We must, therefore, pray at all times.

But, you will ask, *how is this possible?* Have we not other duties to discharge, which occupy the greater part of our time? How, then, can we always pray, without neglecting our other duties? True, if it were necessary to spend all our time in the church, or shut ourselves up in our chambers at home, occupying ourselves exclusively with prayer and meditation, we could not fulfil this command without neglecting our ordinary duties. But without recurring to such expedients, even in the midst of the most various and engrossing external occupations, we can always pray. For, according to St. Thomas, whatever we do to the honor of God is true prayer. What is prayer? Prayer is the elevation of the soul to God; but we cannot do anything to the honor of God without raising our minds to Him and, consequently, without praying. Our blessed Lord Himself confirms this statement. To St. Catherine of Siena He once said in a vision: "Everything that is done from love of God or charity to our neighbor may be called a continued prayer. He who ceases not to do good ceases not to pray." If, then, in your ordinary actions and your various avocations, you always endeavor to have a *right intention*, to do all things for the glory of God, as is, I will not say the pious custom but the duty of good Christians, your life is one of continual prayer, and you fulfil the commandment of Christ always to pray. We must, therefore, in order to fulfil the law of Christ, pray without ceasing. And the easiest and most effectual way of fulfilling this commandment is to have a good intention in all our doings—to do all things for the glory of God, for the attainment of our eternal salvation, or as an atonement for our sins. Thus we change all our actions into so many prayers, and our life becomes a life of constant prayer.

2. Besides this continual prayer, which is practically exercised by a right intention in our actions, we must devote certain *stated times exclusively* to prayer. He who neglects to do so will not fulfil the commandment of God to pray without ceasing. This constant prayer of which I have spoken is itself a grace, which we can secure and preserve only by fervent prayer and frequent communion with God, to the exclusion of all other occupations. He who does not frequently disengage his thoughts from the concerns of this world, and devote them for some time altogether to the practice of prayer, will either not obtain this grace of prayer without ceasing, or, if he should obtain it for a time, is sure to lose it again.

To these prayers, to be practised at stated times, belong, in the very first place, our *daily prayers*—morning and night prayers, prayers before and after meals, and the truly Christian practice of reciting the Angelus at the sound of the church bell, morning, noon, and night. These daily prayers, beloved brethren, are of paramount importance. The most precious graces are attached to their faithful performance. He who faithfully performs his daily prayers will doubtless enjoy a special protection from on high for body and soul. Almighty God will by a special providence preserve him from many grievous temptations; or, if He permits temptations to come upon him, He will surely give him such powerful assistance of grace that he may succesfully resist, and easily overcome them. That bodily evils—diseases, accidents, etc.—are often averted from those who are faithful in their daily prayers is attested by general experience; and no doubt, many of you have made this experience yourselves, or have, at least, seen it strikingly instanced in the case of others. Another priceless fruit of fidelity in our daily prayers is a certain facility in the fulfilment of the duties of our state in a manner pleasing to God—a circumstance which renders our works most fruitful for the life to come, whether as an atonement to God for our sins, or as a rich source of merits and future glory in heaven. And these precious fruits, moreover, are crowned with an inward peace and satisfaction, which not only render us happy ourselves, but make our conduct a source of delight and happiness to others.

On the other hand, he who ordinarily *neglects his daily prayers* greatly endangers his salvation; because he deprives himself of all those graces I have mentioned, and runs the risk of gradually giving up the practice of prayer altogether, or at least to a great extent. Is this, again, not the result of your own experience? Did you not commonly neglect prayer altogether on those days on which you neglected to pray at stated times? And the cause is evident. For we feel ourselves more disposed and incited to say our ordinary prayers, for instance, night and morning, than to say any special prayers during the day. Besides, the Christian is urged on to the performance of those daily devotions by the very habit which he has acquired in his childhood, and strengthened by long continued practice ; he is urged by the general custom and by the example of all good Christians ; he is urged by his sense of gratitude for the many favors which God daily bestows upon him; he is urged by the duty of thankfulness he owes to God for the daily bread which He so liberally supplies for his sustenance ; he is urged by the sound of the bell, which invites him thrice every day to thank God for the benefit of His Redemption, and to salute His heavenly Mother with the angel's greeting words. He who, despite so many and so strong incentives, neglects his daily prayers, will hardly have recourse to special prayers, and thus runs the imminent risk of neglecting prayer altogether, falling into sin, and forfeiting his eternal salvation.

Be always faithful, then, dear brethren, in saying your daily prayers. Let not your work nor your business prevent you from complying with this duty. Prayer has never been a hindrance but always a help to a laborer or a man of business. In prayer he obtains the strength to do his work or manage his business not only successfully, but also in a manner that is fruitful for eternal life. And I would urge upon you particularly never to begin your day's work without giving some time, however short it may be, to prayer. Always rise in such time as to be able to devote at least a few minutes to prayer, and do not omit to offer up the work of the day to Almighty God.

3. We should also pray on *special occasions*, particularly in afflictions and *temptations*. He who neglects to pray in temptations is like a soldier without arms

surrounded by the fiercest enemies; he is like a pilot whose craft, without sail or rudder, is tost on the raging sea; he is like a fortress without a garrison. He is an easy prey to his enemy. Woe is him who prays not in temptation! Let us, then, follow the advice of St. Francis of Sales: "As soon as you perceive the tempter," he says, "do like little children, who, when they see a wild animal, immediately run, or cry for help to their father or mother; so do you, in like manner, hasten to God, your father, or to Mary, your mother, and pray for help, and grace, and mercy." Beloved brethren, it is due to the partial or total neglect of this advice that there are so many unfortunate Christians, who are ever and anon relapsing into the same sins. In temptation, they either neglect to pray altogether, or they do not pray with perseverance. If the temptation does not at once vanish they cease to pray. That is not the way to overcome temptation; we must often renew our prayers, as long as there is danger of consenting to the evil suggestion. He who thus perseveres in prayer will infallibly be victorious. For the Son of God, the Eternal Truth, has pledged His word to that effect.

So much in regard to the times when we should pray; we should pray at all times, that is, do all things with a good intention, for the glory of God and our eternal salvation; we should pray at stated times, that is, say our daily prayers regularly; but, above all, we should pray in temptations, trials, and afflictions.

II. WHERE WE SHOULD PRAY.

With regard to the circumstance of place, we may, and must even, pray everywhere; but the place particularly adapted and set apart for prayer is the church.

1. There are some Christians who seem to think they

cannot pray anywhere but in the church. How absurd this idea is you may perceive from what I have said of the necessity and possibility of praying at all times. For, if all that we do for the honor of God is true prayer; if a right intention transforms all our works—eating, drinking, innocent recreation, the management of our temporal concerns, etc.—into so many prayers, it is evident that we can pray, at least in the more general sense of the word, *in every place*. But prayer, also in the stricter sense, may be practised everywhere, even amid the noise and bustle of the world. For God is present and can hear us everywhere. "The Spirit of the Lord hath filled the whole world; and that which containeth all things hath knowledge of the voice" (Wis. i. 7). Yea, God is present, not only without, but also within us. "For in Him we live, and move, and are" (Acts xvii. 28). The whole world is, therefore, His dwelling-place; and every pious heart is His altar. Wherever we are, there we can always raise our hearts to God and implore His assistance. "Let us not excuse ourselves," says St. Chrysostom, "by saying that it is difficult for one who is incumbered with worldly concerns to pray, because there is no church at hand whither he may retire for prayer. For, wherever we are, we can raise an altar to God. Nor time nor place can prevent us. Though we bow not the knee, though we strike not our breast, though we raise not our hands to heaven, yet, if we offer up a devout heart to the Lord, we have performed a perfect prayer. He who is on his way to the market, he who is walking in the street, may offer many a prayer to God. Even when you are in the working-room, occupied with your needle, you may raise your heart to God. For God has no regard for places; He asks only one

thing of you, a devout heart and recollected mind."
Thus St. Chrysostom.

Accustom yourselves, then, beloved brethren, in the midst of your labors and occupations often to raise your hearts to God. Such short prayers, or *aspirations*, when often and devoutly repeated, have a marvellous efficacy. They preserve us from sin, keep our hearts in the right disposition towards God, and effect that the good intention with which we began the day still perseveres, and, consequently, that all our works are meritorious before God.

2. While we may pray fruitfully in any place, yet *the church* is, by way of excellence, the place for prayer. And why so? For the following important reasons.

a. On account of *the real presence* of Jesus Christ in our churches. Is it not meet that we should often visit Him, who is our Redeemer and the author of all graces and favors; who is present for us in the church, by day and by night, to dispense His graces to us; who invites us Himself, when we labor and are heavily laden, to come to Him, that He may refresh us? Where, then, could we hope to be heard, if not in the church, where Our Saviour Himself has taken up His abode for the express purpose of bestowing His favors upon us! Beloved brethren, if Almighty God chose the Temple of Jerusalem as the place where He loved to communicate His favors to His chosen people, how much more is He disposed to lavish His graces on those who implore them in the temples sanctified by the real and continued presence of His own divine Son!

b. Another reason why we should particularly love to pray in the church is that there everything is calculated to *awaken our devotion*. The tabernacle, where our Lord and Saviour dwells; the altar, on which He daily renews the Sacrifice of Calvary in an unbloody manner for our salvation; the pictures and images of the saints; the solemnity of the divine service; the preaching of the word of God, and the edification of the faithful—all this cannot but arouse our devotion and stimulate us to pray fervently.

c. Moreover, prayer offered *in common* with others has a special efficacy. And such are ordinarily the devotions performed in the church, which is the place where the faithful unite in prayer. Here, if anywhere, we may hope that our prayers will bear the special fruits which Christ promises in the well known words: "Where there are two or three gathered together in My name, there am I in the midst of them" (Matt. xviii. 20).

d. Finally, it is a duty of charity, which is incumbent on all of us, to profess our faith openly, and to give edification to our neighbor by our *good example*. This is an obligation which is overlooked by many, but which, nevertheless, is a sacred duty. Now, the practical means of discharging this obligation is the regular frequenting of the church, and devout behavior in the house of God. Hence we find that those who neglect to go to church are commonly considered as infidels, freethinkers, or at least as bad Catholics, and thus are a cause of great scandal in a community; while, on the other hand, those who frequent the church and behave in a manner becoming the house of God are looked upon as good Christians, and give great edification to the faithful.

Whence you see, beloved brethren, how you are to judge of those who neglect church-going, and, if reminded of their duty, will flippantly answer you that the whole universe is God's temple, that there is no need of churches, that we can worship God anywhere. Where is their faith in the real presence of Jesus Christ? Where their reverence for Christ's Church and her divine service? Where their obedience to the Church's laws? Where are the fruits of their Christian lives? Christ Himself compares them to the heathen and the publican. Let us, therefore, not allow ourselves to be misled by the words and example of such lukewarm Christians, if Christians they may be called. Let us rather look at the example of the early Christians and of the persecuted faithful of more modern times, who practised their religion, frequented their churches, at the risk and even at the cost of their lives. Let us thank God that we enjoy the freedom of practising our religion openly, and let it be our consolation and our pride to frequent our church. Particularly, let us be careful not only to hear Mass but also to frequent the other public services of the church on Sundays and festivals of obligation; thus the blessing of God will attend us, and lead us to the reward of the faithful followers of Christ. Amen.

Fifth Sermon.

APOSTLESHIP OF PRAYER.

"In one Spirit were we all baptized into one body."—I. Cor. xii. 13.

DEARLY beloved brethren, in the preceding discourse I pointed out to you how prayer is to be practised in regard to time and place. It remains for us still to consider how it is to be practised in regard to our neighbor, or to answer the question: for whom should we pray? The practice of prayer for our neighbors is commonly called *apostleship of prayer;* and justly so; for by prayer we may exercise a real apostolate in behalf of our neighbor. With regard to the practice of this apostolic function of prayer, which is to form the subject of to-day's discourse, two things particularly must claim our attention: the motives which should incite us to pray for our neighbors, and the requisites of a truly apostolic prayer. The former will urge us to cultivate this most fruitful kind of prayer; the latter will teach us how to practise it. The subject and division of my discourse will, accordingly, be—

1. *The motives of the apostleship of prayer;*
2. *The requisites for its fruitful practice.*

I. MOTIVES.

There are chiefly two motives which should incite us to the fervent exercise of the apostleship of prayer.

1. The first motive of exercising this apostolate is the duty which is incumbent upon us to promote the *spiritual welfare of our neighbor.* This duty arises from the communion or brotherhood that exists between

all men. We all are children of one and the same Father, who is in heaven. We all are descendants of the same first parents, and are, consequently, brothers and sisters. We all have one common end—that infinite and eternal happiness for which God has created us—one and the same Redeemer, Jesus Christ, the Son of God, who laid down His life for us. Much closer, however, is our relationship to one another as Christians. As Christians we are members of the same family, of which Christ is the head; we are members of the Church, which is the family, the mystical body of Jesus Christ. For the Apostle says: "As in one body we have many members, so we, being many, are one body in Christ, and every one members one of another" (Rom. xii. 4, 5).

This kindred and spiritual *brotherhood in Christ* renders brotherly love, and particularly the concern for our neighbor's spiritual welfare, a sacred duty. For, are not the members of the same family bound to love one another, and to promote each other's spiritual as well as temporal welfare? What does the Apostle St. Paul teach us concerning this duty? "As the body," he says, "is one, and hath many members; and all the members of the body, whereas they are many, yet are one body, so also is Christ.... The eye cannot say to the hand: I need not thy help, nor again the head to the feet: I have no need of you. Yea, much more those that seem to be the more feeble members of the body are more necessary.... God hath tempered the body together, giving to that which wanted the more abundant honor that there might be no schism in the body but the members might be mutually careful one for another. And if one member suffer anything, all the members suffer with it; or if one member glory, all the members rejoice with it. Now you are the body of Christ and members of member" (I. Cor. xii. 12-27). How clearly does the Apostle here show that it is the duty of every one of us to promote the welfare, especially the eternal welfare, of his neighbor; and, accordingly, to exert himself, to the utmost of his power, for the salvation of his neighbor's soul! But as the spiritual welfare of our neighbor is promoted most effectually by the apostleship of prayer, it is manifest that all Christians without exception are called to the exercise of this apostolate.

Hence you see that the practice of prayer for our neighbor has been justly called *an apostleship;* because it springs from that same active and sympathetic love which urged the apostles to the preaching of the Gospel for the salvation of man. Therefore St. Chrysostom says: "Whoever mourns for the sins of others, his heart is filled with apostolic love; he follows the example of St. Paul, who says: Who is weak, and I am not weak? Who is scandalized and I do not burn?" The duty which rests upon us to promote the spiritual welfare of our neighbors, therefore, strongly urges us to the exercise of the apostleship of prayer.

2. The second motive which should impel us to exercise this apostolate is *its efficacy*. This apostolic prayer is like a two-edged sword; it has a twofold efficiency—one for our neighbor, for whom we pray; and one for ourselves, who pray.

a. The efficacy of our prayers *in behalf of our neighbor* is not infallible, it is true; but it is most powerful. For all the prayers we offer for our neighbors, like those we offer for ourselves, will assuredly be heard by Almighty God, unless the person for whom we pray puts an obstacle in the way of God's grace. This is the teaching of St. Thomas; and it is, besides, based on solid reasons. For, if God were not disposed to hear our prayers in behalf of our neighbors, Christ would not have exhorted us to pray for them. "God would not urge us to pray," says St. Augustine, "if it were not His intention to grant us what we ask." But Christ emphatically does exhort us to pray for our neighbors. He Himself practised the apostleship of prayer, and by His example made it a standing institution in His Church. For full thirty years He carried on His own divine apostolate, not by His preaching, but by His prayers and example. Christ's life is a practical instruction on apostolic prayer. But the same instruction we find conveyed in His words. When His apostles asked Him to teach them how to pray, He answered: When you pray, say: *"Our* Father"—not *my* Father—to intimate that they were to pray in the name of all, and for all: Thy kingdom come" (to all men without exception); " give *us our* daily bread "—not give *me my* daily bread—and, in like manner, in all the other petitions He teaches us that our prayers should extend to all men. And thus He Himself prays the night before His passion for His apostles and for all mankind; nay, He prays on the cross even for His enemies: "Father, forgive them, for they know not what they do!" Christ, therefore, by word and example teaches us to exercise this apostolate of prayer.

Therefore the apostles repeatedly exhort the faithful to pray for the spiritual welfare and salvation of their neighbors. Thus St. James writes: "Pray one for another, that you may be saved; for the continual prayer of a just man availeth much" (James v. 16). And St. Paul writes to his disciple Timothy: " I desire, first of all, that supplications, prayers, intercessions, and thanksgivings be made for all men; for kings, and for all who are in high station, that we may lead a quiet and a peaceable life, in all piety and chastity ; for this is good and acceptable in the sight of God our Saviour, who will have all men to be saved, and to come to the knowledge of the truth " (I. Tim. ii. 1-4). Since, therefore, Christ Himself by word and example has instituted the apostleship of prayer, and so emphatically exhorts us by His apostles to practise it, He certainly intends to hear our prayers in behalf of our neighbors, unless, perchance, these themselves place an obstacle in the way of His grace. The prayers we offer for our neighbors, therefore, have the same effect as those we offer for ourselves, provided they do not meet a positive hindrance in those for whom we pray. But even in this case, as St. Alphonsus Liguori teaches, God in His infinite mercy often removes the hindrance and grants them the benefit of our prayers.

b. The second effect of the apostleship of prayer refers to *ourselves.* This efficacy is an infallible one to the full extent of Christ's promises. Our prayers in behalf of our neighbors, though, for the reason stated, they may not be heard in favor of those for whom they have been offered, are always of the greatest advantage to ourselves. For, by praying for our neighbor, we perform a most eminent *work of charity*—a work which has for its object, not the temporal interest, but the eternal welfare of our neighbor. If the cup of cold water which we extend to the thirsty does not go without its reward, what reward may he not expect who daily by his prayers relieves the spiritual necessity of thousands of poor, miserable souls ? Therefore St. John Damascene writes: " Let no one think that what we offer in faith will not meet with its ample reward. It produces its fruits first for ourselves and then for our neighbor. For God is not unjust, that He could be unmindful of our good work."

Another great advantage which accrues to us from the practice of apostolic prayer, an advantage which cannot be over-estimated, is that it renders God more *disposed to hear our prayers* in our own behalf, according to the words of Our Saviour: "Blessed are the merciful, for they shall obtain mercy" (Matt. v. 7).

Finally, with regard to the advantages which we ourselves derive from our prayers for *the dead*, St. Alphonsus says: "I take it for certain that a soul that has been delivered from purgatory by the prayers of a pious Christian continually prays to God: Lord, permit not him to be lost, who has freed me from my sufferings, to whom I owe the blessedness of being sooner admitted to Thy beatific vision!"

The practice of apostolic prayer is, therefore, on the one hand, a sacred duty for all; and, on the other hand, a source of the most precious spiritual blessings, both for our neighbors and for ourselves. It only remains for me, further, to show you what is required for its fruitful practice.

II. REQUIREMENTS.

Now, what is required for the proper and fruitful exercise of this apostolate? Two things: the proper aim or purpose which we should have in view, and the just extent or measure according to which we should practise it.

1. The *aim* which we should have in view in the exercise of the apostleship of prayer is the true spiritual welfare and the eternal salvation of our neighbor. Now, the spiritual welfare and the eternal salvation of the faithful at large depend, to a very great extent, upon the well-being of the Church, and upon her freedom in the exercise of her mission for the salvation of souls.

a. The chief object of this apostolate should, therefore, be the *removal of those obstacles* that trammel the activity of the Church, and thus endanger the salvation of souls. To illustrate the extent and importance of this task, we need only cast a glance at the state of the Church at the present day. We behold her on all sides, like her Divine Spouse, wounded, bruised, heaped with reproaches by her enemies. She, too, is crowned with thorns, laden with the cross, and walks on the sorrowful way of the cross, amid the reproaches, insults, and blasphemies of an infuriated mob of scoffers. The mighty ones of this world arise against her, and not being able to destroy her, clog her activity, and do all they can to impair her vitality. Many of her own children join the standard of the enemies and outstrip them in their hate and fury. And what shall I say of the millions who are still pining in the darkness of paganism, infidelity, and error? What of the numbers of her children who, despite the treasures of grace deposited in her keeping, walk on the way to eternal perdition? All these are obstacles which trammel the activity of the Church and are to thousands of souls the cause of eternal ruin. What a boundless field of action for the apostleship of prayer!

Can we, then, beloved brethren, *look on with indifference* while the Church is thus afflicted, and so many souls run headlong to perdition? Is not the Church our mother? Has she not brought us forth to the life of grace in baptism? Has she not since then watched over us, and provided for us with a mother's tenderness? Are we not indebted to her for our claim to eternal happiness, and the effectual means of obtaining it? Do we not, therefore, owe her the sincerest gratitude? And should we not show our thankfulness, above all, by sympathizing with her in her sufferings? And how can we pay her this debt of gratitude in a more effectual way than by offering constant prayers and supplications to Almighty God, that He may come to the relief and rescue of our holy mother, the Church? But, as to the numberless souls who are treading the path of destruction, are they not our brothers, the children of the same mother, redeemed by the same precious blood of Jesus Christ? Is it not the duty of fraternal charity, therefore, on our part to come to their assistance with our prayers? Pray, then, beloved brethren, for the enemies of the Church, that their pride may be humbled, and that they may be converted to God, in order that the Church may, free and untrammelled, exercise her mission in this world, and bring back to the way of grace and truth the millions that are groping in darkness, and sitting in the shadow of death. The first object of the apostleship of prayer is, therefore, the removal of those obstacles that impede the Church in the exercise of her saving mission.

b. The second object of apostolic prayer is the *furtherance of the Church's efforts* for the salvation of souls. But, as nothing so promotes the work of the Church here on earth as good and zealous bishops and priests, it is especially the task of the apostleship of prayer to implore God incessantly to send good laborers into His vineyard—wise and zealous bishops, and good and worthy pastors, to aid them in their apostolic work—to pray to God, as we are taught in the Litany of the Saints, that He may preserve the Supreme Pastor, the Pope, and all the ranks of the clergy in His holy service. If we consider this twofold function of the apostolate of prayer, we may see that it is nowise inferior to the active apostolate in the Lord's vineyard, and that, consequently, those who exercise it are indeed apostles in the eyes of God. Those who fervently exercise this apostleship will find that, when the day of reckoning shall come, they shall have a copious harvest of souls to present to the Lord of the vineyard.

2. The second requirement of the apostleship of prayer is the *proper measure, or extent*, according to which it is to be exercised. The rule here to be observed is that of charity: viz., that, while we exclude no one from our prayers, we pray for the different classes of our fellow-men according to the closer or more distant relation in which we stand to them.

a. We should *exclude none* from the benefit of our prayers; but, on the contrary, we should pray for all without exception; for all without exception, as we have seen, are our kindred and our brethren. Hence the Apostle exhorts us to pray—to offer supplications, prayers, intercessions, and thanksgivings—for all men.

b. We should, as a rule, pray more for *the faithful*, who are more closely united to us by the ties of spiritual brotherhood, than for those who are outside the fold of Christ. The faithful are the members of Jesus Christ, members of the same mystic body with us, and have, therefore, a stricter claim on our love and spiritual aid than those who do not belong to the communion of the faithful.

c. Others, again, have a still *more special claim* on our prayers. We should pray in an especial manner for our parents, brothers, and sisters; for relatives, friends, and benefactors; for the suffering souls in purgatory; for our enemies, and for all poor sinners. That our first duty is towards our parents is evident; for they are our greatest benefactors. To them next to God we owe our existence and our support. They have made us partakers of the blessings of our religion—of faith, of baptism, and the other sacraments of the Church. In like manner, we should pray for our other temporal and spiritual benefactors. Besides, we have a special duty towards our relatives and friends, owing to the close relation which we bear to them. We are bound to pray for them in the same degree as we are bound to love them. All those claims together, and their miserable and helpless state besides, urge upon us the necessity of praying for the suffering souls in purgatory; while a special command of Our Lord makes it a duty for us to pray for our enemies (Matt. iv. 44). And who does not see that we have a special duty by our prayers to rescue, if possible, the sinner who is walking on the brink of eternal ruin?

In this course of sermons I have endeavored to give you an exhaustive exposition of prayer, as far as it was possible within the prescribed limits of time. We have considered the subject in all its bearings. And you have, doubtless, come to the conviction that in the work of our salvation there is nothing of greater importance than prayer; that prayer is, therefore, not a secondary matter, but a matter of sovereign moment; that, consequently, our life should be a life of prayer; that prayer should be, as it were, the atmosphere in which we should live, and move, and have our being. Let us, then, beloved brethren, henceforth live up to this conviction; let us make prayer the most important matter of our lives. If we do so, its exercise will daily become easier, more agreeable, and more consoling for us. We shall enjoy an unspeakable peace in life; and in death, upon which ultimately all depends, we shall reap solid consolation, the well-grounded and unwavering hope to obtain that everlasting bliss which is pre-eminently the fruit of persevering prayer. Amen.

LENTEN SERMONS.

Second Course.

On Sufferings.

First Sermon.

SOURCES OF SUFFERINGS.

"Through many tribulations we must enter into the kingdom of God."—Acts xiv. 21.

THESE words, beloved brethren, by which St. Luke in the Acts of the Apostles describes the theme of St. Paul's preaching to the newly converted Christians, have their true application to all of us. For there is none amongst us but wishes and hopes once to enter the kingdom of heaven, to save his soul; and, consequently, there is none amongst us who is altogether free from sufferings and afflictions. But suffering alone will not secure for us eternal salvation. If we, on our part, neglect to make our sufferings fruitful, if we fail to accept and bear them in the right spirit, they will be of little avail for our salvation. It is, therefore, of the greatest importance that we look upon the sufferings of this life in the true light, and that we learn to bear them in such a manner as to make them fruitful for eternal life. I have, for that reason, determined to take for the subject of these Lenten discourses *the sufferings of this life*. And I had the less misgiving in making this choice, because Lent, being a season of penance, is the time when we are disposed to occupy ourselves with earnest thoughts.

By sufferings or afflictions I understand whatever is disagreeable to human nature, such as poverty, contempt, sickness, persecution, temptations, and the like. To give the subject as full a treatment as the time assigned me will permit, I shall lay before you successively the *sources*, the *effects*, and the *remedies* of sufferings. In the present discourse the sources of sufferings will claim your attention.

What, then, is the origin of our sufferings, or whence are we ultimately to derive them? From two principal sources—(1) from *God*, who is their author; (2) from *sin*, on account of which He inflicts, or permits them.

I. GOD THE AUTHOR OF OUR SUFFERINGS.

1. The first source, the supreme cause and *author of our sufferings* is God Himself. It is He who in His goodness and providence inflicts them upon us for our own good. So Holy Scripture teaches us. "Good things and evil, life and death, poverty and riches, are from God" (Ecclus. xi. 14). And again: "I am the Lord, and there is none else; I form the light and create darkness; I make peace and create evil; I [am] the Lord, that do all these things" (Is. xlv. 6, 7). In another place we read: "Shall there be evil in a city, which the Lord hath not done?" (Amos iii. 6.) And to omit innumerable other passages, how does the patient and God-fearing Job judge of the origin of his sufferings? Does he ascribe them ultimately to the influence of the evil one? Does he say: God gave, and the devil hath taken away? No; he says: The Lord gave and the Lord hath taken away; as it hath pleased the Lord, so is it done; blessed be the name of the Lord (Job i. 21). Whether our sufferings, then, come directly from natural causes, from our fellow-men, or from the evil spirit, it is He whose voice all things obey, whom we must bless, fear, invoke, and endeavor to appease; for He it is whose zeal, according to the words of Holy Writ, takes up arms, and who arms the creature for the revenge of His enemies (Wis. v. 18). Almighty God, says St. Clement, will come on the Day of Judgment

with power, and in a great pitched battle make war upon the sins and iniquity of the wicked; then shall come that great affliction, which the Lord hath foretold—tribulation such as never has been, and never shall be. But, in order that men might not think that He is now asleep, He from time to time makes inroads into the land of His enemies, and in slight skirmishes inflicts sensitive wounds upon them. Thus He sends pestilence, which carries off thousands; wars, which devastate whole countries; inundations, which sweep down man and beast, and whatever lies in their course; stagnation in business and financial crises, which leave multitudes of men breadless and penniless. Those who know not God take all this, 'tis true, as a mere natural course of events; but they are, none the less, according to the teaching of Scripture, the armed forces of the Most High, that make war upon the vices of men. However, these divine visitations are not of long duration, nor do they utterly disturb the order and well-being of human society; because the day of the great decisive battle has not yet come. God does not yet send His full forces against us; but He commands pestilence, and famine, and the elements of nature, and evil times—all of which are, as it were, His light troops —to sally forth against us; but He recalls them when they have but inflicted a slight chastisement on us.

Hence it is plain that God Himself is the prime author of our afflictions. But it follows, at the same time, that the sufferings of this life are for us the most *salutary penance*, provided we bear them in the proper spirit, with patience and resignation. This penance is the most pleasing to God, because He Himself, the author of our sufferings, imposes it upon us. It is a penance free from all self-love, because it is not of our own choice. It is the most useful and effectual penance, because God in His infinite wisdom best knows that chastisement which is most suitable for us, and in His goodness sends us that which is best suited and most useful for us.

Now, the *best means* to bear our sufferings with patience and resignation is thus to look upon them in the light of faith as coming from God, sent us by Him for our spiritual advantage. In this thought we will always find strength and consolation in our sufferings. And, in fact, what can be more encouraging and consoling than the thought that all our afflictions come from Him who is our loving Father, who, therefore, will permit no trial to come upon us which we are not able to bear, and which is not for our spiritual advantage?

2. It is, moreover, a source of consolation to us to know that all our sufferings have not only God as their author and first cause, but that they are the outcome of that *universal providence*, by means of which He governs the universe. God's all-ruling providence orders and controls the universe in all its details, and even in its minutest operations and movements. The same divine providence directs the free actions of men, so that they ultimately tend to the greater glory of the Creator.

This doctrine is so clearly laid down in *Holy Scripture*, that it cannot admit of a doubt. Thus says, for instance, the Wise Man: "He [God] hath made the little and the great, and hath equally care of all" (Wis. vi. 8). And again: "He reacheth from end to end mightily, and ordereth all things sweetly" (Ibid. viii. 1). And does not Jesus Christ Himself clearly teach us the same truth? "Are not two sparrows," He says, "sold for a farthing? And not one of them shall fall on the ground without your Father. But the very hairs of your head are all numbered. Fear not, therefore, better are you than many sparrows" (Matt. x. 29–31).

But *reason* itself, as well as Scripture, convinces us of the universal ruling of divine providence. For the marvellous order so conspicuous in the universe, that order by which its numberless, varied, and even conflicting elements are harmoniously combined to a most admirable unity—that wonderful order, I say, proves to evidence the existence of an all-ruling providence. For, as St. Athanasius remarks, if you listen in the distance to a harmonious piece of music played on the lyre, will you imagine that the melody is produced by the inert instrument, without the guiding hand of an intelligent artist? Though you see no one, you recognize the ruling of a rational being. How, then, could you attribute the exquisite harmony which pervades this universe to the agency of inert matter or to mere accident, not to the ruling of an all-intelligent cause, that is, a divine providence?

Now, this all-ruling providence is, as it were, the instrument which Almighty God uses to inflict upon us His fatherly chastisements. By this means He sends us not only those sufferings which come upon us without the fault of our fellow-men, but also those that are *unjustly inflicted* upon us by the sins of our neighbors; not that God is the cause or author of sin, which He supremely detests; but He permits sin by the free action of man for the greater good which thence arises. He permits sin, He allows man to abuse his free will and offend Him for the sake of those sufferings which are a source of greater merit to us, and of greater glory to Himself. It is only because by His wonderful providence He knows how to obtain good from evil —good which far outweighs the evil of sin, which enhances His glory more than sin can lessen it—that He can permit sin. Therefore St. Augustine says: "God prefers to bring forth good from evil rather than that no evil should exist." Do we not act on the same principle ourselves? Why do you sometimes cast into the fire the wood, which might still serve for better purposes? Is it not because you see that an advantage arises from burning it that more than counterbalances its loss for other purposes? In like manner, God in His goodness would never permit evil, unless He were able by His wisdom and power to derive greater good from it. Why did God permit so many holy prophets, so many apostles, so many martyrs, nay, His only-begotten Son, to be put to death? Could He not have prevented all that? Without the slightest difficulty; but He did not prevent it. He preferred the inestimable good that was to follow. And how inconceivably great was this good! How great is the glory and bliss of those who suffered! What glory have they not given to God, for whom they suffered! What graces and blessings have not their sufferings brought on the whole world! How many immortal souls have been saved by the passion of Jesus Christ and by the example of the martyrs!

It is, therefore, certain beyond doubt that also the sufferings inflicted on us by the malice of men ultimately come from God through His wise providence for our own greater good. If, then, we suffer slander or detraction or any other kind of injustice from our neighbor, it is most unreasonable on our part to see in this only the malice of men. We must *look beyond the immediate causes* of our wrongs and sufferings; we must see the providence of God, God Himself, the author of our sufferings, who permits this evil for our good. If you do so, beloved brethren, you will not so easily allow yourselves to be carried away by your own passions to impatience, complaints, murmurings, imprecations, anger, hatred, enmities, and revenge. No, you will receive your sufferings as blessings and favors from the hand of God, and bear them with Christian meekness, patience, and resignation.

II. SIN THE CAUSE OF OUR SUFFERINGS.

Though God is the author of our sufferings, yet He does not inflict them upon us for their own sake, or because He delights in our afflictions, but as a chastisement for sin. Sin is, therefore, the cause which moves God to inflict them upon us. God, it is true, could have in the beginning created man, as he now is, subject to sufferings and to death. But in His infinite goodness He created him not in his present state. He chose to elevate him to a supernatural state, and so to endow him with preternatural gifts, that he was exempt from sufferings and death. As the body that is embalmed is preserved from corruption, so the body of the first man was, as it were, pervaded by the supernatural grace of God, so that, though naturally mortal and liable to suffer, it was by the agency of grace rendered immortal and impassible. But by the sin of our first parents this supernatural virtue was lost; sufferings came and brought death in their wake. Such was the bitter fruit of the disobedience of God's law. " God made man from the beginning," says the Scripture, " and left him in the hand of his own counsel. He added His commandments and precepts. If thou wilt keep the commandments, and perform acceptable fidelity forever, they shall preserve thee" (Ecclus. xv. 14-16). Such was the original condition of our first parents.

But they did not keep the commandment, and therefore the commandment did not preserve them. *They sinned*. Now, abandoned to his own nature, our first father soon became conscious of the dread fact that all flesh is perishable. He learned the truth of the words: "Dust thou art, and into dust thou shalt return" (Gen. iii. 19); and, "In what day soever thou shalt eat of it [the forbidden tree] thou shalt die the death" (Ibid. ii. 17). The inevitable sentence of death is pronounced upon him and all posterity. Hence the Apostle writes: "By one man sin entered into this world, and by sin death; and so death passed upon all men" (Rom. v. 12).

What a *terrible chastisement*, beloved brethren! Is this punishment alone not sufficient to reveal to us the dreadful malice of sin? Terrible was the chastisement inflicted on Pharao, when he himself and all his forces were engulfed in the waters of the Red Sea; still more terrible was the judgment executed on the wicked cities of Sodom and Gomorrha; much more terrible was the punishment of the Deluge, that swept man and beast from the face of the earth. But none of these divine chastisements can be compared with that inflicted for the sin of our first father, entailing as it did the death-sentence on all mankind. What a dreadful evil, what a terrible crime is sin, which deserves such a punishment! By this one sin we are all, like so many criminals, under the sentence of death, awaiting the hand of the executioner. Sin, therefore, hath brought death into the world. Since the first sin has been committed death reigns as king in the world. He strides triumphantly over land and sea, and with him the numberless army of ills and afflictions, which make up his following, and execute his orders. How truly, then, does the Apostle say: "The wages of sin is death!" (Rom. vi. 23.) How true is the proverb, "sin maketh nations miserable!" (Prov. xiv. 34.)

Not only the sin of our first parents, however, but

also our own *personal sins* are the cause of our sufferings. If we read the history of the Jewish people and the history of the Church we frequently meet with great chastisements, which are manifestly traceable to the sins of the people at large or of certain classes. And as it is with nations and classes, so it is with individuals. But time does not permit me further to enlarge on this subject.

If, then, beloved brethren, evils befall you; if sufferings and afflictions come upon you, whether it be ill health, or temporal losses, or slander and detraction, or family troubles, or differences with your neighbors; lay not the blame on the elements or on men, but on the true causes, on your own past and present sins. Remember how often you deserved eternal punishment for your sins, and what would now be your lot, had not the mercy of God preserved you from this sad fate. And then ask yourself: what is all I now suffer compared with the pains of hell, which I have so often merited for my sins? Thus did the saints of God; and, therefore, they bore their sufferings not only patiently but magnanimously. And thus you, too, will bear all your afflictions with resignation if you look upon them in this light, and cherish the same sentiments as the saints did. Thus your sufferings will not make you unhappy and discontent with your lot; they will not mislead you to murmurs and complaints, but they will be for you a source of merit and glory, which will triumph over suffering and death; for it is written: "Through many tribulations we must enter into the kingdom of God." Amen.

Second Sermon.
FRUITS OF SUFFERINGS.

"He that is patient is governed with much wisdom; but he that is impatient exalteth his folly."—Prov. xiv. 29.

HAVING in the preceding discourse considered the sources of sufferings—which are God Himself and His loving providence, on the one hand, and sin, both original and actual, on the other—we now proceed to consider their fruits. The fruits of our sufferings are good or evil, according as we bear them patiently or impatiently; as is hinted at in the words of my text: "He that is patient is governed with much wisdom; but he that is impatient exalteth his folly." I shall, therefore, endeavor to show you—

1. *The evil fruits of sufferings borne impatiently;*
2. *The good fruits of sufferings borne patiently.*

I. EVIL FRUITS.

The effects of those sufferings, beloved brethren, which are not accepted with resignation and borne with patience are of a very malicious character. The tree of suffering when planted in such soil commonly produces bitter and poisonous fruits.

1. The first of those bitter fruits is *grief and sadness* on account of the afflictions themselves—at the loss of temporal goods, of fortune, health, reputation, friends, relatives, comfort, etc. And this fruit is the more bitter for the impatient, because their whole heart clings to what they have lost. Their sorrow does not depend on the value of the object lost; for often it is

only a mere trifle of no real value, a matter that has value only in their own fancy, that makes them unhappy. This we find illustrated in the case of Aman in the Book of Esther. Although he occupied the most honorable position at the king's court; although he possessed riches, and honors, and pleasures in abundance, yet one trifling circumstance, viz., that Mardochæus refused to take off his hat to him, sufficed to render him completely unhappy.

2. But more bitter still is the *harvest of sin* which the impatient reap from their sufferings. To what crimes and outrages does not their impatience drive them! For, how often do we not find that infidelity, dishonesty, murder, adultery, blasphemy, and despair have originated from impatience in afflictions! Whence comes it that there are such as doubt or deny the existence of a divine providence? It comes from the fact that they see the wicked prosper, while they themselves and others whom they consider just and pious men are unable to succeed in the world. This the impatient, blinded by their passion, can neither relish, nor understand; and consequently they begin to doubt the existence of an all-ruling, just providence. But impatience in suffering is likewise the source of many other sins. For, whence come so many thefts and dishonesties? From the fact that so many are impatient of the inconveniences caused by poverty and want, and, consequently, have recourse to dishonest practices. What is the cause of so many murders? It is the fact that many are unable to bear up under the violent pressure of the passion of anger and revenge. Whence comes it that so many abandon themselves a prey to the lusts of the flesh? It comes from the sad fact that they have not the patience and perseverance to struggle successfully against their own

concupiscence and the temptations of the devil. And how can we account for the deplorable fact that so many, contrary to the voice of nature, lay violent hands upon themselves? By the mere fact that they have not learned to bear afflictions with patience. They are like shy horses, that, to escape a harmless, but dreaded object, leap headlong down the steepest precipice. Blinded by their impatience and fear of present evils, real or imaginary, they reflect not on their future lot; and, wishing to free themselves from a short-lived affliction, they blindly thrust themselves into the fathomless abyss of misery, from which there is no escape for all eternity. Finally, whence so many curses, imprecations, and blasphemies against God and man? What are these else than the bitter and poisonous outgrowth of impatience in sufferings and afflictions?

3. The third and last fruit of impatience in suffering—the most baneful of all—is *obstinacy in sin*, which leads directly to eternal ruin. As potter's clay is hardened by the scorching rays of the sun, so the wicked become more and more obdurate under the influence of sufferings and tribulations. Thus it was with Pharao. The greater the scourges which Almighty God sent for his correction, the more obstinate he became, until, at last, he lost his first-born, his whole army, his crown and his life, and thus came before the all-just tribunal of God.

Such are the fruits which sufferings produce in those who do not receive them in the right spirit, who do not accept them with resignation from the hand of the Almighty and All-wise. Their lives are embittered with grief and sadness at their losses; they are driven to all manner of crimes and enormities; and, finally, they become confirmed in their wickedness, and walk the broad way to destruction. Are these not bitter fruits, indeed, infinitely more bitter than all the griefs and inconveniences resulting from the sufferings themselves? And should this fact not be for us a powerful motive cheerfully to accept all sufferings from the hand of the Most High, and to bear them without complaint or murmur?

II. GOOD FRUITS.

The sufferings that fall upon good soil and are borne with patience and resignation bear the choicest and most precious fruits. They cleanse us from sin and its effects; they enlighten our understanding; they lead us to the highest degree of Christian perfection.

1. They *cleanse us from sin* and its effects. That sufferings, borne in the true spirit, have the salutary effect of washing away our sins cannot be doubted; for the Holy Ghost Himself says: "God is compassionate and merciful, and will forgive sins in the day of tribulation" (Ecclus. ii. 13). It is peculiar to sufferings to bring man to reflect upon himself; to detach him from the things of this world; to make him enter into his own heart, see his own weakness and helplessness, turn to Almighty God, and seek consolation and strength with Him. This fact we see illustrated in David, who says of himself: "Day and night Thy hand was heavy upon me; I am turned in my anguish, whilst the thorn is fastened" (Ps. xxxi. 4). And what does our blessed Lord say of the prodigal son? After he began to suffer want, "returning to himself," he said: "I will arise and go to my father" (Luke xv. 17, 18). It was only under the pressure of distress and suffering that he entered into himself and resolved to return to his father. And sufferings have still the same efficacy. How often does it not happen that one

who has for many years lived in riot and dissipation, when prostrate on a bed of sickness, or stricken by some other misfortune, at once stops short in his wicked career, and, like the prodigal in the gospel, enters into himself, and seeks reconciliation with God? Are there not perhaps here present some who have thus been brought to a better life; who under the pressure of suffering have been brought to see the errors of their lives; who have thus been reconciled to God by a good confession, and have since lived a truly Christian life? By suffering, therefore, we are cleansed from our sins, that is, we are disposed to receive the Sacrament of Reconciliation worthily, whereby we are finally washed from our sins.

But sufferings, moreover, cleanse us from the effects of sin. In the first place, they wholly, or in part, cancel the debt of *temporal punishment* due to our sins, for which we would otherwise have to satisfy in purgatory. And this is of the greatest advantage for us. To illustrate this truth let us take the following comparison. Two wayfarers come to an inn, where they take up their quarters and make common mess. After they have contracted a certain amount of debt in common, one of them takes his departure without paying his share of the bill. What is the result? The one on hand is held answerable for the full amount, and, if he is unable or unwilling to pay it, is cast into prison until the last farthing is paid off. Now, let us make the application to our own case. The two companions are our body and our soul. They take up their abode, and lead a common life in this earthly mansion; and thus they contract a common debt by their sins, whether these be committed by sensuality, which has its principal seat in the body, or by pride and self-exaltation, which is the peculiar sin of the spirit. Each bears its part of the responsibility. But what happens? Death comes and snatches away the body, which again returns to the dust from which it was taken. Consequently the soul alone is held answerable for the full amount of the debt; and, as it no longer has wherewith to pay, it is detained in the prison of purgatory until it pays off the last farthing, that is, until it has atoned for the entire debt of temporal punishment. What a dreadful misfortune it is, then, to die without having paid at least a portion of the debt of temporal punishment due to our sins! But God in His mercy provides us with means for its payment in this life by sending us sufferings and afflictions. Thus soul and body in common co-operate in the payment of the debt which they have contracted in common. Is this not a signal favor on the part of God? The debt must be paid either in this life or in the life to come. And how much easier is it not to pay it in this life. Here, as I said, body and soul co-operate. Here we do not atone according to the rigor of justice, but according to the sweet law of mercy. Here our sufferings are not only satisfactory, but also meritorious, and will, therefore, add to our future glory. Must not these considerations be for us the strongest motives joyfully to accept from the hand of God those sufferings which are so beneficial to us?

Finally, sufferings not only cleanse us from personal sin and free us from the temporal punishment due to it, but they also purify us from *immoderate passions*. They weaken and check the impulses of that concupiscence, which is the parent of sin and the source of innumerable and grievous temptations. This concupiscence, according to the teaching of St. John (I. ii. 16), is threefold: the concupiscence of the flesh, or sensuality; the concupiscence of the eyes, or avarice; and the pride of life, or the desire of self-glorification. Now, there is no more effectual means of counteracting these immoderate lusts than those sufferings which are diametrically opposed to them. Sensuality is checked and mortified by the sufferings of the body; avarice is restrained by poverty, loss of fortune, and the like; and pride is humbled by humiliation, contempt, reproaches, and insults. There is no doubt, then, but the best means of cleansing and chastening our passions is to test them in the crucible of sufferings and afflictions.

2. The second good fruit of sufferings, borne in a Christian spirit, is true *enlightenment* of the understanding. Sufferings might justly be compared with the fish's gall with which the younger Tobias anointed his father's eyes and cured his blindness (Tob. xi. 13). They are bitter as gall; like the fish's gall they are the product of the sea, of the troublous sea of this world; but if properly used they open our eyes, not, indeed, the eyes of the body, but those of the soul, so that we see those truths that were heretofore hidden from us.

In the first place, we learn from the afflictions and sufferings of this life the true nature of *future punishment*. When we suffer in our bodies, when our limbs are shaken with fever, or racked with pains, it is quite natural that we should ask ourselves: If such a trifling malady or indisposition produces such dreadful pains, what must be the sufferings caused by hell-fire, which tortures not only the body, but also the soul; not only at intervals, but without ceasing and without relief; not only for a time, but for all eternity! Must we not, then, exclaim with the prophet Isaias: "Which of you can dwell with devouring fire? which of you shall dwell with everlasting burnings?" (Is. xxxiii. 14.)

The second lesson which afflictions teach us is the utter *nothingness of the things of this world*, and the consequent folly of those who seek their happiness in them. In the day of affliction it becomes palpable to us how easily all earthly goods can escape our grasp, and, consequently, how unstable and fleeting they are. An hour's illness convinces us of the unstability of health; a slight temporal loss, of the fickleness of fortune; a slanderous attack, of the vanity of earthly honors.

Besides, adversity or afflictions give us a true *knowledge of our fellow-men*, particularly of those with whom we are wont to associate. For in adversity we learn to distinguish our true friends, that is, those who love us for our own sake, from our apparent friends, or those who love us for the sake of our money, or for the pleasures and conveniences which we afford them. Our true friends remain faithful to us in misfortune and assist us according to their ability, while apparent friends abandon us as soon as they perceive that they have nothing more to hope from us.

Lastly, we obtain in afflictions the most valuable of all knowledge—*the knowledge of ourselves*. We learn to know our own weakness, to distrust ourselves, and to pray. As long as everything succeeds according to our wishes we are full of courage and self-reliance, and imagine that there is nothing too hard for us. But as soon as we encounter misfortune and distress, we are humbled, become conscious of our own weakness, and sensible of our insufficiency. Thus distrusting ourselves, and convinced of the incompetency of all earthly means, we take refuge to Almighty God, who alone has the will and the power to aid us. Our help is in the name of the Lord; our refuge is in heaven, not on earth. Thus sufferings really enlighten our understanding; they are our best and most efficient teachers.

3. The third fruit of sufferings, accepted and borne

in a Christian spirit, is *true Christian perfection*. In what does the perfection of a Christian consist? It consists in the love of God. So the Apostle teaches us, when he calls the love of God the fulfilment of the law, and the bond of perfection (Rom. xiii. 10; Col. iii. 14). It is, therefore, the fire of divine love which perfectly cleanses our souls, unites us with God, and makes us perfect. But, alas! the fire of charity is sometimes so weak in our hearts that it is hardly deserving of this name. The reason of this is that besides God our hearts cling to many other things. The heart of one is immoderately attached to his wife and family, or to his friends; that of another, to his fortune; that of a third, to honors and distinction; that of a fourth, to pleasures and amusements. And all these things are loved, not for God's sake, as they aught to be loved, but for their own sake, or for the sake of the gratification they afford, independently of God, to whom all love is due. Our love is, therefore, commonly divided between God and many other objects.

Now, what is the cause of this division, and of this consequent weakness of our love? How is this languor on our part to be remedied? How is the love of God to be strengthened and inflamed in our hearts? The means which Almighty God often uses to gain our whole heart and all its affections are sufferings and afflictions. And these are also the most *effectual means*. Why so? Because they take from us those objects to which our hearts were attached, those objects which divided our affections and deprived God of the love that is due to Him alone. Thus death often takes away those that stood between us and Almighty God; temporal losses and reverses of fortune remove those earthly goods to which our hearts were immoderately attached. Ill health and sickness not only remove the object of our self-love, but also give us a distaste for the pleasures and amusements of the world. Thus you see that sufferings force us to a great extent to detach our hearts from the goods of this world, and to give all our affections to God ; and, therefore, they inflame our hearts with the love of God, which is the summit of Christian perfection.

You see, then, beloved brethren, that sufferings and afflictions, though they are not without their grave dangers for those who do not receive them in the proper spirit, are yet the greatest blessings, provided we make a right use of them; whence you may learn in what light we are to consider them, and how we are to accept and to endure them—namely, as favors from the hands of the Almighty we are to look upon them, and as such we are to accept them with resignation and to endure them with patience. But as we cannot do so without employing the necessary means, you are doubtless eager to learn the means of making your sufferings fruitful for your salvation. The means of making our sufferings productive of eternal life will occupy our attention exclusively in the succeeding discourses. Do not, therefore, fail to be present at all these sermons, and you will find yourselves equipped with all the necessary means of making the sufferings of this life subservient to your eternal happiness. Amen.

Third Sermon.

REMEDIES AGAINST SUFFERINGS.

"Stand, therefore, having your loins girt about with truth."—Eph. vi. 14.

THE remedies against the sufferings of this life will claim our attention in this and the following sermons. By remedies I here understand those arms by which we may either entirely ward off, or considerably diminish our sufferings. These arms of the Christian soldier are summed up by the Apostle in his Epistle to the Ephesians. Having foretold the Christians of Ephesus that evil days, days of trial and tribulation, would come upon them, he exhorts them to put on the armor of God, that they may be strengthened in the Lord and be able to withstand the assaults of their enemies (Eph. vi). He then goes on to explain to them what he understands by the armor of God, and enumerates the various articles of which it is composed. And, first, he says, we should have our loins begirt with truth. The girdle of truth is, therefore, the first article of this divine panoply, and shall form the subject of the present discourse. We shall consider in succession (1) its *meaning*, (2) its *advantages*, and (3) the *means of securing* it.

I. MEANING OF THE GIRDLE OF TRUTH.

What, then, is the Apostle's meaning, when he exhorts us to gird our loins with the girdle of truth? By these words he would exhort us to appropriate to ourselves and secure the holy *virtue of chastity*. This angelic virtue is for various important and instructive reasons aptly compared with a girdle.

1. As it is the office of a girdle to encircle the loins and confine the body within certain dimensions, so this holy virtue of purity controls and *checks the lusts of the flesh*. St. Gregory, in his explanation of the words " Let your loins be girt, and lamps burning in your hands " (Luke xii. 35), says : " We gird our loins when by continence we check the desires of the flesh." Now, as a material girdle may be of two kinds—either a loose or a tight one—so also the girdle of chastity. The looser one is that chastity which is peculiar to married life, which consists in the abstinence from all carnal pleasures except those that are permitted by the law of God to those who live in the wedded state. The tight girdle is that of virginal chastity, which consists in the total abstinence from carnal pleasures. The former is obligatory on all those who live in the married state ; the latter is a strict obligation for all others— boys and girls, young men and young women, widowers and widows—to the same extent and in the same measure as on those who have consecrated themselves to God ; with the only difference that these latter (priests and religious) bind themselves under the special obligation of a vow. Whoever, therefore, will serve under the banner of Jesus Christ, whoever will follow Him, must faithfully wear the one or the other of these two girdles. There is no middle state. Therefore the Apostle addresses all without exception, and exhorts them to have their loins girt with truth, that is, with the girdle of chastity. As the belt was in ancient times the distinctive mark of the soldier, so that his admission to and retirement from the service were expressed by the phrase " to take," and " to lay down the belt," so this girdle of chastity is the characteristic device of the soldier of Jesus Christ. Whatever appearances of piety the impure or the adulterous may present,

though outwardly they may seem to be good Christians, yet they are not true soldiers of Jesus Christ; they do not belong to His active service; they are not of His standard. Hence you see the enormity of the sin of impurity. By this sin the soldier of Jesus Christ throws away the emblem of his Christian profession, becomes disloyal to his leader and untrue to his standard, sacrifices his merits and his honor, and deserves the punishment of a deserter and a renegade.

2. The second reason why the virtue of chastity is symbolized by a girdle is because it renders the Christian a service similar to that which his belt renders to the soldier. For the soldier's belt not only adds to the gracefulness and free movement of the body, but also serves as a convenient support for his sword, that he may have it always at hand and use it when occasion requires. Thus also the girdle of chastity affords the soldier of Christ the facility of always going armed with the *sword of the word of God* and wielding it as necessity demands, as the Apostle exhorts in the words: "Take the sword of the Spirit (which is the word of God)." Nothing contributes so much to the understanding, the appreciation, and the fulfilment of the word of God as does the angelic virtue of chastity. Therefore our Divine Lord says: "Blessed are the clean of heart, for they shall see God" (Matt. v. 8). One of the chief reasons why the word of God is not understood nor received in the right spirit, much less practically applied to their lives, by many, is that their hearts are defiled by impurity. Hence we read in the Book of Wisdom: "Wisdom will not enter into a malicious soul, nor dwell in a body subject to sins" (Wis. i. 4).

3. A third reason why this holy virtue is compared with a girdle is, because it girds us, that is, makes us

free and disentangled for the *following of Christ*. For, what is it that impedes us in the following of Christ? Is it not our passions, our immoderate desires and inclinations? Is it not covetousness, pride, and lust? Now, he who has obtained the mastery over the lusts of the flesh, he who has girded on the belt of chastity, is master of all his passions. For thus he has laid low the strongest of his enemies; and as David after slaying Goliath easily put to flight the rest of the Philistines, so he who has subdued this Goliath among the passions obtains an easy victory over the rest. The girdle of chastity, therefore, removes the hindrances which impede us in the following of Christ, and thus enables us to follow Him with free and unencumbered pace.

The girdle of truth which the Apostle exhorts us to put on may, therefore, be aptly understood to signify the virtue of chastity, which, as I have shown you, is most necessary for all classes, the distinctive emblem of the soldier of Jesus Christ, the inseparable companion of the truly enlightened Christian, and the victory which overcomes all obstacles in the following of Jesus Christ. Let us, further, consider its—

II. ADVANTAGES AGAINST SUFFERINGS.

Holy chastity, beloved brethren, has a twofold advantage in regard to the sufferings and afflictions of this life. First, it preserves us from many and grievous afflictions; and, secondly, it enables us more easily to bear those which it cannot avert.

1. It *preserves* us from many grievous afflictions. Even conjugal chastity, or that peculiar to the married state, has this salutary effect; for it removes the two causes from which the greatest troubles of married people arise, viz., jealousy and immoderate sensu-

ality. Who can recount the numberless afflictions which flow from these two sources? Suffice it to say that these two vices extinguish mutual love in the hearts of husbands and wives, destroy all domestic happiness, are the cause of shameful diseases, poverty, dishonor, implacable enmities, and not seldom even of murder and suicide. Conjugal chastity is a remedy against all those evils; for, if married parties are armed with this virtue, they will foster mutual, chaste, and well-ordered charity; nor will they allow themselves to be carried away by jealousy, much less to be driven to other more atrocious excesses.

But much greater is the protection afforded by the girdle of *virginal chastity*. In the first place, it removes all those evils against which I said conjugal chastity is a preservative. Besides, it preserves its possessors from many other evils and afflictions. It relieves them from the various irksome duties connected with the married life; it exempts them from the obligation of providing for the wants and comforts, and conforming to the wishes and inclinations of another party; it frees them from the grave duty of bringing up children and providing for their maintenance and education; it preserves them from the vice of avarice, which is the source of so many afflictions; for he who has not to provide for a wife and children is easily satisfied with his station in life. Such a one easily finds his consolation and delight in God; and, if God is pleased to call him to a higher state, there is nothing to prevent him from following the divine vocation, abandoning all things, and giving himself entirely and without reserve to Almighty God—a thing which is impossible in the married state. The girdle of chastity, therefore, preserves from a multitude of afflictions.

2. It *moderates* those sufferings which it is unable

to prevent or remove, and thus renders them easy to be borne. Why? Because the virtue of chastity, which can neither be obtained nor preserved without great and continued effort, teaches us self-denial; because this virtue bestows upon us great inward peace and contentment of soul, which more than outweigh all the sufferings and afflictions of this life; because, being the most pleasing to God of all virtues, it secures for us His grace and assistance in an extraordinary measure.

The girdle of chastity is, therefore, in truth a powerful protection against the sufferings and afflictions of this life. But remember, my dear brethren, in order to afford this security it must be a *true* girdle, not a girdle in appearance only. Therefore the Apostle says: "Stand, having your loins girt about *with truth.*" By these words he would imply that we should not be satisfied with mere appearances, but must begird ourselves with genuine chastity. For, if we only wear the outward garb of chastity, if we are chaste only in body, but inwardly foster thoughts and desires of impurity, the girdle of chastity which we wear is not a true, but a counterfeit one, a sham which may deceive the eyes of men, but cannot deceive Almighty God, who looks into the inmost recesses of the heart. Or, if we preserve chastity inwardly and outwardly, but only to gain the approval of men, we do not wear the true girdle of chastity, the belt that signalizes the soldier of Jesus Christ. Or, if the motive which checks us from impurity is pride, avarice, or some other vice, we are not girded with truth; our chastity is not genuine, and cannot be pleasing to God. Who is it, then, that girds his loins with truth? He who, according to the teaching of Our Saviour (Matt. xix. 12), is pure in every regard, in thought, word, and deed, and that to make himself more pleasing to Almighty God. It was of such that the Lord said: "I will give to them, in My house, and within My walls, a place, and a name better than sons and daughters; I will give them an everlasting name, which shall never perish" (Is. lvi. 5). Hence you may see, beloved brethren, that the girdle of chastity is not only most advantageous as a remedy against the ills of this life, but at the same time absolutely necessary for salvation. Being, therefore, of the utmost importance for us, I shall briefly show you—

III. HOW TO SECURE IT.

1. This girdle, or gift of chastity, can be obtained only from Him who is its author, that is, *from God Himself*. Besides Him there is none other in heaven or on earth who can produce or bestow this heavenly gift. What does the Wise Man say of the origin of this virtue? "As I knew that I could not otherwise be continent, except God gave it, and this also was a point of wisdom, to know whose gift it was, I went to the Lord, and besought Him" (Wis. viii. 21). And what does Our Lord Himself say of this gift? "All receive not this word, but they to whom it is given" (Matt. xix. 11); that is, not all understand and follow the divine rule of chastity, but those who have received a special grace from above. The girdle of chastity is, therefore, the word of God, the gift of the Most High. Man of his own natural strength is unable to raise himself to the height of this sublime virtue.

2. While the girdle of chastity is a free gift of God, yet it cannot be obtained without our own co-operation. In order to secure it, we must pray fervently; but this is not enough. If our prayers should be heard, we must also—

a. Guard our senses, particularly our eyes, our ears,

and our tongue. He who neglects this will pray in vain for the grace of purity. For the senses are the gates through which sin, especially impurity, enters the soul. "Death has come up through our windows," says the prophet Jeremias (ix. 21); and again: "My eye hath wasted my soul" (Lament. iii. 51). Modest matrons and young women, says St. Basil, never entirely open the windows of their senses, in order that they may be always ready to close them, should they meet any indecent object. And this, beloved brethren, must be the rule of all to whom the virtue of chastity is dear.

b. We must *avoid the occasion* of sin—the society of the immodest and impure; for evil communications corrupt good manners (I. Cor. xv. 33); and no less carefully the society of bad books, which are even more mischievous. On the other hand, we must cultivate the society of the good and pure, and read pious books—the best means of promoting purity and gaining a distaste and hatred for all that is contrary to this holy virtue.

c. Finally, we must *frequent the sacraments*, especially the sacrament of penance. It is almost incredible, beloved brethren, how easily the malicious plans of the devil are frustrated by the use of frequent confession. As the king of Israel was invincible, as long as he made use of the advice of the prophet Eliseus, who revealed to him the plans of the enemies, so he who resorts to frequent confession, and follows the advice of his confessor, will be victorious over all the designs of the evil one (IV. Kings vi.).

Let us faithfully avail ourselves of these means, and Almighty God will hear our prayers, and encircle our loins with the girdle of true chastity. This precious girdle will avert numberless evils and afflictions from us, or, at least, enable us to bear them with patience and resignation. True, we cannot secure this treasure without effort; we cannot obtain the victory without combat. But let us not despond; let us look forward to the glorious reward, and follow the example of so many millions of Christian heroes and heroines of every age and condition, who have gained this glorious victory over themselves and over their enemies. Thus we, too, shall go forth victorious from the struggle, and shall once join them in the never-ending bliss of the heavenly kingdom. Amen.

Fourth Sermon.

REMEDIES AGAINST SUFFERINGS (CONTINUED).

"Take unto you the helmet of salvation, and the sword of the Spirit (which is the word of God)."—Eph. vi. 17.

THE girdle of chastity, as you saw in the preceding discourse, is an excellent remedy against the afflictions and sufferings of this life. It preserves us from many evils; and, at least, renders more bearable those which it is unable to ward off. But it is not the only remedy. To the armor of God, which the Apostle exhorts us to put on, belong other articles and other weapons, no less efficacious and no less necessary; and among these he next enumerates the *helmet of salvation* and the *sword of the Spirit*. Of these two pieces of the armor of the Christian soldier we shall treat in the present discourse, showing the meaning and use of each.

I. THE SWORD OF THE SPIRIT.

1. We shall begin with the sword of the Spirit, because it is in close connection with the subject of our preceding discourse, the girdle of truth.

a. What is *the meaning* of the sword of the Spirit? By the sword of the Spirit, as the Apostle himself declares, we are to understand the *word of God*. Why? Because the word of God is like a sword; it wounds and kills. It wounds and puts to death the enemies of God, that is, those sinners who rebel against God; or rather their sins and vices—their pride, avarice, and lust. This is the two-edged sword which St. John saw issuing from the mouth of God: "And from His mouth came out a sharp two-edged sword" (Apoc. i. 16). This is the rod of which the prophet Isaias speaks when he says: "He shall strike the earth with the rod of His mouth, and with the breath of His lips He shall slay the wicked" (Is. xi. 4). This is the sword with which St. Peter was commanded to slay the "four-footed beasts, and creeping things of the earth, and fowls of the air" (Acts x. 12, 13), which symbolize the three great classes of sinners—the sensual, the avaricious, and the proud. For the sensual, like the four-footed beasts, have their eyes continually turned down to the things of earth, to the pleasures of sense, while the covetous cling to the earth, like creeping vermin; and the proud, like the birds of the air, extol themselves in self-glorification beyond their natural and God-appointed sphere. These sinners are slain by the sword of God's word, when they cease to resemble irrational beasts; when they begin to live according to the law of reason and the law of God; when, from being sensual, avaricious, and proud, they have become chaste, generous, and humble Christians. It is, finally, of this sword that our blessed Lord speaks when He says: "Do not think that I came to send peace upon earth; I came not to send peace, but the sword" (Matt. x. 34). This is the two-edged sword which He gave into the hands of His apostles, and with which they subdued the whole earth to the dominion of Jesus Christ.

b. But why is the word of God called not simply a sword, but the *sword of the Spirit*? It is called the sword of the Spirit chiefly for the following reasons:

This sword is forged and tempered by the *Holy Spirit*. For no instrument of man's manufacture can pierce the soul, penetrate into the most hidden thoughts, reach unto the division of the soul and the spirit. This efficacy is the work of the Holy Ghost alone.

Therefore St. Peter says of the word of God: "The holy men of God spoke, inspired by the Holy Ghost" (II. Pet. i. 21).

It is also the Holy Ghost who *wields* this sword. He it is who combats vice, puts to death the old man with all his acts, and converts the sinner. The priests, or preachers of the word of God, are only, as it were, His shield-bearers. They are only His mouth-piece. "For it is not you that speak," says Our Lord, "but the Spirit of your Father that speaketh in you" (Matt. x. 20).

The chief reason, however, why the word of God is called the sword of the Spirit is because it is only with the *assistance of the Holy Ghost* that this sword can be handled. But can we not read the Scriptures? And are the Scriptures not the sword of the Spirit? Very true; the Scriptures are a sword, but not a drawn sword. They are a sword sheathed in the scabbard. It is only he who has the understanding of the Scriptures that can draw this sword. But without the assistance of the Holy Ghost no one can gain this understanding. It is only he who understands the Scriptures in the sense in which the holy Catholic Church understands and explains them that is able to wield the sword of the Spirit; for to the Catholic Church alone has been promised and communicated the assistance of the Holy Ghost in the understanding and exposition of the Scriptures. If any one interprets the Scripture otherwise, he does not wield the sword of the Spirit. He handles the sheath, but not the sword. That is the delusion under which non-Catholics labor, whose war-cry is the Scriptures, the Bible; but who, in fact, handle the sheath instead of the sword. Hence it is that, with all their efforts, with all their Bible Societies, and the millions of money which they yearly expend on the circulation of the Bible, they do not effect a single true conversion. And the reason is, because they fight with the sheath, not with the sword.

2. *How are we to use this sword* of the Spirit against the trials and afflictions of this life? Its use must be in accordance with the quality of our sufferings.

a. There are certain sufferings or temptations against which the *fear of God* is most effectual. In these temptations we must, according to the example given us by our blessed Lord in the desert, have recourse to the sword of the word of God, and wield this powerful weapon to inspire ourselves with fear and trembling. If, for instance, the spirit of pride torments you; if it urges you on to the immoderate desire of honors and distinctions; if it inspires you to exalt yourself and despise others, take up the sword of the Spirit; ponder well the words of the Holy Ghost: " Horribly and speedily will He [the Lord] appear to you; for a most severe judgment shall be for them that bear rule. For to him that is little, mercy is granted; but the mighty shall be mightily tormented " (Wis. vi. 6, 7). If it is the spirit of avarice that torments you, and goads you on to heap up riches, remember the words of the Apostle: " They that will become rich, fall into temptation, and into the snare of the devil, and into many unprofitable and hurtful desires, which drown men into destruction and perdition. For covetousness is the root of all evils; which some desiring, have erred from the faith, and have entangled themselves in many sorrows " (I. Tim. vi. 9,10). If it is the demon of impurity that tempts you, alluring you with the bait of sensual pleasures, then take up the sword of the Spirit, and weigh well the words of the Apostle: " Fornicators and adulterers God will judge " (Heb. xiii. 4); and: " Do not err; neither fornicators, nor adulterers, nor the effeminate shall possess the kingdom of God" (I. Cor. vi. 9, 10).

b. But, if our afflictions are such that they cannot be removed, and that we cannot escape them; if they are inevitable evils, such as poverty, distress, sickness, death of parents, children, or friends, and such like casualties; we must, again, take up the sword of the Spirit, not to inspire ourselves with fear and trembling, but *to strengthen and console ourselves*, and to lighten our sorrows. In such cases we must have recourse to those passages of Holy Scripture in which the consoling promises of God and the inspiring examples of the saints are contained. These promises and examples are so numerous that it is unnecessary to make special reference to them. You have only to recall the history of Abraham, Jacob, Joseph, Moses, Job, David, of the elder and younger Tobias. If we consider these examples, and consult our own experience, we must come to the same conclusion with the Royal Prophet: "I have been young, but now am old; and I have not seen the just forsaken, nor his seed seeking bread" (Ps. xxxvi. 25).

Arm yourselves, then, with the sword of the spirit, and use it as a remedy against the sufferings of this life. But do not think that your armor is thus complete, but put on also, as the Apostle exhorts—

II. THE HELMET OF SALVATION.

1. Now, what is *the meaning* of the helmet of salvation? The Apostle himself explains it in another passage, where he exhorts the Christians to " be sober, having on the breast-plate of faith and charity, and for a helmet, the hope of salvation " (I. Thess. v. 8). By the helmet of salvation, therefore, the Apostle understands *the hope of salvation*. And, in fact, the virtue of hope

may be justly compared with a helmet. For, as the helmet protects the head, and leaves the rest of the body unprotected, so hope teaches us to direct our whole attention to Christ, our head, to the disregard of everything else—of fortune, honor, reputation, comfort, and even life itself. This divine virtue teaches us, like the Apostle, to reckon all things to be but a loss, and count them as dirt, that we may gain Christ (Phil. iii. 8). Though we may have been stript of everything else, if only Christ, our head, is secured to us, if His glory is maintained, all is saved; all our wishes are realized. This virtue of hope is, therefore, aptly symbolized by a helmet, and justly called the helmet of salvation.

Hope is a helmet of quite *marvellous virtue*. It not only offers extraordinary resistance against adversity, but, instead of being impaired by the blows of affliction, it is only rendered more impenetrable. For, as the Apostle teaches us, "tribulation worketh patience; and patience trial; and trial hope; and hope confoundeth not" (Rom. v. 3-5). Tribulation worketh patience; for patience is not a thing that, like knowledge, can be learned from books or teachers, but from sufferings and labors, that is, from tribulations. Patience worketh trial; for he who suffers much, and suffers patiently, is approved of God and found worthy of eternal recompense. As a soldier is not tested and found worthy of his reward by the splendor and beauty of his armor, but by his endurance and deeds of valor, so the soldier of Jesus Christ is proved, not by his wealth and natural endowments or acquirements, but by his perseverance in trials and temptations, and by his patience in sufferings and afflictions. Trial worketh hope; for, when a man is conscious of having suffered much, and suffered with resignation, in the cause of his salvation, he has a sort of presentiment of the love and friendship of God, and thus his hope of the eternal reward is strengthened. And hope confoundeth not; because God is all-powerful, and mercifully disposed to grant us even more than we dare to hope.

Hence you see that the blows of affliction, far from shattering or impairing this helmet of hope, only tend to perfect and strengthen it. But, as it becomes more durable and invincible by use, so it also effects that the scourges of adversity are less keenly felt, and that we are less likely to succumb under their pressure. This leads us to the second consideration, viz.—

2. *The use*, or advantages of the helmet of salvation in regard to the sufferings of this life. In the first place, I say, this helmet, or the virtue of hope, effects that, in consideration of the future eternal and infinite reward, we look upon our sufferings as mere *insignificant trifles*. How comes it that the avaricious man disregards the toils and labors which he has daily to undergo in the pursuit of wealth? Is it not the hope of enriching himself that supports him? What is it that encourages the husbandman cheerfully to submit to the greatest hardships, to expose himself without a murmur to wind and rain, heat and cold? Is it not the hope of a rich harvest? What spurs on the soldier bravely to meet the foe, and fearlessly to look death in the face? Is it not the hope of booty, or the hope of glory? If, then, the infirm hope of paltry and perishable gain exerts such wonderful power to make the greatest toils and hardships seem but mere trifles, what must be the power of the unshaken hope of infinite recompense, which rests on the infallible promises of the all-powerful and all-bountiful God? Will this unwavering hope not make all our afflictions, no matter how great they are, look like the merest trifles?

Must we not confess with the Apostle that "the sufferings of this time are not worthy to be compared with the glory to come, that shall be revealed in us"? (Rom. viii. 18.)

The helmet of the hope of salvation also protects the soldier of Jesus Christ against the assaults of his enemy by raising his soul to the contemplation of the divine promises, and thus *sustains him in the struggle* for his salvation. For hope effects not only that we constantly bear in mind the heavenly reward, but also that we do not allow ourselves to be excluded from it by any obstacles, by the dread of any hardships or sufferings. Hence the Apostle St. Paul, writing to the Hebrews, compares hope with an anchor (Heb. vi. 19). For, as the seaman in the storm is wont to cast the anchor in the deep and thus secure his vessel, so also the Christian in the storm of tribulations casts the anchor of hope and finds rest and security on the solid and unshaken foundation of the divine promises. But, while the anchor of a ship is never quite safe, since the cable to which it is fastened may break under the violence of the storm, the anchor of our hope is always reliable; for, as the Scripture says, "a threefold cord is not easily broken" (Eccles. iv. 12). The anchor of our hope is fastened by a triple cord. One is the infallible faithfulness of God, which alone is all-sufficient; a second is the oath which, as the Apostle says (Heb. vi. 17), "God interposed" to confirm His promises; a third is the signature wherewith He sealed the testament of His promises in the blood of His only-begotten Son.

Let us, then, beloved brethren, according to the example of the holy martyrs, in all our afflictions and temptations cast the anchor of hope as an infallible resource in all our sufferings. Let us always bear in mind the exceeding great reward promised to those who persevere in patience, and we will go forth victorious from all trials which it may please God to send us; we will hoard up immeasurable merits in this life, and obtain from the hand of Our Lord the victor's crown, the crown of everlasting glory. Amen.

Fifth Sermon.

REMEDIES AGAINST SUFFERINGS (CONTINUED).

"Stand, ... having on the breastplate of justice, ... in all things taking the shield of faith, wherewith you may be able to extinguish all the fiery darts of the most wicked one."—Eph. vi. 14, 16.

To the armor of the soldier of Jesus Christ belong, besides the girdle of chastity, the sword of God's word, and the helmet of hope, also the *breastplate of justice* and the *shield of faith*. The meaning and the advantages of these two articles of the Christian's supernatural equipment remain still to be considered, and will form the subject of the present discourse.

I. THE BREASTPLATE OF JUSTICE.

1. *Meaning.* What does the Apostle understand by the breastplate of justice? By the breastplate of justice he understands the divine virtue of charity. For in his First Epistle to the Thessalonians he calls it the breastplate of faith and charity, that is, of that faith which is enlivened by charity or sanctifying grace. Therefore he calls it the breastplate of justice; for justice, in its more general acceptation, signifies the virtue of divine love, because it is this virtue which makes us just in the eyes of God. But why is this virtue called a breastplate? For the following reasons.

a. As the breastplate, or cuirass, protects the chest, and thus defends the heart, which is for life the most necessary organ, so the virtue of divine love *defends the very life of the soul*. Upon this breastplate depends altogether the existence of our supernatural life; for, as St. John says, " he that loveth not, abideth in death " (I. John iii. 14).

b. Moreover, as the breastplate or corselet of the soldier in olden times was made of an indefinite number of metallic rings, skilfully linked together into one tissue, so the virtue of charity is the *sum of all virtues*, united in one by this common bond. Where charity is, there no essential virtue of a Christian is wanting. Therefore the Apostle says: " Charity is patient, is kind; charity envieth not, dealeth not perversely, is not puffed up, is not ambitious, seeketh not her own, is not provoked to anger, thinketh no evil, rejoiceth not in iniquity, but rejoiceth with the truth; beareth all things, believeth all things, hopeth all things, endureth all things " (I. Cor. xiii. 4-7).

c. Finally, as the breastplate of the soldier is strong and durable, and wards off all the darts of the enemy, so also the divine virtue of love is endowed with *marvellous power*, endures all things, even the greatest injuries and insults. Whence the Holy Ghost says: " Love is strong as death " (Cant. viii. 6). Yea, it is even stronger than death; for it vanquishes sin, which is stronger than death. Death is so strong that no living being of God's visible creation can resist it. All men and beasts must yield to its power; but sin is still more powerful. For what death could not effect, sin has brought about. It ascended into heaven and unpeopled it of the legions of its immortal spirits. But love is more powerful than sin and death; for, as soon as it enters into the heart of man, it not only casts out sin, but annihilates it. Nay, love has such power that, in a certain sense, it overcomes the Almighty Himself. Once God, enraged at the idolatry of His people, had resolved to destroy them; but the love of His servant Moses intervened in their behalf. " Moses besought the Lord saying: Why,

O Lord, is Thy indignation enkindled against Thy people, whom Thou hast brought out of the land of Egypt, with great power and with a mighty hand? Let not the Egyptians say, I beseech thee: He craftily brought them out, that He might kill them in the mountains, and destroy them from the earth; let Thy anger cease, and be appeased upon the wickedness of Thy people "(Exod. xxxii. 11, 12). And God was appeased and spared His people, overcome by the love of Moses. The love of His servant had staid the hand of the Almighty. So love triumphs over the wrath and justice of God. Hence the Almighty besought Moses not to intercede for the people. "Let Me alone," He says, "that My wrath may be kindled against them, and that I may destroy them" (Ibid. 10). Such is the power of divine love over our own passions, over sin, over all the enemies of our souls, over Almighty God Himself. Is it not, then, aptly called the breastplate of justice?

2. How great must not, therefore, be the *advantages* of this invincible piece of spiritual armor against the sufferings of this life?

a. First of all, it begets *patience*, according to the words of the Apostle: "charity is patient." And is it not evident from the character of patience that it is the daughter of charity? For, how does patience obtain the victory? Is it by force and violence? No; it conquers by meek and inoffensive endurance, by gently and fearlessly submitting to insult and injury. It is by the wounds which he receives, by the death which he endures, that the patient man triumphs over his enemies. Is that not the victory of Christ and of His holy martyrs and saints? And yet, what victory is greater than theirs? Now, it is evident that only a heart glowing with divine love can achieve such a victory, can display such heroic constancy in suffering.

Patience is, therefore, the daughter of charity; and where this divine virtue exists, patience cannot fail. He whose heart is inflamed by the love of God will, therefore, infallibly be patient in sufferings.

b. But charity effects that we not only endure our sufferings with patience, but also with *cheerfulness.* For under the influence of charity we look upon our sufferings and afflictions in quite a new light. He who does not possess this virtue looks upon affliction as a burden and an evil; and therefore he finds it disagreeable, and naturally grows impatient under its pressure. On the other hand, he who is in possession of this virtue looks upon his sufferings as so many opportunities of proving his love to Almighty God; consequently he bears them not only patiently, but even joyfully.

c. Such is the effect of divine love that it, by no means seldom, makes us altogether *disregard our sufferings.* Love has the power of so transporting the soul that it becomes quite unconscious of its afflictions. As wine gladdens the heart of man, and makes him forgetful of his cares and sorrows, and of all his miseries, so divine love—that wine which inebriated the apostles on the day of Pentecost, that wine with which the martyrs and saints of God were drunk—makes us rejoice in the midst of tribulations and forget all our sufferings. For fourteen years the patriarch Jacob served Laban, his father-in-law, to obtain the hand of his daughter Rachel. Such was the severity of his service that day and night he had to bear the heat and the cold, and that sleep had fled from his eyes. Yet for the greatness of his love to Rachel these years of toils and hardships seemed to him but a few days (Gen. xxix. 20). If natural love has such power to overcome sufferings and hardships, what must be the virtue of supernatural love, of the love infused by the

Holy Ghost, which so enraptures the soul! Transported with this love, the apostles once, after being scourged by the Jews, went forth from the presence of the council rejoicing, because they were accounted worthy to suffer reproaches for the name of Jesus (Acts v. 41). Transported with this divine love, St. Paul and Silas, after being beaten with rods, joyfully sang the praises of God in their prison dungeon (Acts xvi. 25). Transported with this love, St. Laurence, while his body was being roasted on a red-hot iron, so forgot his sufferings, that he made light of his tortures. If, then, beloved brethren, our hearts thus glow with the love of God, like the apostle St. Paul we shall abound with joy in the midst of our tribulations.

The breastplate of charity is, therefore, the most powerful defence against afflictions. But as our love is often weak and insufficient, and hardly deserves to be called by the name of love, we must also take up the shield of faith, which completes the armor of the soldier of Jesus Christ.

II. THE SHIELD OF FAITH.

1. What the shield of the soldier of Jesus Christ here *means* is sufficiently evident from the words of the Apostle, who calls it the *shield of faith:* " In all things taking the shield of faith, that you may be able to extinguish the fiery darts of the most wicked one." That faith is one of the ordinary weapons by which we are to ward off the assaults of the enemies of our salvation, we learn from many passages of Holy Scripture. Thus St. Peter says: " Be sober and watch, because your adversary, the devil, as a roaring lion, goeth about, seeking whom he may devour; whom resist ye strong in faith " (I. Pet. v. 8, 9). And, again, St. John: " This is the victory which overcometh the world, our

faith" (I. John v. 4). Faith is, therefore, the weapon with which we are to fight against the fury of Satan, and against the spirit of this world.

Faith is most *aptly compared* with a shield in the combat of salvation; for it renders the same services to the soul as the soldier's shield renders to the body. As the shield protects the body from all assaults of the enemy, so faith wards off every assault and every temptation from the soul, from whatever source it may chance to come, and of whatever quality it may be. Therefore the Apostle exhorts us to take up this defence, not only in certain cases and against a certain kind of assaults, but in all things, that we may be able to extinguish all the fiery darts of the enemy. Such is briefly the meaning of the shield of faith.

2. Now, with regard to its practical *use* against the sufferings and afflictions of this life, it consists chiefly in recalling to mind and considering well certain great truths, which our faith teaches us.

a. The first of those truths is *that the greatest of all evils is sin*. If, therefore, poverty, sickness, persecution, or any other affliction weighs heavy upon you, and is the occasion of temptations to impatience, dishonesty, intemperance, or even despair, then take up the shield of faith and oppose it to the darts of the enemy. Remember, if you yield to the temptation, you only add to your present affliction an incomparably greater evil—the boundless evil of sin. If you do so, you will not fail to see that it is much better to suffer the lesser evil, and to endure your afflictions with patience.

b. The second truth which we should call to mind in affliction is that as long as we love God and continue to be His children, all our sufferings, from whatever source they may come, will be useful and *salutary* for us. For, on the one hand, every affliction that befalls us comes from the hand of God; and, on the other hand, He loves His children with unspeakable tenderness. Could, then, God, who loves His children so tenderly, and is able to avert all evils from them, permit afflictions to come over them, which would prove injurious, not advantageous for their salvation? Suppose you had an enemy who had resolved to poison you, but could not execute his design without manifesting his intention to, and obtaining permission of your parents, would you not consider yourself free from danger? Or could your parents give their consent to such a heinous crime? But the love of God is infinitely greater towards us than the love of our parents. And, on the other hand, no power on earth or in hell can hurt us without the knowledge and permission of Almighty God. Is it not evident, then, that, as long as we are the children of God, no affliction can befall us which will not be for our greater good? And is this consideration not well fitted to dispose us to receive all our afflictions and sufferings with resignation from the hand of God?

c. The third truth which we should bear in mind in our afflictions is that the sufferings of this life, if borne with patience, will *preserve us* from incomparably greater sufferings in the next life. For we are all sinners. "In many things we all offend" (James iii. 2). And "if we say that we have no sin, we deceive ourselves, and the truth is not in us; if we say that we have not sinned, we make Him [God] a liar; and His word is not in us" (I. John i. 8, 10). We are all sinners, therefore, and our sins must be atoned for either in this life, or in the life to come. It is much easier to satisfy for our sins in this life than to suffer for them in the next. Should we not, therefore, willingly and joyfully accept the afflictions of this life as a penance for our sins, and say with St. Augustine: "Here burn, here cut, O Lord, that Thou mayest spare me in eternity!"

3. Moreover, in our afflictions we should weigh well the truth that in poverty, in bodily ailments, or in sufferings of any kind, *there is no disgrace*. For Christ our Lord, by His example and teaching, has removed from them whatever reproach or ignominy human prejudice had attached to them.

By His *example* He has removed all disgrace from human sufferings, for He chose for Himself the most humiliating of all sufferings, and thus not only sanctified, but ennobled them. As soon as a certain kind of dress, no matter how simple and common it may be, has been worn by persons of high rank, no one is any longer ashamed to wear it. Why, then, should Christians be ashamed to wear that poverty and humiliation, those hardships and sufferings, with which Christ clothed Himself as with a garment? Sufferings, therefore, are a right royal apparel, of which every Christian should be proud, not ashamed.

And what is Christ's *teaching* concerning sufferings and their contraries? "Blessed are the poor in spirit; for theirs is the kingdom of heaven. Blessed are they that mourn; for they shall be comforted. Blessed are they that suffer persecution for justice' sake. Be glad and rejoice, because your reward is very great in heaven" (Matt. v. 3-12). And of those who abound in the good things of this world He says: " Woe to you that are rich; for you have your consolation! Woe to you that are filled; for you shall hunger! Woe to you that now laugh; for you shall mourn and weep!" (Luke vi. 24, 25.)

4. Lastly, we should bear in mind that sufferings, far from being dishonorable, are among *the most valuable gifts of God*. For they are the true way that

leads to heaven ; they are the price at which the greatest treasures and the highest honors are procured. Has not Christ Himself purchased His eternal glory at the price of His sufferings? Did it not behoove Him to suffer, and thus enter into His glory? Is this not the way upon which the saints of God walked to glory? Of what infinite value, then, are sufferings, since they lead to such a glorious end! Such is the use we are to make of the shield of faith as a remedy against the trials and sufferings of this life.

Thus, beloved brethren, I have finished the task I proposed to myself in this course of sermons. It remains for me only to ask you seriously to reflect upon the truths I have put before you. The holy time upon which we are about to enter—the season which is especially devoted to the consideration of the passion of Our Lord, offers a suitable opportunity for such serious reflection. Make your Crucified Lord the subject of your thoughts during these days, and consider how He practised in this life all those truths which I have been endeavoring to impress upon you. This consideration of the passion of Our Saviour will strengthen you in the good resolutions you have made, and enable you to bear up under the sufferings and afflictions of this life. Thus the tribulations of this present time will be for you a source of merit in this life, and of infinite bliss in the next. Amen.

TRIDUUM

FOR THE

Adoration of the Forty Hours.

Jesus the Good Shepherd
IN THE
Most Holy Sacrament of the Eucharist.

First Day.

THE GOOD SHEPHERD DWELLS AMID HIS SHEEP.

"Take ye and eat; this is My body."—Matt. xxvi. 26.

THE chief aim of the Forty Hours' Adoration, beloved brethren, as you are aware, is the renewal of the faithful in the devotion to the Most Holy Sacrament of the Altar. It will, therefore, be my endeavor in these discourses to contribute what little I can to this end. Now, as there is nothing that tends to increase our devotion more than a true love and veneration for its object, I shall endeavor to awaken in your hearts an intense love and reverence towards Jesus in the Blessed Sacrament.

Of all the figures under which our blessed Lord is represented to us in the Gospel there is, to my thinking, none better suited to elicit our love than that of the Good Shepherd; and therefore I have determined in these sermons to show you how Jesus Christ in the Blessed Sacrament acts the part of the Good Shepherd. What is the part of a good shepherd? The good shepherd, who loves his sheep, dwells among them, feeds them, and, if necessary, sacrifices his comfort and convenience and even his life for them. And this is precisely the threefold function which our blessed Lord performs in our behalf in the Most Adorable Sacrament of the Altar. He dwells amongst us by His continual presence in the tabernacle of our altars; He gives Himself as the spiritual food of our souls in holy Communion; He offers Himself as a holocaust for us in the holy sacrifice of the Mass. In the present discourse we shall confine ourselves to the consideration of the first of these three functions of the Good Shepherd. Jesus Christ, the Good Shepherd, continually *dwells amid His flock* in the Most Holy Sacrament; and thus He manifests His love for us in a twofold way: (1) by *the very fact* that He has taken up His abode amongst us; and (2) by *the manner* in which He abides with us.

I. FACT OF THE REAL PRESENCE.

Has Jesus Christ, the Good Shepherd, really taken up His abode with us? Yes, beloved brethren; Jesus Christ, the Son of God made man, is really, truly, and substantially present, is wholly and entirely present—with His Godhead and Manhood, with His body and His soul, with His flesh and His blood—in the Most Holy Sacrament of the Altar, which is preserved in our tabernacles. This is an article of our faith, the explicit teaching of the infallible Church; this doctrine is clearly laid down in Holy Scripture as well as in Tradition, and is at the same time altogether consistent with reason itself.

1. And first, with regard to *Holy Scripture*, I say that the real presence of Jesus Christ under the appearances of bread and wine could not be put in clearer terms than those which our blessed Lord Himself used in the institution of this Most Holy Sacrament at the Last Supper. After having celebrated the pasch, which was a figure of this sacrament, with His apostles, and having washed their feet to signify with what purity of heart and fraternal charity they should approach this sacred banquet, He took bread and blessed it, and broke and gave it to them, saying: "Take ye and eat; This is My body. In like manner, taking the chalice with wine, He blessed it, and said: Drink ye all of this;

this is My blood." What He took into His hands, therefore, was bread and wine; but what He gave to His disciples was His body and blood. This is the obvious meaning of the words: "This is My body; this is My blood." What follows from this? It follows manifestly that the bread and wine which He took into His hands were changed into His body and blood—into His living body and blood, as they then existed, united with His soul and Divinity. Consequently, Jesus Christ Himself was at that moment wholly and entirely present under the appearances of bread and wine, and was really, truly, and substantially received by His disciples. The entire Christ is, therefore, truly present in the Most Holy Sacrament under the appearance of bread as well as under the appearance of wine. Could, then, Christ our Lord express Himself more clearly than by saying: "This is My body; this is My blood"? Could His words possibly have any other sense than that He is really present under the sacramental species?

2. And thus, in fact, He was understood by His apostles and by the Church in all ages, as we see from the evident and universal teaching of *Tradition*. The testimonies of the holy Fathers of the Church are so numerous and so extensive upon this point that they could not be condensed even within the bounds of an entire sermon. I shall, therefore, refer only to a few from the very earliest ages of the Church. St. Ignatius, Martyr, the disciple of St. John the apostle, in the beginning of the second century, writing to the Christians of Smyrna, raises his warning voice against those who denied the real presence of Jesus Christ in the Blessed Eucharist. Some fifty years later, St. Justin Martyr, in his Apology to the Roman Emperor, writes: "We receive the Holy Eucharist not as ordinary

bread and ordinary drink, but, as we have been taught to believe, we receive it as the flesh and blood of Jesus, God made man." Similar passages, no less explicit on this belief, might be quoted from St. Irenæus, from Tertullian, Origen, and many other Fathers and Doctors of the Church, from the earliest centuries to our own times.

3. This manifest teaching of Scripture and Tradition is altogether consistent with sound *reason*. True, reason cannot prove this truth, because it is a strict mystery, which we can learn only from divine Revelation. But, after it has been once revealed, reason teaches that it is highly in keeping with the divine attributes and with God's merciful dealings with man. For the real presence of Jesus Christ in the Most Holy Sacrament tends both to the supreme honor of God and to our own greatest advantage.

Nothing tends more to the *glory of God* than the manifestation of His unspeakable love and mercy to us, poor unworthy sinners. But His love and mercy are manifested in the most conspicuous manner in the mystery of the real presence of Our Saviour in the Blessed Sacrament. For what else than His infinite love and mercy could move Him not only to send His only-begotten Son into this world to save us, but also to devise this wonderful means, whereby He might remain with us, sinful men, unto the end of the world?

But the real presence of Jesus Christ, at the same time, tends to *our own greatest advantage;* for, if there is anything suited to promote our spiritual welfare, and to secure our eternal salvation, it is certainly the continued presence of our Divine Lord. And, in fact, what can more efficaciously restrain us from sin, or stimulate us on the path of virtue, than the consciousness that the God-man, Jesus Christ, who gave His life for us, and who will once come to judge us, personally abides in our midst, and is witness of all our doings? If this consideration of the presence of Our Lord would fail of its effects upon us, our condition would be, indeed, a most lamentable one. You see, then, beloved brethren, that reason itself combines with Holy Scripture and Tradition to confirm our belief in the real presence of Jesus Christ in the Adorable Sacrament of the Altar. May we, then, not say more truly than Moses: "Neither is there any other nation so great, that hath gods so nigh them, as our God is present to all our petitions"? (Deut. iv. 7.) Does not Jesus Christ here prove Himself the Good Shepherd, who abides with His flock? His delight is to be among the children of men. But let us, further, consider—

II. THE MANNER IN WHICH HE IS PRESENT.

Christ our Lord dwells in our midst in a way which is most befitting His character as Good Shepherd, and at the same time best calculated to attach us, the sheep of His fold, to His sacred Person. Nothing is more apt to inspire us with a great attachment for the person of our Divine Saviour than His extraordinary humility, meekness, and love. But by the manner of His presence in the Most Holy Sacrament He displays the profoundest humility, the most admirable meekness, and the tenderest love.

1. *Humility.* Jesus Christ in the Blessed Sacrament displays the profoundest humility; for here He conceals not only the splendor of His Godhead, but also the glory of His Manhood, under the lowly species of bread. That blessed Humanity which is transfigured in heaven, which sits at the right hand of the Eternal Father, which is adored and praised without ceasing

by all the angels and saints in heaven, which is a source of endless bliss to all the inmates of the celestial mansions—that same glorious Humanity is hidden under the sacramental veil. And how great is the glory that Jesus Christ conceals under this lowly garb! He once gave a glimpse of this glory to His apostles at His Transfiguration on Mount Tabor. And what were the effects produced upon the apostles? They were so transported with joy at the sight of His glory that, forgetful of everything else, they desired only to remain there and always to contemplate Him in His glory. To St. Teresa it was once granted, as she relates in the history of her own life, to behold in a vision the hands of our Divine Lord; and such was their glory that she was rapt in ecstasy at the sight. What, then, must be the glory of the Humanity of Our Lord as contemplated by the angels and saints in heaven! And all this glory He conceals under the lowly appearance of bread. How great, then, is the humility He displays in the Blessed Sacrament, in which by miracle He veils under such humble garb the unspeakable glory of His Humanity! In consideration of such humility of the Shepherd of our souls, must we not exclaim with St. Cyril: "O condescension, which no thought can comprehend!"

No less conspicuously does our blessed Lord display His boundless humility by the fact that He deigns to dwell amongst us, *despite our unworthiness*, and despite the unworthy treatment He receives at our hands. Who are we that the Son of God should condescend to take up His abode amongst us? We are all poor, weak, sinful creatures. And how do we receive Him? What kind of mansions do we prepare for Him? How poor and lowly are not often the abodes in which He is constrained to reside? Houses of wood and huts of clay are often the residences where the King of heaven and earth abides among men. And what is the grandest cathedral but a miserable hovel for Him whose court is heaven, whose tent is the starry firmament? Must not those who have reared the grandest temples for Jesus Christ exclaim with Solomon: "If heaven and the heavens of heavens cannot contain Thee, how much less this house, which I have built?" (III. Kings viii. 27.)

Add to this the humiliating circumstance that our blessed Lord is often so utterly *abandoned* in our churches. While the places of business and the haunts of pleasure and amusement, which are dedicated to the worship of mammon and the service of Satan, are crowded to overflowing, the churches, where Jesus Christ has taken up His permanent abode, are deserted day and night; as if no one had any business there, as if the salvation of men, for which Our Lord resides on earth, were a matter of no concern—and all this, despite the urgent invitation He extends to us in the loving words: "Come to Me, all you that labor, and are burdened, and I will refresh you" (Matt. xi. 28). And yet, Jesus Christ in His patience and long-suffering does not abandon us, but continues to abide amongst us. Does this circumstance not give evidence of an unfathomable humility on the part of the Son of God?

2. *Meekness.* The meekness displayed by Our Lord in the Most Holy Sacrament is no less marvellous than His humility. Meekness is shown particularly in the patient endurance of outrages; and the greater the outrages are, and the more patiently they are endured, the greater and more heroic this meekness appears. But what outrages are committed against Our Lord in the Blessed Sacrament! What insults are inflicted upon Him. I will not say by infidels and heretics, but

by Christians and Catholics! How many there are among Catholics who absent themselves from divine service, even on Sundays and holy-days of obligation; or, what is no less an outrage against the real presence of Jesus Christ, who come too late, to the great scandal and annoyance of the whole congregation! How many there are who in the house of God, in the awful presence of Jesus Christ, even during the august sacrifice of the Mass, behave in a way that is not only unworthy of the sacred edifice, but altogether irreverent towards the divine presence! How many there are who display such indifference towards the Son of God in the Blessed Sacrament that they seldom—at most once a year—approach to receive His body and blood! And are there not, again, such as commit the outrage of outrages against His divine presence, who approach in the state of grievous sin, commit a terrible sacrilege against His sacred Person, and, to use the words of the Apostle, eat and drink damnation to themselves? Are these not terrible outrages, beloved brethren—thus to abuse the love and condescension of the benign Shepherd, to heap insult on His divine Person?

And *how does the Good Shepherd bear these outrages?* With what admirable meekness! He who possesses all power in heaven and on earth bears all this with patience, in silence, without a murmur; and, what is still more to be marvelled at, generously pardons these insults to those who are penitent and contrite of heart; nay, while His Sacred Heart is thus grieved by the sins of men, His blood cries to heaven for mercy and forgiveness more eloquently than the blood of Abel did (Heb. xii. 24). His blood pleads, as once He pleaded upon the cross: "Father, forgive them; for they know not what they do!" He offers up the ransom of His blood for them to His heavenly Father;

He extends forgiveness to them, if they will only accept it with repentance. What inconceivable meekness does the Good Shepherd display towards His wayward sheep!

3. *Love*. The immense love of the Good Shepherd towards His sheep is manifested by the circumstances as well as by the fact of His presence amongst them. Which are the most striking *circumstances* in connection with the real presence of Our Lord? They are, as we have seen, His self-abasement, and the many and grievous outrages which He has to endure. Now, why does He submit Himself to such humiliation, and expose Himself to such insults? Is it to exercise Himself in humility and meekness? He has no need of the practice of these virtues; He is meek and humble of heart; He is humility and meekness in person. He practises these virtues, therefore, not for His own sake but for our sake. Does He not thus display His infinite love for us?

But by *the very fact* of His real presence, apart from the circumstances connected with it, He displays the greatest love for us. For why did He determine to take up His abode amongst us? First, He wished to be near to us; He wished to afford us easy access to Him, that we might come to Him for aid and comfort in all our spiritual wants and in all our afflictions, according to the words: "Come to Me, all you that labor, and are burdened, and I will refresh you." But He intended, also, to open for us in this Most Holy Sacrament an inexhaustible source of graces; for in His real presence we possess not only the necessary graces for our salvation, but also the fountain from which all graces flow. However, then, we may consider the real presence of Jesus Christ, whether in itself or in its circumstances, it discloses to us in the clearest light the infinite love of our Lord and Saviour. Whence this Sacrament has been justly styled by the holy Fathers of the Church the Sacrament of Love.

You see, then, beloved brethren, that Jesus Christ has not only taken up His permanent abode amongst us, but that He has done so in a way which is well suited to attach our hearts to His sacred Person, to unite us most intimately with Him by the bond of charity. If there is anything calculated to win our affections and attach our hearts to a true friend, it is a truly humble, meek, and loving behavior on his part. And does not Our Lord by His presence in the Blessed Sacrament prove Himself such a friend? Does He not herein act the part of the good shepherd? Let us, then, be grateful to our good Lord; let us return Him love for love. Let us prove that, as it is His delight to abide so lovingly with us, His sheep, so it is our delight to be with Him, our Good Shepherd. And let us show our love and gratitude by often visiting Him in the Blessed Sacrament, not only on Sundays and festivals of obligation, when we are strictly bound to do so, but as often as an opportunity is offered us. Thus we shall not only give joy to His loving Heart, but also obtain many graces from Him, especially the grace to follow the guidance of the Shepherd of our souls on the true pasture of eternal life, and thus once, associated with the elect of His flock, to enter with Him in triumph into the mansion of everlasting bliss. Amen.

Second Day.

THE GOOD SHEPHERD FEEDS HIS SHEEP.

"Thou didst feed Thy people with the food of angels."—Wis. xvi. 20.

JESUS CHRIST, the Good Shepherd, dwells in our midst in the Most Holy Sacrament with infinite humility, meekness, and love. That was the subject of the preceding discourse. But a good shepherd not only dwells among his sheep; he also feeds them. It is my intention in the present discourse to show you how our Lord and Saviour acts also this part of a good shepherd in the Blessed Sacrament. We shall see that He performs also this function in a way that characterizes Him as the most loving Shepherd of our souls. We shall, therefore, consider—

1. *The food which He offers us;*
2. *The end for which He gives it;*
3. *How we should receive it.*

I. THE FOOD OF OUR SOULS.

The food which the Good Shepherd gives in the Most Holy Sacrament for the nourishment of our souls, and which we actually receive in holy Communion, is so precious that no earthly food can be brought into comparison with it. It is none other than His own most sacred body and blood. Thus He Himself, the Eternal Truth, assures us. For, after declaring to His disciples that He is the living bread that came down from heaven, He says: "My flesh is meat indeed, and My blood is drink indeed" (John vi. 56).

The food which is here presented to us is, therefore, a supernatural, divine food.

1. *It is supernatural:* supernatural in its origin, for it is of heaven, not of earth—the living bread that came down from heaven, not by creation, but by the greatest of all miracles, the incarnation of the Son of God in the womb of the Immaculate Virgin, by the intervention of the Holy Ghost. It is supernatural as the food of the soul; for no natural food can nourish the soul; no earthly food can perfect, augment, strengthen our inward spiritual faculties; no material nourishment can enlighten the understanding and strengthen the will of man. It is supernatural in its effects on the recipient, for it is not, like ordinary food, transformed into our flesh and blood; but, on the contrary, it transforms us, in a spiritual manner, into itself, by making us members of Jesus Christ, according to the words: "He that eateth My flesh, and drinketh My blood, abideth in Me, and I in him. He that eateth Me the same also shall live by Me" (John vi. 57, 58). Therefore he that eateth of the flesh of the Son of Man and drinketh of His blood is a member of the mystic body of Jesus Christ, lives the life of Jesus Christ, is spiritually transformed into Jesus Christ, so that he may truly say with the Apostle: "I live, now not I, but Christ liveth in me" (Gal. ii. 20).

2. But this heavenly food, with which the Good Shepherd nourishes His sheep, is not only supernatural; *it is also truly divine.* The body of Christ, which we receive in holy Communion, is not only His living and glorified body, but is, at the same time, inseparably united with the Second Person of the Most Holy Trinity. Therefore, it is truly the body of the Son of God, a divine body. Hence it is that the sacrifice of the cross which Christ offered for our sins was of infinite

value, because the blood that was shed was the blood of the God-man, because the life that was laid down was the life of the Incarnate Son of God—and, consequently, the victim was truly divine. Hence it is that some of the greatest divines maintain that the contemplation of the glorious body of Jesus Christ, without the beatific vision of the Divinity, would suffice to constitute the eternal happiness of the blessed. Hence it is that this heavenly bread, as the true body of the living God, inseparably united with the Godhead, claims not only our reverence and honor, but our *adoration* in the strictest sense, that is, supreme divine worship. Therefore it is called the Adorable Sacrament of the Altar. Therefore the priest after the Consecration raises the sacred host as well as the chalice of the blood of Jesus Christ for our adoration. Therefore it is preserved and exposed in our churches, and borne in procession, for the adoration of the faithful. But supreme adoration is a species of worship which is due to God alone, the sovereign and infinite Lord of all things. The food that is given us in the Most Holy Sacrament is, therefore, divine. It is God Himself, the Second Person of the Adorable Trinity, the Son of God made man, wholly and entirely present under the appearance of bread. Is not this food truly divine?

You see, then, beloved brethren, with what marvellous love, with what wonderful providence, Jesus Christ fulfils the second function of a good shepherd; how He feeds His sheep with heavenly, supernatural, divine food—His own most sacred flesh and blood. How doleful, therefore, is the condition of those who, through their own neglect, or because they do not belong to the fold of the Good Shepherd, are deprived of this heavenly nutriment of the soul! This sad fact will be still more evident to us when we consider—

II. THE END OF THIS HEAVENLY FOOD.

Now, what is the end for which the Good Shepherd gives us this heavenly food? His object is one that is altogether worthy of the Shepherd of our souls. It is to promote our true spiritual well-being, to secure our eternal salvation. Let us, then, briefly consider how this divine nourishment, which we receive in holy Communion, really promotes our spiritual welfare and thus tends to secure our salvation. Herein we shall, again, have occasion to admire, to praise, and to bless the bounty and mercy of the Good Shepherd.

The use of this heavenly food promotes the work of our eternal salvation chiefly by *the intimate union* it establishes between us and Jesus Christ, our head. This mystic union is no less intimate than that which exists between head and members, since by holy Communion we are made members of Christ. True, Our Lord remains bodily present with us only so long as the species of the sacred host remains unchanged. The spiritual union, however, and the supernatural influence of the divine presence remain after the sacramental species are destroyed. But, since it is impossible, as the Roman Catechism remarks, to enumerate all the salutary fruits of holy Communion, I shall confine myself to a few of the chief ones. These few will be sufficient to convince us of the wonderful efficacy of this divine food of our souls, and to show us how its devout use promotes our spiritual well-being.

1. The first fruit which results from our union with Jesus Christ in the Most Holy Sacrament is *the preservation and increase of sanctifying grace.* For, how could we receive our Divine Saviour bodily within our bosom without partaking to a large extent of the infinite riches of His spiritual life? But by this participation of the spiritual life of Our Saviour our own

spiritual life, that is, sanctifying grace, is not only preserved, but also augmented. Therefore the Council of Trent teaches (Sess. xiii. cap. 2) that it was the intention of our blessed Saviour in the institution of the Blessed Sacrament that by this heavenly food the supernatural life of the soul, which consists in sanctifying grace, should be strengthened and increased.

2. Another fruit of this intimate union with Christ is *the weakening of our evil inclinations*, the greater relish for the practice of virtue, and energy in the performance of good works; whence Christian life, the observance of the commandments of God, and the exercise of Christian virtue, become easy and pleasant to us. For by holy Communion, as we have just seen, sanctifying grace is increased; and with every increase of sanctifying grace is connected a corresponding increase of all supernatural virtues, most particularly of the virtue of charity. But in the same proportion as the love of God is increased in us, as St. Augustine aptly remarks, the inclination to what is displeasing to God diminishes, in other words, our inclination to evil is weakened. Hence arise, at the same time, the eagerness and the energy for doing good. For, by the increase of the love of God and of the other supernatural virtues, new strength and ardor are infused into the soul, which produce an ardent desire to embrace the will of God, and the power to execute it. The more a servant loves his master the more cheerfully and energetically he applies himself to his service. In like manner, the greater the love of God within our hearts, the more fervently and faithfully we shall serve Him. By this increase of grace and love, therefore, the union with our blessed Lord in the Most Holy Sacrament subdues our evil inclinations, and infuses into our souls new ardor and new strength in the service of God.

3. A third fruit of our union with Jesus Christ in holy Communion consists in *cleansing the soul from sin.* It purifies the soul from venial sin, and preserves it from mortal sin. For, according to the teaching of St. Thomas, by the worthy reception of the Holy Eucharist the souls of the faithful are awakened to fervor and devotion, filled with ardent love of God and intense sorrow for sin, and stimulated to do penance for their sins. And it is by such acts mainly that venial sins are cancelled apart from the sacrament of penance. But holy Communion also preserves us from grievous sin; for by the increase of charity the temptations to sin are weakened, and our power of resistance is increased. Besides, it secures us a special providence and protection of God, which shields us against the dangers of sin and the many temptations that beset us. Hence, it is that holy Communion worthily received is a pledge of eternal salvation, according to the words of the Saviour: "He that eateth this bread shall live forever" (John vi. 59).

If we consider all these precious fruits of holy Communion—the preservation and increase of sanctifying grace, the victory over our evil propensities, the ardor and energy communicated to the soul, the purification of the soul from venial sins and its perseverance in the grace of God—must we not acknowledge that our union with Christ in the Most Holy Sacrament is the most powerful means for the advancement of our spiritual welfare and for the securing of our eternal salvation? Is not holy Communion, then, truly a pledge of eternal life? As a pledge of a glorious resurrection and of everlasting life, the Good Shepherd has given us this spiritual nourishment of our souls. How great is, then, the love of the bountiful Shepherd to us, His flock! And how great would not be our ingratitude, nay, how reckless our folly, if we refused to receive this heavenly food from His loving hand! How eager should we not be, on the contrary, often and worthily to partake of this bread of eternal life! And how careful should we not be to receive it not only worthily, but also fruitfully! Let us, then, consider—

III. HOW WE SHOULD RECEIVE THIS HEAVENLY FOOD.

The infinite sanctity of this heavenly food, which the Good Shepherd offers us for the spiritual nourishment of our souls, demands that we approach, not rashly or thoughtlessly, but that we present ourselves after due preparation, receive it with reverence, and return thanks for the infinite bounty shown to us by the loving Shepherd of our souls. For a worthy and fruitful Communion, therefore, three things are required: preparation, devout reception, and thanksgiving.

1. *Preparation.* Our preparation for holy Communion must be partly internal, partly external. It must extend to the body as well as to the soul.

a. First, as regards the *soul*, it must be cleansed, at least from all grievous sins, by a good confession. For, if the soul is in the state of mortal sin, that is, deprived of the supernatural life of grace, this divine food can be of no more service to it than material food is to a dead body. On the contrary, as you are well aware, this supernatural food would only add to the damnation of the soul that is in grievous sin. But, while it is required as an essential condition that we be free from mortal sin, we should endeavor, at the same time, as far as possible to cleanse our souls from all venial sins; for venial sin, though it does not render our Communions unworthy, yet impedes their efficacy, because it defiles the soul and thus renders the union with Jesus Christ less intimate. And as the fruits of holy Communion, as I have said, are produced by this union with Christ, it is manifest that venial sin, which loosens this bond, prevents to some extent the fruits which it is intended to produce in our souls. What must we do, then, to obtain in full the fruits of this divine banquet? We must endeavor in our confessions to cleanse our souls from all venial sins, not only by confessing them fully, to the best of our ability, but particularly by a true and perfect contrition and a firm purpose of amendment.

b. With regard to the external preparation, or the disposition of the *body*, the law of the Church strictly commands that he who approaches holy Communion is fasting, that is, has abstained from all food and drink from twelve o'clock of the preceding night. Those, however, are excepted who are dangerously ill and receive the Holy Sacrament by way of viaticum. The reverence due to Our Lord in the Most Holy Sacrament requires also that those who approach it are decently dressed; for, if common decency requires that we appear in decent attire when we present ourselves before a person of respect, how much more is this attention due to the Divine Majesty before whom we present ourselves and whom we receive in holy Communion. Our dress, however, need neither be rich nor elegant. It may be ever so poor, provided only it be cleanly, modest, and becoming. The poorer and simpler it is, the more becoming it is, because it renders us the more like Him whom we receive.

2. *Reception.* When the happy moment comes when we are to approach the Communion-rail, we should approach and receive with reverence and devotion. Our outward behavior, our gait and carriage, should be such as bespeak our inward sentiments of lively faith, profound humility, ardent longing, and inward devotion.

At the moment when the priest raises the sacred host and pronounces the words: "The body of Our Lord Jesus Christ preserve thy soul unto eternal life," we should adore Our Saviour in the Blessed Sacrament, and say to Him: My Jesus, come to me; my soul I give to Thee, or some such pious aspiration, which our devotion will suggest; and then we should with profound reverence receive the adorable body of Our Lord. Then follows a no less important, but, alas! much neglected duty—

3. *Thanksgiving.* After receiving holy Communion we should spend at least about a quarter of an hour in thanksgiving. By thanksgiving we are here to understand familiar converse with our blessed Lord, who now dwells personally in our hearts; for, although all this time is not necessarily to be employed in giving thanks, but also in other pious acts of devotion, yet it is appropriately called thanksgiving, because the motive of our devotions after Communion is gratitude for the unspeakable benefit conferred upon us by the union with Jesus Christ in the Holy Eucharist. This thanksgiving after Communion is of the greatest importance, because the fruits of the Blessed Sacrament depend upon it to a great extent. For, on the one hand, God is the more disposed to be liberal towards us in the dispensation of His graces, the more solicitous we are to thank Him for His favors; and, on the other hand, He is at no time more inclined to hear our prayers, and to lavish His graces upon us, than at the moment when Jesus Christ is personally present in our hearts, and most intimately united with us in holy Communion. St. Teresa says that after Communion our blessed Lord resides in our hearts, sitting, as it were, upon a throne of grace, prepared to enrich our souls with all His blessings. From this throne of mercy He asks us: "What wilt thou that I should do to thee? Behold,

O beloved soul, for no other end have I descended from heaven, and come to thee, than to enrich thee with My graces! Ask of Me what thou wilt and as much as thou wilt. All graces shall be given thee."

Thus, beloved brethren, we should approach the Holy of Holies, Jesus Christ in the Most Holy Sacrament, with due preparation, with great reverence and devotion, and with thanksgiving proportioned to the greatness of the favor conferred upon us. These are the conditions under which we may receive Our Lord not only worthily, but also fruitfully. They are the conditions under which Jesus Christ offers Himself to us as the food of our souls. And in putting these conditions He only consulted our own spiritual welfare; He only intended that this heavenly food should be the more fruitful of eternal life. You see, then, beloved brethren, that our blessed Lord proves Himself the good shepherd not only in the choice of this heavenly food which He gives us, and the loving purpose for which He gives it, but also by the disposition and sentiments with which he requires that we should receive it. Should not this generous and self-sacrificing love of the Shepherd of our souls fill our hearts with love and gratitude towards Him? And should we not endeavor to show our appreciation of His goodness practically by often and worthily receiving this heavenly food? In the presence of Jesus Christ, therefore, who looks down upon you from His throne of mercy upon the altar, make now this firm resolve frequently and worthily to receive Him in the Most Blessed Sacrament. Thus the Bread of Life will be for you a sure pledge of salvation; the prayer of the priest in the administration of the Blessed Sacrament will be realized in you: the body of Our Lord Jesus Christ will preserve your souls unto life everlasting. Amen.

Third Day.

THE GOOD SHEPHERD SACRIFICES HIMSELF FOR HIS SHEEP.

"The Good Shepherd giveth His life for His sheep."—John x. 11.

JESUS CHRIST, the Good Shepherd, as I have already shown you, dwells among His sheep, and feeds them with His own most precious body and blood in the Most Holy Sacrament of the Altar. But this is not all. "The Good Shepherd giveth His life for His sheep." He sacrifices Himself for them. He offered Himself for them once as a bleeding victim on the cross; but, not content with this, He instituted a permanent sacrifice, in which He daily offers Himself in an unbloody manner as a living holocaust for His flock. Our devotion to the Blessed Sacrament would be very defective, and our knowledge and love of the Good Shepherd imperfect, if we had not a full appreciation and a great esteem and reverence for the adorable sacrifice of the Mass. Therefore I have determined to take this third loving function of the Good Shepherd in the Most Holy Sacrament for the subject of this closing discourse of the Triduum of the Forty Hours. And in order to bring home to you, as far as possible, the love displayed by the benign Shepherd in this holy mystery, I shall endeavor to show you—

1. *That the Good Shepherd really offers Himself as a true sacrifice for us;*
2. *With what love and condescension He offers this sacrifice for us.*

I. A TRUE SACRIFICE.

It is an undoubted revealed fact, beloved brethren, that Jesus Christ in the Most Blessed Sacrament offers Himself as a true sacrifice: for, in the first place, it is certain that the holy Mass is a sacrifice in the strictest sense of the word, and, secondly, that in this sacrifice it is Christ who offers Himself as a victim for us.

1. *The Mass is a sacrifice in the strictest sense.* Whatever we do for the service of God in this world may, in a certain sense, be called a sacrifice, and is so called according to the usage of Holy Scripture as well as in the language of the faithful. But a sacrifice in the strict sense of the word, as we are here to understand it, is the offering to God of a visible gift in acknowledgment and adoration of His supreme dominion over us and over all things. Now, if the holy Mass were not such a sacrifice in the strict sense of the word, there would be in the New Law, as all, even those outside the Church, agree, no true and permanent sacrifice at all. For the sacrifice of the cross, though a true sacrifice, was not a permanent, but a transient one, that was offered but once; because Christ, having died once, can die no more. But the New Law instituted by Christ as well as the Old must have a permanent sacrifice, not a mere passing sacrifice that is offered only once. This follows—

a. From the *excellence of the Christian religion*, which is the most perfect of all religions, both on account of its divine origin and its sublime destination. Now, since the essence of religion consists in divine worship, it follows that in every true religion there must be a true sacrifice. And the reason is that sacrifice, being an actual acknowledgment of the supreme dominion of God, is the highest act of divine worship. And such it has been considered at all times and by all nations who possessed any form of divine worship. Could, then, the religion of Jesus Christ be wanting in this highest and most essential feature of divine worship?

b. The same truth is manifest from *the relation between the Old and the New Law.* The Old Law was the figure of the New. The New Law is the fulfilment of the Old. Therefore, since in the Old Law daily sacrifices were offered according to the prescription of God, so also in the New there must be a permanent sacrifice; else the Old Law, which was but the figure of what was to come, would be more perfect than the New Law, which is the fulfilment and reality.

c. But the most convincing proof of the existence of a true permanent sacrifice in the New Dispensation is that God expressly *promised and foretold* the institution of such a sacrifice.

He promised it. By the mouth of the Royal Prophet God addresses the following words to Jesus Christ, His Son: " Thou art a priest forever according to the order of Melchisedech " (Ps. cix. 4). Now, according to these words, the priesthood of Melchisedech is characterized by the Holy Ghost as the type and figure of the priesthood of Jesus Christ. But what was peculiar in the priesthood of Melchisedech was that he offered a sacrifice of bread and wine to the Most High. Christ, therefore, who is the fulfilment of this figure, must offer sacrifice under the appearance of bread and wine, and that not only once, or for a time, but forever: " Thou art a priest forever." For, as the priesthood of Christ is to last forever, that is, to the end of the world, and as it is the essential function of a priest, according to the Apostle (Heb. viii. 3), to offer sacrifice, it follows that Christ, being a priest according to the order of Melchisedech, will at all times, even to the consummation of the world, offer sacrifice under the appearance of bread and wine.

He foretold its institution. The prophecy of such a permanent sacrifice is no less explicit than the promise. Thus God speaks through the Prophet Malachias to the Jewish priesthood: " I have no pleasure in you, saith the Lord of hosts; and I will not receive a gift of your hand. For from the rising of the sun even to the going down, My name is great among the gentiles; and in every place there is sacrifice, and there is offered to My name a clean offering" (Mal. i. 10, 11). By these words the Lord plainly declares that the sacrifices of the Old Law will be abolished, and that in the New Law a new sacrifice will be offered, a clean offering be made to His name, all over the world. Now, where is this new sacrifice? Where is this clean oblation? It is evidently the sacrifice of the Mass, as no other true and permanent sacrifice was ever heard of in the Christian Dispensation. Therefore the Council of Trent, in accordance with the constant tradition of the Church, solemnly declares that the prophecy of Malachias is fulfilled in the institution of the holy sacrifice of the Mass, which is the unbloody sacrifice of the New Law, having for its object to apply to the faithful the fruits of the bloody sacrifice of the cross. And the contrary teaching of the heretics is condemned under anathema (Sess. 22. can. 1). The holy Mass is, therefore, the true and permanent sacrifice of the New Law.

2. And in this sacrifice *Christ offers Himself as a victim* for us. This is manifest from the circumstances of the institution of the Blessed Sacrament. Our blessed Lord took bread, gave thanks, broke it, and gave it to His disciples, saying: " This is My body, which is given for you" (Luke xxii. 19). In like manner, He took also the chalice, saying, " This is the chalice, the new Testament in My blood, which shall be shed for

you." And He adds: "Do this for a commemoration of Me" (Ibid. 20). With these last words Christ manifestly gave charge to His apostles to do the very same thing He had just done Himself. Now, what was it that He had just done? He had given His own flesh and blood to His apostles under the appearance of bread and wine; in other words, He had offered Himself as a sacrifice in the strictest sense. For what is a sacrifice in the strict sense of the word? It is, as we have seen, the offering of a visible gift in acknowledgment and adoration of the Divine Majesty. According to ancient custom, and according to the precepts of God, the victim or gift that was offered was destroyed, or submitted to a change that was equivalent to destruction, in order to signify the supreme dominion of God over man and all his possessions, and even over life and death. And to such an annihilation or change in acknowledgment of the supreme Divine Majesty Christ submitted Himself by putting Himself under the appearance of food and drink. The state which Christ assumed, therefore, thus imprisoned under the species of bread and wine, was equivalent to the state of death, as it was only by a new miracle that He could in this state exercise the functions of life. In this change, therefore, which Christ undergoes by the fact of His real presence in the Blessed Sacrament, we find all those features which essentially belong to a true sacrifice in the strictest sense. And of this sacrifice He Himself is both the priest and the victim. Therefore He truly offered Himself at the Last Supper as a victim for us to His heavenly Father.

This same truth is manifest from the *signification of the words* which Jesus Christ used in the institution of the Holy Eucharist, and which He ordained to be used in the consecration of His body and blood in the holy

Mass. These words in the original text, both in reference to His sacred body and to His precious blood, are expressions peculiar to sacrifices of food and drink. The chalice of His blood is represented as being actually poured out as a libation, that is, as a sacrifice of drink; and His sacred body not only as being delivered up for us, but also as being served for us as a sacrificial feast. From the words used by Our Lord, therefore, as well as from the change of existence to which He submits Himself, apart from the teaching of the Church and Tradition, it is evident that He offered Himself for us as a true sacrifice at the Last Supper, and empowered and commanded His apostles and their successors to do the same in the words: "Do this for a commemoration of Me." And lest any doubt should remain concerning the permanency of this holy sacrifice in His Church, according to the testimony of St. Paul, He added: "As often as you shall eat this bread and drink this chalice, you shall show the death of the Lord, until He come" (I. Cor. xi. 26)—that is, you shall celebrate this mystery, and commemorate My passion and death in so doing, until I come at the end of the world to judge the living and the dead. The holy Mass is, therefore, a true and permanent sacrifice, instituted by Jesus Christ at the Last Supper, in which He offered Himself for us as a victim to His heavenly Father, continues to offer Himself daily, and will continue unto the end of time. Let us, further, consider the Good Shepherd's—

II. LOVING CONDESCENSION IN THIS SACRIFICE.

The love and condescension of self-sacrifice in general are manifested most conspicuously by the exalted character of him who sacrifices himself, by the lowly condition of those for whom he sacrifices himself, and by the value of those goods which he secures for others by his self-devotion. Let us apply this principle to the true sacrifice of Jesus Christ in the holy Mass, and we shall see that His is a sacrifice of infinite love and condescension.

1. *Who is He* who sacrifices Himself for us? It is Jesus Christ Himself, the eternal Son of God. The priest, who stands at the altar, is only His representative. Therefore, at the consecration, in virtue of which the sacrifice is consummated, he speaks not in his own name, but in the name and in the person of Jesus Christ. He does not say: This is the body of Christ; this is the blood of Christ; he says: This is *My* body; this is *My* blood. Jesus Christ Himself is, therefore, the sacrificing High Priest. How infinitely sublime is, then, the character of Him who here sacrifices Himself for us! What grand titles are not given Him by the Holy Ghost Himself in Holy Writ! He is called the Most High, the Son of the living God, the Light of the world, the Author of life, the Way, the Truth, and the Life, the Judge of the living and the dead; He in whose name every knee shall bow in heaven, on earth, and in hell. He it is who condescends to offer Himself for us as a living holocaust under the lowly species of bread and wine. Can we imagine greater condescension than that from the glorious throne at the right hand of the Eternal Father to the altar, to the tiny host, to the chalice?

2. And *who are we*, on the other hand, for whom He thus sacrifices Himself? What are we of ourselves? Of ourselves we are nothing. We have nothing that we can call our own. Whatever we have we have received from God, who has given us our being, our lives, and all we possess. But, being nothing of ourselves, we have rendered ourselves worse than noth-

ing in the eyes of God. For what does not exist is not hateful to God; but we by our sins have converted ourselves into an object of God's hatred and abomination, and therefore rendered ourselves viler and more contemptible in the eyes of the Most High than nothing itself. And for such miserable and hateful creatures the Son of God sacrifices Himself on the altar! Oh, what merciful, what loving condescension!

3. Finally, *what are the goods* which our blessed Lord secures us by His sacrifice? First of all, by the adorable sacrifice of the Mass He procures for us the possibility and the facility of paying to the Divine Majesty *a tribute of honor* which is worthy of His infinite greatness and sanctity. For the holy sacrifice is an act of homage of infinite value on account of the infinite dignity of Jesus Christ, who is both the High Priest and the Victim in this august sacrifice. However unworthy, then, the visible ministering priest may be, the honor paid to God in this adorable sacrifice is infinite, because the priest who stands at the altar, as I have said, is only the representative and, as it were, the instrument of Jesus Christ, the supreme High Priest.

This divine sacrifice is so pleasing to God that it more than outweighs all the offences committed against Him all over the world. If, therefore, God, despite the innumerable sins that daily cry up to Him for vengeance, has thus far spared the world, and has not abandoned it to destruction, we may safely attribute this merciful fact to the infinite *atonement* that is daily rendered Him by the constant offering of this divine sacrifice of propitiation. Hence you may conclude, beloved brethren, what a boundless treasure we possess in the holy sacrifice of the Mass. Hence you may conceive what implacable hatred the infuriate arch-enemy of God and man bears towards this august mystery, and how he triumphs in his victory when he has succeeded to alienate the faithful from this inexhaustible source of grace.

Besides, by the holy sacrifice of the Mass we are enabled daily to assist at that *self-same sacrifice that was once offered on Calvary*. For the sacrifice of our altar is the renewal of the sacrifice of the cross, the only difference being in the manner of offering. Both are essentially the same, as both have the same supreme High Priest and the same saving Victim, Jesus Christ, the God-man. Nor does the difference in the manner of offering destroy the identity of both sacrifices. In the holy Mass, therefore, we assist at the sacrifice of the cross, and may derive the same graces from it as if we stood with the Mother of Jesus and St. John at the foot of the cross. Should not this circumstance fill us with love, reverence, and esteem for the thrice holy sacrifice of the Mass? Should we not consider it a very special grace and privilege to assist at Mass, and endeavor to appropriate to ourselves as much as possible of its boundless spiritual treasures?

From the fact of its identity with the sacrifice of the cross it is evident that the holy sacrifice of the Mass is *an inexhaustible source of graces* and blessings. For, since, according to the teaching of the Council of Trent, it has been instituted to apply to us the infinite treasure of the merits and satisfactions of the sacrifice of the cross, it must needs be an ever-flowing fountain of supernatural favors, from which we may daily draw plentiful graces for the sanctification and salvation of our immortal souls. Whether we wish to give due honor and praise to God, to thank Him for His favors, to atone for our sins, or to secure God's grace, the divine sacrifice is a most powerful and infallible means of obtaining our purpose. Here it is not our prayers that move Almighty God to confer His graces upon us, but the infinite honor and atonement rendered Him by His own divine Son, in whom He is well pleased.

The merciful Shepherd, therefore, sacrifices Himself for His sheep. He daily on thousands of altars lays down His life anew for them in a mystical way in the most adorable sacrifice of the Mass. And with what love and condescension does He offer this sacrifice! What profound self-abasement! What mercy towards us poor sinners! What bounty in the dispensation of His graces and favors! Does He not here, again, prove Himself in truth a good shepherd?

You see, then, beloved brethren, from what I have said to you during these days, that Jesus Christ in the Most Holy Sacrament of the Altar truly acts the part of a good shepherd. He dwells among His sheep; He feeds them with His own flesh and blood; He lays down His life for them. What, then, could He do for His sheep that He has not done? What greater love could He show us than that displayed in the Sacrament of Love? What an inestimable favor, what a priceless boon do we not possess in this Most Holy Sacrament! Should we, then, not show our gratitude to the divine Shepherd of our souls for this proof of His infinite love? But, instead of gratitude, does He not reap ingratitude? Is not His love often returned with insults, or at least with coldness and indifference? Therefore, beloved brethren, it is but meet that we should close this Adoration of the Forty Hours with a public act of reparation to the loving Shepherd for the outrages or neglect of which we ourselves and all men have been guilty against His divine presence in this Adorable Sacrament. Kneel down, then, and recite for yourselves devoutly the words which I will now address to our outraged Lord, who in the sacred host is really, truly, and substantially present before us.

O Jesus, Son of the living God, our Good Shepherd and loving friend, full of confusion and sorrow we prostrate ourselves at Thy feet. O merciful Saviour, great, exceeding great is the ingratitude with which we have returned Thy infinite love and unspeakable favors. We are heartily sorry for the coldness and indifference with which we have thus far grieved Thy loving Heart. O merciful Jesus, we beseech Thee by the infinite love of Thy Sacred Heart, forgive us our offences! Forgive us the irreverence we have shown to Thy all-holy presence! Forgive us that we have so rarely, so indevoutly—yea, perhaps unworthily, received Thy body and blood! Forgive our indifference or neglect in assisting at holy Mass, the sacrifice of Thy incomprehensible love! O Jesus, Friend of our souls, it is our unshaken purpose henceforth to love and honor Thee in this Sacrament of Love. Thy Love has triumphed over our hearts. Henceforth, O sweet Jesus, the Sacrament of Thy love shall be our joy and our comfort, the centre of all our affections. But Thou, O merciful Lord, give us Thy blessing as a pledge of Thy forgiveness. Come, O Jesus, and bless us, that in all future we may as the obedient sheep of Thy fold joyfully follow Thee, the bountiful Shepherd of our souls, and be eternally united with Thee in Thy glory! Amen.

INDEX.

ADVENT, Sanctification of, I. 11.
Alms-giving, I. 306.
Angels, Guardian—Devotion to, II. 233.
Annunciation of the B. V. M., II. 80.
Apostleship of prayer, II. 313.
Assumption of the B. V. M., II. 194.
Avarice, I. 378.

BAPTISM, II. 141.

CHARITY, Attributes of, I. 386.
  A remedy against sufferings, II. 362.
Chastity, a remedy against sufferings, II. 344.
Children, Duties of, I. 61.
Christ, Following of, I. 186.
  Birth of, II. 14.
  Passion of, II. 88.
  Resurrection of, II. 102.
  Ascension of, II. 120.
Christmas Day, II. 14.
Church, The, I. 105.
  St. Peter, the head of the, II. 183.
  Dedication of a, II. 262.

Communion, Holy, II. 383.
  Fruits of Holy, I. 79.
Conception, the Immaculate II. 5
Confession, I. 196.
Conscience, Remorse of, I. 315.
Contrition, Perfect, I. 323.
Conversion, Delay of, I. 37.
Corpus Christi, II. 158.

DEAF and Dumb, Healing of the, I. 333.
Death, Preparation for, I. 442.
Dedication of a church, II. 262.

EASTER Monday, II. 112.
  Sunday, II. 102.
Eucharist, The Most Holy Sacrament of the, I. 79, II. 158, 373, 383, 393.

FAITH and good works, I. 299.
  Effects of, I. 350.
  Vocation to the, II. 43.
  A remedy against sufferings, II. 362.
Forgiveness of injuries, I. 424.
Friday, Good, II. 88.

GENEROSITY of the Blessed Virgin, II. 80.
God, Image of, I. 434.
　Presence of, I. 28.
　Love of, I. 386.
　The Author of sufferings, II. 325.
Goods, Unequal distribution of earthly, I. 219.
Grace, Workings of Divine, I. 229.
　Loss of, I. 255.

HEART, The devotion to the Sacred, II. 171.
Heaven, I. 153, II. 120.
Hell, I. 407.
Holy Ghost, Mission of, II. 131.
Hope, a remedy against sufferings, II. 353.
House of God, II. 262.
　The place for prayer, II. 308.

IMPURITY, I. 161.
Incarnation, I. 46.
Injuries, Forgiveness of, I. 424.
Injustice, I. 359.
Intention, Good, I. 273.

JESUS, Sacred Heart of, II. 171.
　Holy Name of, II. 53.
Joseph, St., II. 72.
Judgment, The last, I. 450.

LOVE of God, Attributes of the, I. 386.
Lukewarmness, I. 292.

MARY, The Immaculate Conception of the B. V., II. 5.
　The Purification, II. 62.
　The Annunciation, II. 80.
　The Assumption, II. 194.
　The Nativity, II. 222.
Marriage, I. 71.

Mass, The holy sacrifice of the, I. 281, II. 393.
Michael, Feast of St., II. 213.
Mortification, Christian, I. 170.

NATIVITY of the B. V. M., II. 222.
　Of Our Lord, II. 14.

PENANCE, I. 20.
　Virtue of, I. 264.
　Sacrament of, I. 196.
Peter, St., the Head of the Church, II. 183.
Prayer—Why our prayers are not always heard, I. 238.
　Necessity of, II. 273.
　Efficacy of, II. 284.
　Requisites of fruitful, II. 293.
　Time and place of, II. 303.
　Apostleship of, II. 313.
Presence of God, I. 28.
　The Real, II. 158, II. 373.
Providence, Discontent with Divine, I. 53.
　Cause of sufferings, II. 325.
Punishment, Belief in eternal, I. 407.
Purgatory, II. 252.
Purification of the B. V. M., II. 62.

READING, Dangerous, I. 135.
Religion, Zeal for the honor of, I. 415.
Remorse, I. 315.
Respect, Human, I. 246.
Resurrection of Christ, II. 102.
　Our own, II. 112.
Rosary, The holy, II. 222.

SACRAMENT, The Blessed. *See* Eucharist.

Saints, Feast of All, II. 243.
Salvation, I. 209.
Sanctity, Reward of, II. 243.
Scandal, I. 97.
Self-sacrifice of the Mother of God, II. 62.
Shepherd, The Good, in the Blessed Sacrament, II. 371.
   Abides with us, II. 373.
   Feeds us with His own flesh and blood, II. 383.
   Sacrifices Himself for us, II. 393.
Sin, I. 367.
   Habitual, I. 178.
   Venial, I. 395.
   Proximate occasion of, I. 88.
Slander, I. 342.
Souls, Devotion to the suffering, II. 252.
Stephen, Feast of St., II. 23.
Suffering of this life, II. 323.
   Sources of, II. 325.
   Fruits of, II. 334.
Suffering, remedies against, II. 344, 353, 362.

TEMPTATIONS, I. 145.
Time, Good use of, II. 32.
   For Prayer, II. 303.
Trinity, Feast of the Most Holy, II. 149.

VIRGIN, The Blessed. *See* Mary.

WHITMONDAY, II. 141.
Whitsunday, II. 131.
Word of God, Hearing of the, I. 124.
   A remedy against sufferings, II. 353.
Works, Faith and good, I. 299.

YEAR, New, II. 32.

ZEAL for the honor of religion I. 415.

END OF VOLUME II.

www.ingramcontent.com/pod-product-compliance
Lightning Source LLC
Chambersburg PA
CBHW022121290426
44112CB00008B/760